Also by Garry Wills

Saint Augustine
John Wayne's America: The Politics of Celebrity
Certain Trumpets: The Call of Leaders
Witches and Jesuits: Shakespeare's Macbeth
Lincoln at Gettysburg: The Words That Remade America
Under God: Religion and American Politics
Reagan's America: Innocents at Home
Nixon Agonistes
The Kennedy Imprisonment
Inventing America
Cincinnatus: George Washington and the Enlightenment
Explaining America
Lead Time
Chesterton
Politics and the Catholic Freedom
Roman Culture
Jack Ruby
The Second Civil War
Bare Ruined Choirs
Confessions of a Conservative
At Button's

GARRY WILLS

A
NECESSARY
EVIL

A History of American Distrust of Government

Simon & Schuster

SIMON & SCHUSTER
Rockefeller Center
1230 Avenue of the Americas
New York, NY 10020

Designed by DEIRDRE C. AMTHOR

Manufactured in the United States of America

10 9 8 7 6 5 4 3 2 1

Library of Congress Cataloging-in-Publication Data

Wills, Garry, [date]
    A necessary evil : a history of American distrust of government / Garry Wills.
        p.   cm.
    Includes bibliographical references.
    1. United States—Politics and government.   2. Dissenters—United States—History.
    3. Government, Resistance to—United States—History.   I. Title.
E183.W57   1999
973—dc21   99–35879
                                                                                CIP

ISBN 0-684-84489-3

Acknowledgments

Again I am indebted to my peerless editor (Alice Mayhew) and agent (Andrew Wylie). Also to John C. Wills, who brought me (belatedly) into the computer age with this book. Readers who were particularly helpful were Gordon Wood of Brown University on the founding period and Steven Lubet of Northwestern University Law School on matters constitutional.

To the Unicorn symposiasts

for all they teach me

Contents

Key to Brief Citations

AF   *The Complete Anti-Federalist*, edited by Herbert J. Storing (Chicago: University of Chicago Press, 1981), vols. 1–7

CC   *Letters to Members of the Continental Congress*, edited by Edmund C. Burnett (Washington, D.C.: Carnegie Institution of Washington, 1921–36), vols. 1–8

F   *The Federalist*, edited by Jacob E. Cooke (Middletown, Ct.: Wesleyan University Press, 1961)

FC   *The Records of the Federal Convention of 1787*, edited by Max Farrand (New Haven: Yale University Press, 1937), vols. 1–4

J   *The Papers of Thomas Jefferson*, edited by Julian P. Boyd et al. (Princeton: Princeton University Press, 1950–90), vols. 1–23

JL   *The Writings of Thomas Jefferson*, edited by Andrew A. Lipscomb and Albert E. Bergh (Washington, D.C.: Thomas Jefferson Memorial Association, 1903–1904), vols. 1–20

JW   *Thomas Jefferson: Writings*, edited by Merrill D. Peterson (New York: Library of America, 1984)

L   *Abraham Lincoln: Speeches and Writings*, edited by Don E. Fehrenbacher (New York: Library of America, 1980), vols. 1–2

M   *James Madison, Papers*, edited by William T. Hutchinson, William M.E. Rachal et al. (Chicago: University of Chicago Press, 1962–91), vols. 1–17

MH   *The Writings of James Madison*, edited by Gaillard
                  Hunt (New York: Putnam, 1900–1910), vols. 1–9
R   *The Documentary History of the Ratification of the*
                  Constitution, edited by Merrill Jensen et al. (Madi-
                  son: State Historical Society of Wisconsin,
                  1976–86), vols. 1–4, 8–10, 13–16
RL   *The Republic of Letters: The Correspondence Between*
                  Thomas Jefferson and James Madison, 1776–1826,
                  edited by James Morton Smith (New York: Norton,
                  1995), vols. 1–2

Introduction

Henry David Thoreau put in extreme form what many Americans want to believe about their government:

> I heartily accept the motto, "That government is best which governs least"; and I should like to see it acted up to more rapidly and systematically. Carried out, it finally amounts to this, which also I believe, "That government is best which governs not at all."[1]

Government is accepted as, at best, a necessary evil, one we must put up with while resenting the necessity. We want as little of it as possible, since anything beyond that necessary minimum instantly cancels one or other liberty. There is more to this attitude, in our culture, than the normal and universal resistance to authority. Americans believe that they have a government which is itself against government, that our Constitution is so distrustful of itself as to hamper itself. The great Supreme Court Justice Louis Brandeis pronounced, in 1926, that "the doctrine of the separation of powers was adopted by the Convention of 1787, not to promote efficiency but to preclude the exercise of arbitrary power."[2] So common is the assumption that the Constitution is deliberately inefficient that Chief Justice Earl Warren could echo Brandeis in 1965, saying that the Constitution was "obviously not instituted with the idea that it would promote governmental efficiency."[3]

Actually, as we shall see, efficiency was precisely the aim of the drafters of our Constitution. But in this whole area we live with a mythical history and jurisprudence. There is a positive determination to see even in the organs of government itself only anti-governmental values. Our whole history is read and invoked in this light. Hardly a modern controversy arises without instant recourse to the founding fathers, and to a heavily distorted version of what they were up to when they drafted and ratified the Constitution. *The Federalist,* written mainly by James Madison and Alexander Hamilton, is not just yesterday's scholarship but today's weapon—as useful to the National Rifle Association as to U.S. Term Limits. We are pious toward our history in order to be cynical toward our government. We keep summoning the founders to testify against what they founded. Our very liberty depends so heavily on distrust of government that the government itself, we are constantly told, was constructed to instill that distrust.

Our government does this by checking and balancing itself, each of its three major parts being so equal that deadlock occurs unless all three are brought into guarded or grudging agreement. According to this view, said Walter Bagehot, the British constitutionalist, "a good whole is constructed not simply in spite of but by means of the counteracting defects of the constituent parts."[4] Eminent historians of ideas, including the founder of that discipline, Arthur Lovejoy, inform us that the American Constitution expresses a pessimistic view of human nature, of its inevitable corruptibility by power.[5] Since human nature cannot be trusted, power must be so insecurely seated that even slight opposition to it can stymie it.

We are faced with a zero-sum game. Any power given to the government is necessarily subtracted from the liberty of the governed. This formula is of continual service. Are Americans less protected against threats to their health than other citizens of industrial democracies? Say that is so—but are we to purchase health at the price of liberty? For that is what giving power to the government would mean, including power to provide medical care. If government has the power to take away guns, all our liberties are gone. If the states, as lesser units of government, cede power to the central government, tyranny impends. The power to regulate businesses is a power to crush them. Increasing the size of government inevitably decreases freedom.

I shall be arguing, in this book, that the historical and constitutional evidence constantly used in these debates is largely bogus. But that just raises another question. Whence comes this determination to distort the history of our legal system? The distortion began very early, when the arguments of Antifederalists *against* the Constitution were said, only a decade or so after that document's ratification, to be embodied *in* the Constitution. People could stay loyal to the Constitution only if they felt it was structurally disloyal to itself.

The American attitude toward central power is rooted in the fact that the founding colonies had no central organ of expression. They had been established on different bases, with exiguous ties to each other through the distant British Crown. Differences of religion separated them, different economies, different cultures. Other peoples have had, from their earliest history, a central city or shrine, sanctified by long associations, belonging to the entire population. When our Constitution provided for an artificial capital to be imposed on the scene, sectional interests struggled over its placement. It was a source of discord rather than of unity, and its grubby appearance for a long time deflated rather than enhanced national pride (which was fitting in the eyes of many). The American separation of church and state, meanwhile, precluded agreement on a central shrine or symbol of worship. Our culture would not be centripetal but centrifugal— distrusting cities, yearning out toward nature's free space, to the frontier. Self-government by the individual was so intensely desired that government by others—even by legitimately chosen representative others—was, in many incremental ways, delegitimated.

Thus, to the arguments about the shape of our government and our history are added, always, certain attitudes that tend to come in a cluster, each reinforcing the other. After studying the ways our fear of government has found expression, I was struck by the persistence, through these different forms of opposition, of values that not only recurred but recurred in relatively stable proximity to each other. At times, these values uphold liberal positions, at times conservative ones. They can show up on the left or on the right; but wherever they show up, they bring along all or most of their fellows. They can be found in a hippie commune or a modern militia camp. These are all good American values, and it is no wonder that people want to uphold them, especially if they believe (as they often do) that government would weaken or obliterate them. That sincere belief is behind much of the need to oppose any increase in government.

Here are the values we shall find recurring wherever government is opposed: a belief that government, as a necessary evil, should be kept at a minimum; and that legitimate social activity should be provincial, amateur, authentic, spontaneous, candid, homogeneous, traditional, popular, organic, rights-oriented, religious, voluntary, participatory, and rotational.

Values contrasting with those are not polar opposites, but distant points on the continuum of approaches to government—namely, a belief that government is sometimes a positive good, and that it should be cosmopolitan, expert, authoritative, efficient, confidential, articulated in its parts, progressive, elite, mechanical, duties-oriented, secular, regulatory, and delegative, with a division of labor. Ideally, I suppose, government should combine all these values in a tempered way, since the one set does not necessarily preclude the other. But as a matter of empirical fact I find that group after group in our history does treat the first cluster of values as endangered by the second, under siege from them. And a recognition of this fact helps explain things that look merely perverse or irrational unless one sees what values are at work and what are their interconnections.

When Martin Luther King Jr. demonstrated against segregation, he came up against fierce opposition, not only from bigots but from ordinary southerners who felt that segregation was so built into the fabric of their lives that it would ravel out everything they held dear, even their religion, to make such a fundamental alteration in the world their ancestors had given them. Tradition was at stake, the conception that they had treated blacks well despite the misunderstanding of outsiders. One of Ronald Reagan's favorite doctrines was that local government is best because the citizens at that level have the best grasp of their own complex circumstances. Outsiders will take an abstract view of what is organically related in the lives of people over many generations. It is arrogant for others, people not in the situation themselves, to judge and dispose of those who are in it. So all of the anti-government values I listed above were engaged in the defense of segregation. To southerners, neat arguments about equality, legality, and progress seemed beside the point.

This was an example of the clash between what Carol Rose, of the Yale Law School, calls "the ancient constitution" and the "plain vanilla" (or fits-all-sizes) constitution.[6] The former is made up of a dense weave of legal custom, immemorial practice, practical compromise, and shared memories. Its burdens do not seem burdens (at least to the local majority) because they are one's *own* practices. Government at this level does not have the impersonal air of dictation—what Thoreau called a decision by people he never met about the use of his tax money for purposes he never authorized. What I shall be calling anti-governmentalism is opposed to government in Thoreau's sense, the form of government that achieves efficiency by ignoring the messy particularities of everyday life. Such anti-governmentalism grew, originally, out of the localisms of colonial history and was prolonged into an anti-governmental reading of the Constitution. In conjunction, these two factors proved formidable allies, calling into question any accretion of power, making "big government" hostile to life as it is really lived. They helped create a Lockean orthodoxy in our political thinking, which equates the *forming* of any reputable government with the *limiting* of government. To question that orthodoxy is to be for unlimited government— that is, for despotism.

There is good reason to be suspicious of any approach to American history that sees it as a recurring clash between two principles. Some people— Henry Cabot Lodge, for instance, and Claude Bowers, and Franklin Roosevelt—used to maintain that America reenacts over and over the disagreement between Jeffersonians and Hamiltonians.[7] That claim has an element of truth, but it puts the matter too narrowly. Professor Rose comes closer, I think, with her clash between the concrete and the abstract experiences of government. We have to begin with an observable thing we *can* call a constant in American history—the fear of government, sometimes sensible, sometimes hysterical, but always pronounced. To call this Jeffersonian is to miss some of the related values I listed—religion, for instance, or traditionalism (neither a strong concern of Jefferson). What I am suggesting, and what has to be tested empirically in examples over a broad range of time and regions, is whether these values tend to occur in connection with each other. To do this, I have sifted the forms taken by the anti-governmental impulse in our past—by nullifiers, seceders, insurrectionists, vigilantes, by those who withdraw from government or commit civil disobedience—to see if the same attitudes recur in similar clusters. And if the anti-government values recur in this way, so do the pro-government values. When, for instance, sixties radicals adopted the anti-government values of authenticity and spontaneity and participation (and even religion of various mystical forms), the southern conservatives who normally espouse those values switched for a while to the whole cluster of government values, wanting duties imposed on the rebellious by authoritative efficiency and confidential expertise (i.e., FBI spying). Those who denounced out-siders for coming into their community now wanted the government, both local and federal, to infiltrate and break up the communes and demonstra-tions of the hippies.

Certain anomalies in our history are better understood if we recognize in them the power of anti-governmental values, even when they are illog-ically invoked. America's business culture, for instance, lives by the values of the governmental attitude—efficiency, division of labor, impersonal ex-pertise, the mechanics of the market, secular progress, and so on. But in re-sisting some forms of government regulation, the business community portrays itself as defending spontaneity and freedom (anti-governmental values). Thus its defenders insensibly attach most of the other values in that cluster. That is why men like William Buckley or Michael Novak can feel that religion is embedded in the very nature of capitalism, as southern-ers thought that religion was embedded in the very nature of segregation. The things they value are so deeply lodged in their hearts that they feel there must be some necessary link between them outside that enclosing chamber.

So traditionalists end up defending that ceaseless engine for change, capitalism. They portray the free market as spontaneous, giving a chance to the amateur inventor or aspiring amateur, when it imposes specializa-tion and rewards expertise. They think of it as provincial, enriching a lo-cale or the nation, when it is cosmopolitan, going wherever profit takes it. Thus big government and big business, which are partners more often than foes, are seen through distorting lenses, with preachers like Pat Robertson damning the former as heartily as they praise the latter. These confusions are not the result of rigorous analysis but of the tendency of the anti-gov-ernmental values to cling together—take one and you are likely to end up with most or all of them. Or so I hope to demonstrate, using a wide variety of examples of the phenomenon.

I cannot, of course, treat all the manifestations of the fear of govern-ment in a history so rich with examples of that fearful attitude as to make it an American tradition (almost, but not quite, *the* American tradition). What I have sketched out is a typology of examples, treating salient episodes to show the persistence of trends and attitudes. The same values, differently filtered through moral concerns, underlie such active resistance to government as bombing an abortion clinic (see Chapter 18) and such passive resistance as refusing to vote (see Chapter 22). The same concerns can motivate civil disobedience from the right or from the left. In the 1980s, the anti-abortion activist Randall Terry told me that he took the civil rights demonstrators of the sixties as his model. In 1998, Paul Weyrich of the right-wing Free Congress Foundation told me that he, too, was considering sixties-like protest against his own party's moral indifference. The religious journal *First Things* could combine reverence for the founding fathers with a belief that the American "holocaust" (of unborn babies) might call for imitation of Dietrich Bonhoeffer (the Lutheran minister who considered assassinating Hitler).

Of course our ingrained fear of government does not normally take such extreme form. But many people find themselves surprised at the sympathy they can feel for even outrageous opponents of government—as was demonstrated when popular support blossomed for the anti-government forces holed up with David Koresh at Waco, Texas, or with Randy Weaver, who defied the FBI at Ruby Ridge, Idaho. I remember filmmaker Oliver Stone's telling me how much he sided with those underdogs. After all, much of what those groups said was just the equivalent of the Jefferson tee shirt worn by Timothy McVeigh, the bomber of Oklahoma City's federal building. But the real victims of our fear are not those faced with such extreme action—not even the 168 people killed (and many more injured) by McVeigh. The real victims are the millions of poor or shelterless or medically indigent who have been told, over the years, that they must lack care or life support in the name of their very own freedom. Better for them to starve than to be enslaved by "big government." That is the real cost of our anti-government values.

Before I can address the typology of resistance to government, I must address the misreadings of history that seem to give authoritative warrant to that resistance. I began this book in 1994, when the fear of government manifested itself in the off-year election of a Republican majority to Congress. Led by Newt Gingrich, and waving a Contract With America, the Republicans promised to dismantle whole agencies, undo regulatory boards, abolish long-term government service, and cut off government subsidies to the arts, to farmers, to welfare recipients. They grabbed the fallen banner of Ross Perot, who wanted to replace politicians and bureaucrats with citizen amateurs. Though some people called these moves hard-hearted, their defenders cited the founding fathers' support for freedom from government interference and regulation.

Other concerns of that time were also centered on the founding period. Militias, for instance, were not only springing up in the anti-governmental culture but being studied and defended in new ways by legal scholars—and all this busy activity looked back to the famed minutemen of our Revolution. So did the National Rifle Association's defense of an unlimited right to private possession of firearms. As I began looking for parallels to such modern developments in our past, I noticed that the anti-governmental values are almost always buttressed, on the level of argument, by widespread but mistaken interpretations of the Constitution and its authors. The term limits movement, for instance, asserted that the founders had such a low opinion of politics that no honest man could make it his profession. These are good test cases of the connection between the anti-governmental values and arguments based on the founding period. Before sorting out various types of resistance to government, therefore, I look at the view of the Revolution and the Constitution that underlies most of them.

I.

Revolutionary Myths

Though I take up anti-government attitudes in a rough chronological order, as they manifested themselves in our history, the order is not genetic—later things did not necessarily grow out of earlier ones, despite shared attitudes expressed in them all. Nonetheless, events that surround the establishing of our Republic are brought up again and again by later opponents of central authority, since they are part of a national mythology we have all absorbed. If the nation's founders held a particular opinion, that is a strong incentive for us to adhere to it as well, like dutiful sons and daughters of our glorious forebears.

But our view of the founders' opinions is filtered through later attitudes, which both obscure and magnify certain aspects of their world. In particular, the revolt against king and Parliament in England has been romanticized as a revolution against central authority in general. So great was the Americans' impatience with being told what to do that they won their war and set up their government without needing a counter-authority to direct them. In a spontaneous and amateur way, they fought as individuals united by love of hearth and locality, not by external discipline. Though some political coordination was needed, it was provided by ad hoc committees of correspondence, in which ordinary citizens served for a time, taking turns at positions of trust, not forming a permanent class of rulers. The national government set up after the Revolution was meant to be just an extension of this kind of citizen activity, first under the Articles of Confederation, then under a Constitution drawn up by another ad hoc committee of men making a recommendation to the states and then dissolving itself.

Thus were born the complementary myths of the amateur soldier and the amateur politician, the Minuteman and the Short-Term Man.

1.

Minutemen

One of the dramatic developments of the 1990s was the emergence of self-styled militias training for guerrilla war against the federal government. Proudly patriotic, these organizations presented themselves as the true guardians of Jeffersonian values, as heirs to the Revolution's minutemen. It was hard to judge the extent or depth of the movement, but some of the literature it relied on was an apparent inspiration to Timothy McVeigh when he blew up a federal building in Oklahoma City, killing 168 people. His action echoed, in fact, an event in William Pierce's 1978 book, *The Turner Diaries*, which imagines a war on government beginning with a fertilizer bomb that destroys a federal building.[1]

It may seem absurd for small bands of men to think they can defy a federal government they describe as vast in its power and ruthless in the use of it. But the militias drew on a claim that was routinely accepted in circles less extreme than their own. The Vietcong, they argue, defied the same United States government and bested it by guerrilla "insurgency."[2] This is an analogy that Wayne LaPierre, at the time the executive vice president of the National Rifle Association, used in order to argue that gun owners in general could successfully defeat tyrannical measures taken by the government.[3]

The view that the Vietcong prevailed by guerrilla tactics is a belief widespread but fallacious. The conclusions drawn from a panel of military and academic experts have been amply confirmed in later studies: "The North Vietnamese finally won by purely conventional means. . . . In their lengthy battle accounts that followed Hanoi's great military victory, Generals [Vo Nguyen] Giap and [Van Tien] Dung barely mentioned the contribution of local forces."[4] But surprisingly large numbers of people have been tempted, in recent decades, to believe in an almost magic power of "people's war" to prevail against the odds. Colonial populations hoped they could launch revolutions "on the cheap."[5] And their opponents hoped that "counterinsurgency" could also be scaled to smaller challenges. John Kennedy, recoiling from the Eisenhower era's doctrine of "massive retaliation," turned to "flexible response," relying on covert action, "psywar," and Green Beret derring-do.[6] It was the era of small-time operators promising big results, of spooks like John Paul Vann and Edward Lansdale. (Lansdale tried to psych out the enemies in Vietnam by tampering with their astrological predictions.)[7] The militias of the 1990s were inheritors of such illusion.

Renewed interest in the tactics of limited war led some people to recast our history in terms of the fad. Even some professional historians yielded to the rhetorical elation of the period. The military historian Don Higginbotham confessed that he had exaggerated the importance of militias to the Revolution when he succumbed to the excitement of the 1960s, responding to a timely "preoccupation with irregular war."[8] During the bicentennial celebrations of the seventies, William Casey, the future head of the Central Intelligence Agency, toured Revolutionary battlefields and wrote a book that said our forebears won the Revolution, just as the Vietnamese won their struggle, "by irregular, partisan, guerrilla warfare."[9] The misreading of the one war prompted a misreading of the other, and indicates why Casey, when he became the head of the CIA, thought that Oliver North was an appropriate sponsor of guerrilla Contras in Nicaragua. In the early 1960s, John Galvin, who would serve in Vietnam before becoming the commanding general of NATO, wrote *The Minute Men*, describing the Revolutionary minutemen as an elite rapid response team, just what the Pentagon was dreaming of.[10]

Vietnam-era romanticizing of militias served the 1990s extremists well. No matter how nutty the latter might seem, they had legitimate forebears in our history. Some of the groups even called themselves minutemen. NRA publicist Tanya Metaksa met with militiamen. Congressional officeholders and candidates defended them. Respected law professors argued that the Second Amendment had authorized a "genuine" militia, not the tame National Guard that swears allegiance to the federal government.

But Gary Hart, the former senator, argues in his 1998 book, *The Minute-man*, that the National Guard could be trained to become "citizen guerillas" for our time.[11] The glorification of militias reached such a pitch that Akhil Reed Amar, Southmayd Professor at the Yale Law School, collaborated with a journalist on a book proclaiming that the right to serve in a militia was one of the three most fundamental guarantors of constitutional freedoms.[12] This is not far from Charlton Heston's statement, on behalf of the NRA, that the Second Amendment is the most important part of the Constitution, since it equips people to defend all their other rights with guns.[13]

Even some who do not agree with Heston's assessment of the Second Amendment are willing to accept a rosy depiction of the colonial and Revolutionary militias. They represent, for most of us, a high ideal of citizen response to threats against our liberty. We honor Daniel Chester French's statue *The Minute Man* at Concord's battlefield in Massachusetts. The rallying of other towns to the defense of Lexington was a great moment in American history. But before we get too carried away by the cult of the militias, we should reflect on claims for them that cannot stand a close inquiry.

One of the principal boasts of the militias' admirers is that they exhibited a democratic inclusiveness. Every free white male of military age had to serve, regardless of class or social standing. That was rarely the case in colonial times. There were many exemptions—for conscientious objectors (Pennsylvania had no pre-Revolution militia because of its Quaker population), attendance at college, engagement in important business. The socially prominent could usually avoid service if they wanted to, often by paying others to go in their place. (If the militias were truly universal, there would be no "spare" men to be paid for joining.) The military historian John Shy notes that John Adams, just the right age to take up a musket in the French and Indian War of 1756–63 (when all men were supposed to be in the militias), never even considered doing so.[14]

But there is an even more sweeping fact that made universal service impossible throughout the colonies. There was a drastic shortage of guns. This goes against everything we have assumed about our pioneer forebears—that they vindicated their own liberties with their own arms. But there is overwhelming evidence that a majority of males did not own usable guns. The colonies repeatedly legislated that all men should get or be given guns, and just as repeatedly complained that this had not been accomplished. In the French and Indian War, a contingent of two hundred Virginia militiamen went to the front bearing only eighty muskets, and British officers in Massachusetts, amazed that so few colonials possessed muskets, were even more surprised to find that many had not even fired one.[15] At Lexington and Concord, the opening battles of the Revolution, despite the fact that the Massachusetts militia had spent months desperately trying to arm itself, some contingents showed up at the front unarmed.[16] A captain of the New Hampshire militia reported in 1775 that "not one-half our men have arms," and a militia officer in Virginia said that he had a stand of a thousand guns, but that none of them worked.[17] The New York Committee of Safety refused to send troops to the field because "they have no arms."[18] Thomas Jefferson, Virginia's governor, had to defend his state's militia when, lacking guns, it stole a consignment purchased by the Continental Army; and he consoled one of his commanders with the philosophical reflection that "the subsequent desertions of your militia have taken away the necessity of answering the question how they shall be armed" (J 3.224–27, 640).

If every man had his gun for militia drill, why did so many go off to battle without a musket, not only militiamen, but Continental Army soldiers too? Patrick Henry would later use the dearth of guns as a reason for refusing to ratify the Constitution. The new government promised to arm the militias, but the state of Virginia had been promising to do that for years, *and had never done it*. How could Virginians expect the federal government to do what they could not do for themselves? Henry told the Virginia ratifying convention in 1788 that "we have learned, by experience, that, necessary as it is to have arms, and though our Assembly has, by a succession of laws for many years, endeavored to have the militia completely armed, it is still far from being the case." In an earlier session of the convention he had asked: "Of what service would militia be to you when, most probably, you will not have a single musket in the state? For as arms are to be provided by Congress, they may or may not furnish them" (R 9.957, 10.1273).

If Congress would not supply arms, what prevented each man from taking down his musket from over the mantel? We have all been taught that the guns were there. But they weren't. In one of the most important (but neglected) studies of the colonial frontier, Michael Bellesiles went through over a thousand probate records covering the years 1763 to 1790 from western sectors of New England and Pennsylvania. Though these were inheritance lists for white males (those most likely to own guns), and though belongings were listed in great detail (down to broken mugs), only 14 percent of the men owned guns, and 53 percent of those guns were broken or unusable.

How can this be? We have always known or assumed that men in the colonial period had to hunt for food. Bellesiles shows that this, too, is a myth. Hunting for food—with a musket, inaccurate enough when aimed at a man and generally hopeless against a rabbit; or with a rifle whose loading (after each shot) was slow and difficult—could not be an efficient use of the ordinary person's time. Though most meat consumed was from domestic animals (pigs or cows), the supplementary provisions were best caught with the trapper's or the fisherman's net.[19] People's defense came from their living in communities, with select militias to guard them, using what guns were available. These guns came mainly from Europe, and the typical village's blacksmith was not very good at repairing them. (Much of the smith's time went into forging farm and transportation gear.) Though some guns were made in America, M. L. Brown established that this was "an infant, homespun, widely dispersed, and distinctly disorganized American industry" when the Revolution began.[20] The European source for arms was cut off by British embargo during the Revolution, and was only partially restored when the French entered the fray on the Americans' side.

Guns for both militias and the Continental Army were so scarce that George Washington fills page after page with laments for his inability to get them—and he meant muskets as well as the even scarcer cannon and artillery. If guns were not omnipresent, then obviously the skill in their use was not widespread either. Why were so many guns broken or unusable in the probate records? It was not only that the blacksmiths in small communities were not gunsmiths. Guns were mainly made of iron at the time, and interior rusting of barrel and parts would take place unless guns were cleaned and maintained. Obviously, not enough people kept them in regular use to prevent this from occurring. Though some mastered the difficult handling of the long rifle, few became truly expert. Brown quotes Benjamin

Thompson, a Continental soldier expressing the "common sentiment" about riflemen attached to the army as skirmishers:

> Instead of being the best marksmen in the world and picking off every Regular that was to be seen, there is scarcely a regiment in camp but can produce men that can beat them at shooting, and the army is now universally convinced that the continual firing which they kept up by the week and month together has had no other effect than to waste their ammunition and convince the King's troops that they are not really so formidable.[21]

The famed American rifle was not of much use in war, and its wielders, according to historians George Scheer and Hugh Rankin, were "more noisy than useful." They were wielding an instrument never intended for battle:

> The rifle used by these "irregulars" was practically unknown to the New Englanders, accustomed to the smooth-bore musket and fowling piece. Long in barrel, small in bore, light in weight, and perfectly balanced, it was the weapon of the professional hunter and woodsman, the man who eschewed every ounce of unnecessary burden and could not afford to waste a single charge. Its barrel was spiral-grooved to give spin to its bullet, and its effective range more than doubled the musket's sixty yards. Its greatest disadvantage was that in order to benefit from its rifling, its bullet had to be fitted so tightly that it had to be forced home with an iron ramrod and a wooden mallet, a slow process. It had other disadvantages for line firing: the weather more easily rendered it useless; it had no bayonet, so that its users could not deliver or stand a charge; and surrounded by the smoke of a battle line, the riflemen could not aim carefully enough to take advantage of their weapon's unbelievable accuracy.[22]

The American army found even less use for pistols than for rifles.[23] British cavalrymen and naval officers carried them as signal guns and for defense against a rebel in their ranks, but they were an ornament that Americans forbore: "Few pistols were domestically produced, for cavalry generally performed a minor role in the Continental Army, operating primarily in the southern campaigns, and preferred the carbine and blunderbuss to the saber and the pistol."[24] Pistols, which gentlemen used for duels, were not handy in combat, since one had to get out one's powder and ball and load the things for each shot. In private life, knives were a quicker and more wieldy weapon, and they accounted for most individual killings in the eighteenth century. Bellesiles shows statistically that not until the industrial revolution of the nineteenth century, not until the Colt company's great output and advertising, did gun ownership spread dramatically in America—and then it never stopped spreading. There was one gun for every ten people in the colonies. Now there is more than one for every man, woman, and child in America, with three for every adult male of the population. Yet this latter situation is justified by appeal to the former.[25]

We must give up, then, the idea that every man in the colonies turned out for militia service bearing his own gun or one supplied him. But other factors prevented the militias from being universal. John Shy, the special master of this subject, says that militia composition differed from state to state and from period to period for a variety of social and economic reasons. It is best to consider the militias in four stages—before the Revolution, at its beginning, during its course, and at its end.

1. In the first settlements, short on manpower, everyone did everything possible for the common defense—women, children, slaves, friendly Indians. That condition could recur later, at times of maximum emergency. In response to the British march on Concord, the women of Pepperell township set up militia patrols after their men left town. Blacks warned households that "the Regulars are out." An old woman, "Mother" Batherick, took six unresisting prisoners in the British retreat from Lexington.[26]

But when the pressure of crisis eased, in the colonies before the war, training sessions for the militias were cut back, and attendance was low at them. In the first half of the eighteenth century, Virginia's "militia virtually ceased to exist," since "a handful of semi-professional rangers could watch the frontier."[27] Later, as the slave population grew, and grew restive, the militias were drilled as a police power to intimidate and control the slaves.[28] The militias were becoming "more social than military organizations."[29] Officers held military rank as part of their general influence. Here was the birth of all those "colonels" who have dotted the southern landscape. When a time for actual fighting arose, the poor and vagrants were bribed or dragooned into service. "Tidy colonial laws, imposing a military obligation on almost every free adult white male, became less and less an accurate mirror of military reality, particularly in times of danger."[30] That is, times of crisis—for which the militias were supposed to be trained— were precisely the times when they were least in evidence. This explains the poor performance of the militias in the French and Indian War, when the British acquired a contempt for the American fighting man. Historians James Kirby Martin and Mark Edward Lender respond to that contempt by pointing out that "these provincial soldiers were not militia, but rather outcasts from middle-class society, unfortunates who had been lured or legally pressed into service through promises of bounty payments and decent food and clothing."[31]

Even when vagrants were not being lured to replace militiamen, genuine members of the militias usually volunteered for actual fighting, under the encouragement of special rewards, as if they were not already obliged to service. The militias had become a kind of manpower pool from which volunteers could be sought, rather than a force already formed. The men dispatched to do real fighting were not normally the militia units that were supposed to have trained together, but a collection of those who could leave home with least disruption to the community. They were selected out, becoming the very thing modern celebrants of the militias say that universal citizen service was meant to prevent. They were a "select militia." And the very principle of their selection guaranteed that they would largely be untrained, undisciplined, unskilled in the use of arms, and ready at any minute to desert. That was the type of soldier who served with British Regulars in the French and Indian War, the colonial war waged just before the Revolution.

George Washington, trying to lead those militia forces, said they made him ashamed for his countrymen. His biographer describes the situation he faced as that earlier war began:

Virginia had trained no officers, had kept no troops, had organized no wagon train, and possessed few arms. The militia, as the Governor had phrased it, were in "very bad order." In Frederick, a more nearly accurate word would have been "non-existent." Lord Fairfax apparently had no roll of the men liable to military duty; he possessed no facilities other than those of the tax-lists for preparing a roster; he had raised none of the fifty men George was supposed to find ready for him.[32]

2. If that was the condition of the militias in the 1750s, why did the colonies entertain such high expectations of their performance at the beginning of the Revolution in the 1770s? The pressure of the mounting crisis of the 1760s, when Parliament imposed new taxes like the Stamp Act, made the colonies take their militias more seriously. As the break with the mother country occurred, the units were forced to reorganize. Some of their former officers were Tories, not to be trusted in a fight with British troops. Most of them had been appointed by the royal governors of each colony. Clearly, new arrangements had to be made. The units were formed on ideological lines. Whig officers would now be elected by the troops themselves, and Whig loyalties would be demanded of the troops. In New England, the new bands were formed by covenant (a powerful concept the Puritans had borrowed from the biblical covenant God made with his people).[33] In Pennsylvania, where Quakers had earlier prevented the formation of a militia, newly formed bands were called The Association, and men in it were Associators.

Even when the threat of war made some recall the ideal of universal service, not everyone could be on constant call. In Massachusetts, select teams were formed to be on ready alert—the minutemen, with their own organization, the "minute companies." (They did not operate as individuals, as our myth has it.) The minutemen constituted between a fifth and a fourth of the covenanted force, and they were generally younger and more mobile than the others. They had to serve for a specified period (ten months in the case of Concord), keep arms by them at all times, and be part of a network for early response to any threat. It was through this network that Paul Revere spread the news that "the Regulars are coming out" when the British marched toward the arsenal at Concord. These minutemen's preparedness made them able to stream in from other townships to set ambushes for the British who had been broken and sent into headlong retreat from Concord back to Boston. On the other hand, it was not the minutemen who fought in the towns of Lexington and Concord, but the whole force of each township. Little Lexington, with a militia of forty men or so, had not even set up a minuteman corps and Concord had been late in picking its own elite band.[34]

The euphoria over the Massachusetts militia's early victory bred an illusion that native "virtue" was bound to prevail over hireling coercion in the British ranks. A Pennsylvania militia officer told his men, "The English army derive all their strength from a close attention to discipline, with them it supplies the want of virtue."[35] When the conditions of Lexington and Concord recurred during the war, militias often performed admirably—when, for instance, the Americans were forewarned and prepared, when they were fighting on their home ground, when they were facing small numbers of British troops penetrating that ground, when those troops were acting on a plan that did not foresee organized resistance. But those conditions were not to be the normal ones, and in a long war fought over a vast territory, spasms of local animation were of minor use.

3. The militias soon began to display all the marks of their earlier (inglorious) service. Their lack of discipline made them careless of sanitation (in war, disease competes with combat as a killer). Their staggered and short enlistment times were interrupted even more by their desertion rate (over 20 percent), which gave Washington grounds for some scathing comments on the militias' performance.[36] As his generals struggled to create conditions of discipline in the Continental Army, the use of auxiliary forces from the militias broke down what had painfully been built up. Even people who began with high praise for the militias were disabused of their admiration. Samuel Adams, who had been at Lexington on the day of the glorious clash, would later write, "Would any man in his senses, who wishes the war may be carried on with vigor, prefer the temporary and expensive drafts of militia to a permanent and well-appointed army?"[37] And General Charles Lee, who had desired to lead militia forces, ended up saying, "As to the minutemen, no account ought to be made of them" (and minutemen were the *elite* corps).[38] Jefferson, whose calls to the militia were met with "detestation" and defiance, said that "no possible mode of carrying it [the war] on can be so expensive to the public and so distressing and disgusting to the individuals as by militia" (J 5.34). His fellow southern governor Thomas Burke of North Carolina had begun the Revolution as an enemy of central government, but his experience with the militia convinced him "that every dodge was used to escape military service," and he

tried to set up a regular army at the state level (though that was forbidden by the Articles of Confederation).[39]

Despite some important exceptions, when the militias fought well, their overall battle record is judiciously summed up by Don Higginbotham:

> As an institution, however, the militia proved deficient. The law-making bodies of the colony-states were never able to bring these military organizations up to meeting their responsibilities. . . . When required to stay for extended lengths of time in the field far from home, when mixed closely with sizable bodies of Continentals, and when performing against redcoats in open combat, the militia were at their worst. Nothing in their modest training, not to mention their normally deficient equipment and supplies, prepared them for these duties.[40]

The fervor of the early days in the reorganized militias wore off in the long grind of an eight-year war. Now the right to elect their own officers was used to demand that the men not serve away from their state. Men evaded service, bought substitutes to go for them as in the old days, and had to be bribed with higher and higher bounties to join the effort—which is why Jefferson and Samuel Adams called them so expensive. As wartime inflation devalued the currency, other pledges had to be offered, including land grants and the promise of "a healthy slave" at the end of the war. Some men would take a bounty and not show up. Or they would show up for a while, desert, and then, when they felt the need for another bounty, sign up again in a different place (so much for the claim that the militias were made up of neighbors who all knew each other). This practice was common enough to have its own technical term—"bounty jumping."[41]

One of the more laughable contentions of those modern politicians who romanticize the early American militias is that they prevented the corruptions of a standing army by serving voluntarily, not by compulsion, and freely, not for pay—unlike mercenaries on the other side. But the draft often had to be resorted to by governors unable to get the militia to serve without it, and the draft was often ineffective without the addition of bounties. Even after bounties were raised, evasion or defiance of the draft was common. A North Carolina militia officer told General Nathanael Greene that fifty-six of fifty-eight men drafted in one place claimed they had a disabling hernia, and Jefferson complained that when he tried to send Virginia militiamen out of the state "I had as many sore legs, hipshots, broken backs etc. produced as there were men ordered to go."[42] Bidding to drive bounties higher was engaged in by Continentals as well as militia, by officers as well as their subordinates. Historian Charles Royster calls the active bidding around recruitment the greatest source of corruption in the Revolution.[43]

Yet it would be entirely wrong to say that the militias made no contribution to the Revolution. They played a vital part in it—but not the part their current fans pretend they played. They did not prevent corruption or obviate the need for a standing army. They did not defeat the foe by insurgent tactics. They did not prove superior to trained armies by force of their patriot virtue. What did they do, then? They were crucial to what was called, in the eighteenth century, the internal police.[44] At a time of great turmoil, the stay-at-home militias kept order. The British tried to foment slave rebellions. The militias kept a close watch on the slave population. The British also used Indian allies to raid American communities. The militias, which did have a tradition of active rangers on guard against Indians, repelled them. Roving British marauders, hoping for plunder in American villages, often found the militias there to repel them. Loyalists could have become a fifth column in many communities. But attempts on their part to agitate or denounce the war effort, or to communicate with the enemy, were subject to close scrutiny by the militias—close enough to have made them, at times, a kind of thought police. The lookout for men of suspect allegiance even led Albany County in New York to establish a Committee for Detecting and Defeating Conspiracies, a partial forerunner of the Cold War's House Committee on Un-American Activities. There is a delicious irony in this. Modern defenders of the militias value them as a force that can defend the people from authority, but the Revolutionary militias were put in the position of defending the war authority against dissidents (the Loyalists).[45]

What might be called this home-front importance of the militias had paradoxical results. It was at once a moderating and a radicalizing experience—moderating because it kept a measure of law and order through the paroxysm of revolution, and radicalizing because it put "new men" in the position of disciplining those who had been their social betters. Shy notes both of these effects.[46] By keeping order at the local level, the militias helped maintain that legalism Pauline Maier finds in the Revolution, setting it off from mere mob action.[47] But by breaking down patterns of deference, the militias gave citizens a new sense of control over their lives, especially, as Steven Rosswurm notes, among the Pennsylvania Associators. In fact, one of the most common complaints about the militias as a *military* force—that the men and officers disobeyed commands not to their liking, and were ready to go back to their own states—was an important *social* force for the future.[48]

4. The militias' contribution to this new political atmosphere at the local level explains why so many people, at the end of the war, remembered the militias' performance with a kind of fondness, despite their spotty or disgraceful record on the battlefield. Besides, when the militias did act well in war, it was often when the war came into the locale of the state forces, where the troops were fighting on familiar terrain, under the eyes of their neighbors. In those circumstances, the inhabitants of the region tended to exaggerate the contribution of the militia, playing down the achievement of the Continentals with whom the militia had fought the local battle. The Continental Army was seen as a protector of the states, but also as their dominator. It seemed always to be demanding provisions, paying for them often with promises or with devaluing currency. It drew men off from the home scene for service at a distance.[49] Besides, in the course of the war, it had to depend on the same bounty system that filled ranks with vagrants and dragooned men. Joseph Reed, the president of Pennsylvania's executive council, noticed that the "jealousy" between provincial forces and the Continentals replicated the frictions between the militia and the British Regulars during the French and Indian War.[50]

The difference between militia "vagrants" and Regulars of the same class was that, by the end of the war at least, enlistment in the Regulars was for three years, and distance from local politics gave Washington and his generals the opportunity to create discipline and cohesion in the core groups of officers and men. But even that was held against them. Weren't they taking on the characteristics that had always been feared in a standing army?[51] They were loyal to their own (it was alleged) rather than to the larger society they were defending.[52] These tensions came to a climax at the end of the war, when the Continental officers demanded half-pay pensions for life and set up the Society of the Cincinnati to honor their own wartime deeds. Why should the states pay national taxes to give Continentals a pension when their own militia officers received none, and the noncommissioned men in both forces were ignored? In the emotion of the moment, some expressed regret that the Continental Army had ever been formed, contending that the militias could have done the job if Congress had just stuck with them. Jefferson and others were harshly critical of the Cincinnati for introducing a hereditary aristocracy into America. (Washington agreed to abolition of the hereditary feature, though his stand was ignored by the local Cincinnati groups.)

What is important for our purpose is not the right or the wrong of these particular controversies, but the way they fit into the pairing-off of values listed in my introduction. People were not defending just the record of their own militias but that whole array of values that had become attached to them. I shall not keep repeating the list of clustered values with each chapter, but it is worth listing them here, to notice how readily the militia-vs.-Regulars conflict fits into this schema. Run down the left-hand list with the militias in mind, or the right-hand with the Regulars in mind, and this will be clear except for two apparent exceptions:

Anti-governmental Values	Governmental Values
Provincial	*Cosmopolitan*
Amateur	*Expert*
Authentic	*Authoritative*
Spontaneous	*Efficient*
Candid	*Confidential*
Homogeneous	*Articulated*
Traditional	*Progressive*
Populist	*Elite*
Organic	*Mechanical*
Rights-oriented	*Duties-oriented*
Religious	*Secular*
Voluntary	*Regulatory*
Participatory	*Delegative*
Rotating labor	*Dividing labor*

The apparent exceptions are the religious-secular pairing and the candid-confidential one. But religious backing of the militias was important on the local front, while Washington opposed the Congress's attempt to appoint brigade chaplains for the Continental Army: "Among many other weighty objections to the measure, it has been suggested that it has a tendency to introduce religious disputes into the army."[53] There are already, in his words, the seeds of the separation of church and state that Virginians would accomplish.

As for the candid-confidential polarity, the militias chose their own officers and demanded explanations from them for the military actions they were contemplating. If the officers refused to give them satisfaction, they complained to their state assemblies, which conducted their business in open sessions. But Congress held its deliberations in secret, and appointed Continental officers without explaining their choices, while the officers chosen expected unquestioning obedience from their men, one of the many differences in ethos between the militias and the Continentals. I could go through the whole list of anti-government values to show in detail how each value was exemplified in this case, but it will be more useful to single out two pairings.

1. *The spontaneous vs. the efficient.* If ever a society wants to be efficient, it is in time of war. Wastefulness here not only loses time or money. It loses lives—can even lose the national identity or independence. War imposes many disciplines on the citizenry as well as the fighting units. The claims on society made by the Continental Army were justified in terms of efficiency. But men resented those claims nonetheless. They asked whether they might win the war and lose their cause. Local militias might fight poorly, but they did it for the right motives, free and unforced. They were fighting for their hearth and household gods (*pro ara et focis*). The Continental Army was at a remove from those fierce motives. Professionalism for its own sake contended with or displaced patriotism in the eyes of "localists." It was symptomatic, and ominous, that the Continentals had to depend on foreigners to acquire their new disciplines—Baron von Steuben and the Chevalier de Mauduit du Plessis for battlefield drill (the titles alone were a giveaway), Casimir Pulaski for cavalry instruction, Louis Duportail and Jean Baptiste Gouvion and Lewis de la Radière for engineering standards. The Continental Army's demands may have been necessary in

war, but, like government itself, they were a necessary evil, one that should not be continued, or excessively honored, in peacetime. The militias' faults, by contrast, existed in wartime but could be profitably forgotten in peacetime, when other services they performed were still worth commemorating. Efficiency, let it be granted, won the war on the field. But the spontaneous displays of virtue in the citizen soldiers made the war worth winning.

2. *Rights-oriented vs. duties-oriented.* George Washington, who led the army without pay, embodied the classical republican ideal of virtuous service to one's country. But men of his class, though espousing an ethic of duty, were also prickly about their rights, their social honor. They asserted the latter by virtue of the former. They deserved public status because they performed public service. But some of the men serving under them, in the army and in the militias, learned in the course of the war to assert *their* rights, *their* honor. Why should officers receive pensions, and not those who fought alongside them? One of the complaints against the militias was that they disobeyed when they did not like any commands or any officers issuing them. When affronted, state contingents would just pull out of the ranks and go home. This makes for lousy war-waging, but it had an attractive air of independence at a time when independence was the cause being asserted. War is not usually a time for the vindication of individual rights within the ranks of fighting men, but after the war it was easy to excuse men who were a little too bold in asserting their rights. Within the concept of citizen soldiers, the soldier should serve the citizen, not vice versa. On this point, at least, the militias maintained that they performed better than the Continentals, who sometimes subjected the citizen to the soldier.

If one looks at the militias in terms of the values they asserted, instead of looking only at their actual record of performance, it is easy to see why modern holders of a militia ideal honor the Revolutionary units. Those units did not do most of what their admirers attribute to them. They were not individual minutemen each grabbing his own gun to vindicate his liberties. They did not prevail by the kind of guerrilla war William Casey imagined. They exerted almost as much political force upon their own people as military force upon the enemy. Yet their myth does embody the values that modern militias think they are preserving. That commonalty of ideals, rather than any real historical resemblance, connects our contemporaries with their imagined forebears. This is the first of many cases we shall be considering where, when real history conflicts with symbolic history, the former is subsumed within the latter. Modern militias do not see any gap between ideals and performance where the early militias are concerned. They use the fake history to support the real values. If the minuteman of legend did not exist—well, in terms of what we hold dear, he should have. So let's just pretend that he did.

2.

Term Limits

I intended, at first, to call this chapter "Citizen Politicians," but that formulation would have been considered contradictory in our early history. Since government was at best a necessary evil, one who sought its power, enjoyed it, became professional at wielding it, was bound to be tainted by its evil aspects. Already in 1800 the word "politician" was denigrative, contrasted with terms like "public servant."[1] A servant has to be impressed into service. That is why it was considered unseemly to make an open bid for office. The proper way to accept office was with a genuine or feigned reluctance. The proper way to leave it was with expressions of relief and gratitude—as when Benjamin Franklin, leaving office, said (FC 2.288) that he was happy to return to the ranks of the employers (the people) by leaving those of the employed (their servants). In the deferential world of the eighteenth century, both the reluctance and the relief were sometimes sincere, since the ideal was of *gentlemen* officeholders, men who had rank, authority, and obligations apart from governmental honors. The wish to return to one's plantation or commercial empire could be a heartfelt one. George Washington, who personified the old ethos of gentlemanly service by taking no pay during the Revolution, was genuinely eager to get back to Mount Vernon, which had been deteriorating in his absence.

Franklin wanted to continue the gentlemanly tradition by making the President of the United States draw no salary (FC 1.81–85). But the Revolution was bringing forward a different ideal, that of the citizen legislator. Government was still evil, in fact more so; but people of middling social status might also hold office (with some provisos). To protect them from the corrupting influence of office, a number of devices were invented to keep them detachable from it—short terms, possible recall during the terms, voter instruction on what actions they should take while in office, ineligibility to fill the same office after a certain time, divided responsibilities (as in plural executive branches), restriction of each person to one office at a time, staggered elections (to keep changing the makeup of bodies like the state assembly). Though these features of the first state constitutions were modified later, the fear of government expressed in them was retained. The aim was to have as little government as possible, and Alexis de Tocqueville, when visiting America as late as the 1820s, thought its citizens had succeeded so well that they had almost no government. His prime exhibit on this matter was the New England town meeting, which did away with representatives by the exercise of direct democracy:

> In New England the majority act by representatives in conducting the general business of the state. It is necessary that it should be so. But in the townships, where the legislative and administrative action of the government is nearer to the governed, the system of representation is not adopted. There is no municipal council; but the body of voters, after having chosen its magistrates, directs them in everything that exceeds the simple and ordinary execution of the laws of the state.[2]

Though this arrangement would later be looked on as highly egalitarian and participatory, in the colonial period a group of religious and military leaders had established a ruling class that was deferred to, making the town system what has been described as "a speaking aristocracy in the face of a silent democracy."[3] Indeed, what Tocqueville observed of the states, in their freedom from an intrusive federal government, was even truer of the town meetings—that a social conformity resulted from the isolation of the unit from outside check, with a tendency toward a "despotism of the majority." Town meetings in these Congregational areas had supported measures like the exiling of Anne Hutchinson and Roger Williams, or the burning of witches and hanging of Quakers.

Since power in the meeting was less than it seemed, attendance in normal times was very low, "normally in the range of 10 to 30 percent of adult males."[4] Though attendance increased at times of controversy or crisis, the very scale of the business might cause the state legislature (in Massachusetts, the General Court) to assume responsibility. When the Revolution impended, real power was assumed by ad hoc committees of correspondence or committees of safety, and the town meetings, if used at all, had to be manipulated so that they would not get in the way. Even earlier (by the 1720s), manipulation of the meetings had led to the invention of a characteristically Bostonian device, the caucus—a secret earlier meeting to rig the speakers' lineup and concerted voting strategies. In 1763, two years before the crisis with Britain took hold, John Adams thought that the caucus had usurped the town meeting's major functions (like choosing the selectmen who administered the town's services):

This day [I] learned that the Caucus Club meets, at certain times, in the garret of Tom Dawes, the Adjutant of the Boston Regiment [so the militia was in on the scheming]. He has a large house, and he has a movable partition in his garret which he takes down, and the whole club meets in one room. There they smoke tobacco till you cannot see from one end of the garret to the other. There they drink flip, I suppose, and there they choose a moderator, who puts questions to the vote regularly; and selectmen, assessors, collectors, wardens, fire-wards, and representatives are regularly chosen, before they are chosen in the town. Uncle Fairfield Story, Ruddock, [Samuel] Adams, Cooper, and a *rudis indigestaque moles* [raw unshaped lump] of others are members. They send committees to wait on the merchant's club, and to propose and join in the choice of men and measures. Captain Cunningham says they have often solicited him to go to those caucuses; they have assured him benefit in his business, etc.[5]

Adams's grandson Charles Francis had a similarly realistic view of town meetings, which he contrasted with the idealistic view Tocqueville picked up from a few New Englanders:

Since De Tocqueville brought it into world-wide notice, this New England institution has been often described and infinitely lauded; but it may well be doubted whether one in ten of those who have philosophized over town meetings ever attended one, much more ever took part in one. Yet, without having done so, it is as difficult to understand the practical working of the system as it is to describe war without ever having served in an army or seen a battle. The ideal town meeting is one thing; the actual town meeting is apt to be a very different thing.[6]

But in the nineteenth century a romantic racism connected town meetings with a favorite preoccupation of historians in that period—the Aryan forest meetings which were supposed to have been the origins of democracy.[7] And even in our day the self-governmental halo around the very term "town meetings" has led to its being applied to almost any kind of forum, no matter how rigged, in which some people who are not officials do some speaking. Few people drew the lesson of the caucus from the meetings' colonial history—the lesson that attempts to prevent open government often lead to secret and even less accountable arrangements for manipulating the populace. Samuel Adams would take the caucusing strategy with him to the Continental Congress in 1774, and caucuses would have far more influence in our national history than did town meetings.[8]

The Continental Congress suggested that the colonies about to break away from England should set up provisional governments. These were soon made permanent by state constitutions which expressed the anti-government feelings of the time. These constitutions had weak executive branches (some of them diffusing responsibility in executive councils). They had short terms (usually of a year). They had rotation (what is now called term limits). Each of these features proved in time unworkable. Yet so important did short terms seem to the constitutions' framers that they imposed one year's service even on those representatives each state sent to the Continental Congress. This caused innumerable difficulties. Usually given brief notice of their appointment, the delegates took up part of their year getting ready to travel to the Congress. They sometimes had to rush back to take care of public or private business in their state (remember that the Revolutionary War was going on, and it surged into their areas while the delegates were away). They found excuses to leave early, without finishing their term (brief as it was).

The states' problem in getting delegates to the Congress and keeping them there is suggested by Governor George Clinton's frustration in New York. In 1778 he tried to send back to Congress New York's official ratifica-

tion of the continental constitution, the Articles of Confederation. At first
he asked delegate-elect Philip Livingston to take it with him to the Congress. That was on February 25:

> The great inconveniences which arise from the want of a more ample
> representation from the different states in Congress induce me to wish
> ours as complete as possible and therefore that it may be convenient
> for you to set out for Yorktown as early as the day you proposed when I
> last had the pleasure of seeing you.[9]

But by March 11 he had heard nothing from Livingston and had to write
him again, saying he was doing it at the request of the legislature, which
was disturbed at Livingston's nonresponsiveness. On March 27, Philip
Schuyler was appointed to take Livingston's place. Again the governor got
no answer, and had to repeat his plea: "The necessity there is of your
speedy attendance . . . induces me to . . . beg you to repair to Yorktown
with as much expedition as conveniently may be." This time Schuyler
wrote back—but only to say that his family feared a British approach and
he could not abandon them.

   This kind of pleading with delegates was almost as constant as the beg-
ging of militiamen that they would accept a bounty and serve in the war.
The result was a ragged and thin attendance at the Congress, which often
could not do business because it lacked a quorum. In 1783, when mutinous
Pennsylvania troops marched on Philadelphia, the Congress sitting there
could not order Washington to send a force to control them, since they did
not have a quorum to act in their official capacity. The members had to
send an informal request to him.[10] By 1785, when the body's fecklessness
under the Articles was becoming apparent, the Congress flared up at times
into official existence, only to fade again as people left it for home. They
went where they could do important business.

> Congress was plagued as much by absenteeism during the winter of
> 1786–1787 as during the previous year. No quorum could be obtained
> in the new federal year until January 17, when seven states were at last
> represented. The very next day attendance dropped, and not until Feb-
> ruary 2 was there another quorum. Attendance was sufficient to main-

tain a Congress for the next four months, but when a number of delegates left for the Convention in May Congress could not muster a quorum until July 4, when the North Carolinians and Georgians came up from Philadelphia.[11]

The absurdity of this situation can be properly weighed only when we remember that the Congress was both a legislative and an executive body, and therefore had to have year-round sessions—the result of the anti-government feeling that refused to create a separate executive body with powers of its own. Not only was the Congress always in peril of losing its official status for lack of numbers, but the rate of attendance also discriminated against some states.[12] Though each state had only one vote, it could send several delegates and, as a result, the bigger and wealthier states were the ones most likely to have delegates present whenever a quorum was reached. Also, by having more delegates on hand, these states filled the committees in disproportionate numbers or were given diplomatic tasks because of the absence (or the marginal representation) of men from the smaller states.

If short terms were making it hard for the Continental Congress to struggle back into existence, year by year, short terms and rotation of office were creating even more havoc at the state level, especially for the state governors. Fear of a strong executive, and hatred for the royal governors in their last days of power over the colonies, made the state constitutions opt for a weak executive. That would have caused some difficulty at any time, but the fact that the states were engaged in war made it all the more paralyzing. The one power most governors had was as commander of the militia, but their weakness in other areas made it hard for them to discharge this duty well. As we saw in the last chapter, most governors could not even appoint the officers under them—those were elected by the men. When to these factors was added a short term, sometimes not renewable, maintenance of effective war policies became extremely difficult. It is not surprising, then, that the most effective war governor was George Clinton, who was able to hold office from the very beginning of the war to its end because the New York constitution did not rotate that office.

A more typical condition was that of Virginia in the transition from

Patrick Henry's governorship to Thomas Jefferson's. Henry was elected the state's first governor in 1776, under the new constitution that weakened the governor by making him act in concert with an advisory council. Henry asked for certain wartime powers, and he was backed by some in the assembly but thwarted by others. Jefferson, writing five years later, at a time when he had conceived an intense hatred of Henry, said that the first governor aimed at a dictatorship (JW 252). Though few historians have agreed with him on that point, Henry clearly did chafe at the restrictions placed on his office, at a time when the assembly was distracted by the war, militias were not responding to the governor, and arms and supplies could not be acquired by strict and energetic policies. Henry pushed at the limits of his constitutional power, ignoring the council at times when swift action was needed (even to assemble the council often took many days). Through it all he maintained his popularity and was reelected twice, the limit set by the constitution. But then, by the rules of rotation, he had to go.

Jefferson was elected to succeed him, a man of very different temperament and of nice scruples in the wielding of power. He observed the letter of the law, refusing to act without the council, always using the plural of his executive authority, not the royal "we" but "the council and I." His legalisms infuriated some who had to work with him. General Friedrich von Steuben, sent to Virginia by Washington to organize southern defenses, advocated fortifying a narrow in the James River, to intercept any British naval force sailing toward the capital at Richmond. When he asked Jefferson for forty laborers to build a rampart, Jefferson said that he had no authority to take slaves away from their masters for the task, or to assign militiamen to manual labor, but that he would pass the request on to the assembly. The assembly, about to adjourn, did not act, with the result that Benedict Arnold's raiding force sailed up the James unimpeded and sacked Richmond.[13] Steuben asked Washington how he could do anything useful if the government could not supply any workers for an essential task: "The executive power is so confined that the governor has it not in his power to procure me forty negroes. . . ."[14]

Steuben was even more disgusted later, when he proposed to join the Virginia militia with Nathanael Greene's troops in a strike at General George Cornwallis's forces in North Carolina. Steuben had won approval

for this plan from the Marquis de Lafayette, his immediate military superior, as well as the approval of Washington, Richard Henry Lee, Nathanael
Greene, and the general (George Weedon) in charge of Virginia's militia
war board. Steuben went before Jefferson and his council to defend the action, but the executive turned it down for fear that the troops Steuben
asked for would take too many scarce guns out of the state. Since shortage
of guns was endemic in any case, Greene interpreted this as just another
state refusal to join in the Continental effort, and even General Weedon
criticized "the executive who have not an idea beyond local security"
(J 5.276). Dumas Malone, Jefferson's sympathetic biographer, admits, in
speaking of Steuben's plan, that "he must bear the blame for its unfortunate rejection."[15] Steuben now sought to get away from Jefferson and Virginia, convinced that his hands were tied so long as he remained in their
jurisdiction.

This occurred in 1780, during Jefferson's second year as governor.
When the state was invaded, Jefferson's sense of his own impotence made
him resolve not to ask for another term. To demands for more men and
more guns he could respond only with descriptions of his inability to do
more than issue calls to which no one responded. He wrote to Steuben:
"We can only be answerable for the orders we give and not for their execution. If they are disobeyed from obstinacy of spirit or want of coercion in
the laws it is not our fault" (J 5.120). To Lafayette, who was in Virginia
pleading for reinforcements to his troops, he had written: "I shall candidly
acknowledge that it is not in my power to do anything more than to represent to the General Assembly that unless they can provide more effectually
for the execution of the laws it will be vain to call on militia" (J 5.644).
The executive power was asking the legislature to execute the laws. Logically, all this can mean is that Jefferson is asking for more powers to be
given him by the legislative body—the very thing he had criticized Henry
for doing. Despite his own attacks on Henry for wanting the rule of one
man, Jefferson had become so desperate for a solution by one man that he
asked Washington to leave the rest of the war and rush back to defend his
native state:

Were it possible for this circumstance [the invasion of Virginia] to justify in Your Excellency a determination to lend us your personal aid, it

is evident from the universal voice that the presence of their beloved countryman, whose talents have been so long successfully employed in establishing the freedom of kindred states, to whose person they have still flattered themselves they retained some right, and have ever looked up as their dernier resort in distress, that your appearance among them I say would restore full confidence of salvation, and would render them equal to whatever is not impossible (J 6.33).

Jefferson admits that Washington has other concerns, but suggests that "the danger of this state and its consequence for the Union [may] be such as to render it best for the whole that you should repair to its assistance." Though the militia has failed to respond to Jefferson's calls upon it, if Washington returned to the state "the difficulty would then be how to keep men out of the field." Jefferson adds that he will, in several days, act on "a long declared resolution of relinquishing" the governorship, but that he hopes "as an individual citizen I should feel the comfortable effects of your presence."

Jefferson was not able to submit the resignation he had been looking forward to. His term ended on June 2, 1781, but that fell on a Saturday, so the assembly postponed its session till Monday. At dawn on Monday, however, a courier arrived with news that the British Colonel Banastre Tarleton was making a swift lunge toward Charlottesville (the temporary capital). Most (but not all) of the assemblymen escaped the town, and Jefferson escaped his mansion above the city, leaving Monticello to British occupation. Jefferson went to his home farther in the west, Poplar Forest. When enough of the assembly could be gathered behind the Blue Ridge Mountains to form a quorum, the body not only elected the ranking officer of the militia, Thomas Nelson, as the new governor, but also decreed an investigation of Jefferson's service in office, to see if the disasters that had befallen the state came in any measure from his negligence. To Jefferson's great personal distress, he had to defend his behavior before a specially created committee at the next formal session of the full assembly (J 6.89, 106–07, 135–37). He was exonerated there, but no one could say that he had been an effective governor. Governor Nelson assumed emergency powers, accomplishing what Jefferson said could not be done under the constitution. So far was Nelson from being hampered by his council that he went, despite its urgings, to be with the Virginia troops at the siege of Yorktown.[16] One cannot imagine Jefferson, with his unmilitary temper, doing any such thing.

Jefferson's flight from his home was used by his critics, then and later, to suggest that he showed cowardice. There is no evidence of that. But it is typical of the legalism he brought to office that he considered himself discharged from all further duty or action on the day his term ended. He did not seek out the other members of the council or the assembly to improvise any emergency action.[17] Jefferson went instantly into private life, in a retreat where he would be hard to reach, and put public cares behind him. (Notified that he had already been chosen to go to the Continental Congress, he turned down the appointment.) Contrast the behavior of John Rutledge, the governor of South Carolina. When that state was overrun by the British and its assembly was scattered, there was no legal way for him to be reelected governor, but he continued to serve nonetheless, assuming emergency powers.[18] It is true that the South Carolina legislature, on the point of breaking up without knowing when or where it could reassemble, granted to Rutledge as an individual, with only that part of the council (if any) he could find, "power to do everything necessary for the public good except the taking away the life of a citizen without public trial."[19] But this is exactly the kind of emergency power Jefferson had condemned Henry for entertaining. Thomas Burke of North Carolina also ignored his state's assembly to work more closely with the Continental Army.

To us it is surprising how often people urged or acknowledged the assumption of dictatorial powers in the Revolution. People at that time knew the office was an accepted part of the Roman Republic's constitution. In time of need, temporary powers were granted to an individual, who could take whatever measures he deemed necessary to the salvation of the state. Cincinnatus, the great model for George Washington, was a dictator. Julius Caesar was condemned not for having accepted a dictator's commission, but for refusing to surrender it at the end of the emergency. Madison called special grants of power given to the Pennsylvania executive "dictatorial."[20] Friends as well as critics of Washington said that he exercised a dictator's power at certain junctures of the war. When Edmund Randolph asserted that, Patrick Henry agreed with him:

> In making a dictator, we followed the example of the most glorious, magnanimous, and skilful nations. In great dangers, this power has been given. Rome had furnished us with an illustrious example. America found a person for that trust; she looked to Virginia for him. We gave a dictatorial power to hands that used it gloriously; and which were rendered more glorious by surrendering it up (R 9.983, 1058).

Henry, in fact, had called for Washington to take on the powers of a dictator in 1780, a year before Richard Henry Lee made the same proposal.

The reason people turned to thoughts of a dictatorship was that the state constitutions had made their governors too weak to manage the multiple crises of a war. The need for annual reelection, and for rotation in some of the states, broke the continuity of response to long-term problems. That is why many states came to strengthen their executives and remove or extend the rotation times. Jackson Turner Main, though he was an enthusiast for the first state constitutions, admits that support for the principle of rotation was undercut after six of the most effective wartime governors were forced to retire, at a time when the electorate would clearly have returned them to office.[21]

Once again, Virginia supplies an illustration. When Henry had to step down as governor, he went into the Virginia assembly, where many people still looked to him for leadership, allowing him to second-guess Jefferson's actions, to become an informal counter-authority to the man who replaced him. Jefferson envied Henry's popularity, which he felt was based on glibness—he wrote a year after leaving office that the man was "all tongue without head or heart" (J 6.205). Among Henry's "crooked schemes," Jefferson felt certain, was the move to censure him for his conduct as governor, even though George Nicholas had made the motion for an inquiry:

> The trifling body [Nicholas] who moved the matter was below contempt; he was more an object of pity. His natural ill will was the tool

worked by another hand. He was like the minners [minnows] which go in and out of the fundament of the whale. But the whale himself was discoverable enough by the turbulence of the water under which he moved (J 6.143).

That kind of rancor would not have arisen if the voters had been able to keep Henry in the place where they clearly wanted him, doing a job for which he was better suited than Jefferson was. But in the early days of the Revolution, too many men were called on to run their governments on anti-governmental principles. Even Jefferson, whose two-year attempt at governing his state had been so unhappy, learned an important lesson by 1783. In his 1776 draft for the original Virginia constitution, he had proposed a one-year term for the governor (J 1.359). But seven years later, in his draft for revising the constitution, he changed that term to five years (J 6.298).

By 1810, after eight years as president (including a second term, against which he had inveighed when the Constitution was being ratified), Jefferson had gone even further in the direction of Patrick Henry: "A strict observance of the written laws is *one* of the high duties of a good citizen, but it is not the highest. The laws of necessity, of self-preservation, of saving our country when in danger, are of higher obligation. To lose our country by a scrupulous adherence to written law, would be to lose the law itself, with life, liberty, property and all those who are enjoying them with us; thus absurdly sacrificing the end to the means" (JW 1231). He adduces a Revolutionary example for this doctrine—not his predecessor as governor, Patrick Henry (that would be going too far toward an old enemy), but his successor as governor, Thomas Nelson: "While the army was before York, the governor of Virginia took horses, carriages, provisions and even men by force, to enable that army to stay together till it could master the public enemy; and he was justified" (JW 1231).

Others had reached similar views long before Jefferson did:

By 1783 most people had perceived the perils of withholding essential executive powers and recognized the benefits that a strong government could bestow. . . . The revolutionary reaction against the monarchical principle had run its course, and would give way now to a resumption of authority.[22]

In 1780, Massachusetts retained rotation in the Declaration of Rights that preceded the Frame of Government, a declaration whose Article VII said, in its entirety:

> In order to prevent those who are vested with authority from becoming oppressors, the people have a right at such periods and in such manner as they shall establish by their frame of government, to cause their public officers to retire to private life; and to fill up vacant places by certain and regular elections and appointments.[23]

In 1992, George Will used that ringing proclamation to argue that adopting term limits now would be nothing but a return to our founding principles.[24] But Will seems not to have read further than the opening declaration. If he had, he would have noticed an odd thing. After saying that they have a *right* to put such a provision in their Frame of Government, the Massachusetts framers nowhere did it. This is a fine example of the American instinct for hanging on to anti-governmental principles even when they have proved impracticable. Those crafting the Declaration of Rights wanted to *believe* they believed in a creed, but they did not want to live by it.

The effort to run the Revolutionary War on anti-governmental principles was a noble but a feckless one. It displayed the range of values listed as anti-governmental in my introduction, most especially these:

1. *The amateur vs. the expert.* Since long tenure of power can corrupt, some believe that it is better to have men of pure intent, who may lack some professional skills, than to have bad men using power all too well. The amateurs may not have time to acquire effective managerial expertise, but neither will their integrity have been worn away by a long course of compromise. Jefferson was an embodiment of such principle when he refused to bend the law in order to give Steuben the forty men who might have prevented, and would surely have slowed, the invasion of Richmond.

2. *The populist vs. the elite.* By letting some men wield power with superior skill, one may dismiss the mass of humans as incapable of directing their own affairs. But exaggerated emphasis on this truth can prevent a society from performing necessary tasks. That is why Massachusetts, while

continuing to proclaim the importance of rotation (as part of its whole cluster of anti-governmental instincts), refused to put rotation of office into its constitution—and continued that omission after the war was over and peacetime conditions had returned. The gap between principle and practice was, as usual, ignored.

II.

Constitutional Myths

Though the myths of the Revolution have their own glamour, they cannot compete, so far as influence is concerned, with constitutional myths. The Constitution is always with us, as the basis of our laws. And the basis of the Constitution—lying beneath it, as it were—is its philosophy, as that has been explained to us over the years. We interpret the document in terms of concepts and words that are not in the document. Nowhere, for instance, does the Constitution mention checks, or balances, or separation of powers, or co-equal branches (or even branches) of government, or states' rights (or *any* rights in the original, unamended document).

The reason for this, we are assured, is not far to seek. There was such unanimity on these fundamentals of our constitutionalism that they went without saying in the Constitution—although what went without saying *was* (supposedly) being said all around the framing and discussing and ratifying of the document. Well, most of these items *were,* in fact, thoroughly aired, but by the enemies of the Constitution (known as Antifederalists) bringing up things *not* contained in the document: there were no real checks, no balances, no separation of powers, no equality of the branches, no protection of rights (whether those of the states or those of individuals).

How, over time, did all these attacks on the Constitution become descriptions of it? Was this a matter of the Federalists co-opting the rhetoric of their critics, or of the Antifederalists smuggling their values into a host body that was originally hostile to them? Actually, it was more a matter of anti-governmental values distorting the record, to make the government more acceptable by turning it against itself. This is one of the most successful mythologizings of a large historical sequence that can be found in all of history. What it has produced is an extraordinary consensus on what the Constitution was meant to do. There are six articles to this creed:

1. Our Revolution was fought by sovereign states which set up a government, under the Articles of Confederation, meant to guarantee their sovereignty.

2. When a stronger government had to be adopted (by the Constitution), it was kept from being too efficient, lest it entirely cancel the states' sovereignty.

3. To make sure that this self-checking would be self-perpetuating (like a machine that would run of itself) the government was articulated into three co-equal functional units.

4. This express competition of the governmental units encourages an ethos of competing power centers, pitting factions against themselves in a self-correcting process described by Madison in the defense of the Constitution he wrote with Alexander Hamilton and John Jay, *The Federalist*.

5. To make assurance doubly sure, a Bill of Rights was added to the original Constitution, restraining its powers even more strenuously.

6. Part of this Bill of Rights (Article II) guaranteed independence to the states by entrusting them with their own militias.

As I have found over the years in discussions with my students, these points are so easily assumed—or at least the first five are—as to need no defending or argument. They are the very constitutional air we breathe when we think at all about our government. They establish the entire texture of discussion, with the putatively beneficial effect of focusing all later debate. At least we have a common starting point. Whatever our later disagreements about specific laws or acts of government, we must all agree on these bedrock first principles.

Or must we? I take up the six articles of the creed in the next six chapters.

3.

Sovereign States

The term "sovereign states" rings proudly through our history. My own earliest memory of televised political conventions is of the roll call at the end, when the heads of delegations rose to declare that "The sovereign state of X casts its votes for . . ." Ronald Reagan liked to say that the states were more important than the federal government since they had preceded and formed it.[1] John Adams, who thought that *should* have been the case, lamented, during the actual process of declaring independence, that it was not happening that way. A month before the Declaration of Independence was signed, he wrote to Patrick Henry:

> It has ever appeared to me that the natural course and order of things was this: for every colony to institute a government; for all the colonies to confederate, and define the limits of the continental Constitution; then to declare the colonies a sovereign state, or a number of confederate sovereign states; and last of all, to form treaties with foreign powers. But I fear we cannot proceed systematically . . . (CC 1.471).

What actually happened is better described by President Lincoln than by President Reagan:

> Our states have neither more nor less power than that reserved to them in the Union by the Constitution—no one of them ever having been a state *out* of the Union. The original ones passed into the Union even before they cast off their British colonial dependence; and the new ones each came into the Union directly from a condition of de-

pendence, excepting Texas. And even Texas, in its temporary independence, was never designated a state (L 2.255).

Lincoln had important predecessors agreeing with him—James Wilson, Elbridge Gerry, Nathan Dane, John Quincy Adams, Joseph Story, Daniel Webster, and Andrew Jackson.[2] Nonetheless, most people today assume that Reagan was right. They can argue that (1) some states drew up governments even before the Declaration of Independence was issued, (2) the states formed the Continental Congress by sending their delegates to it, and (3) the states directed their delegates to vote for independence. Pauline Maier devoted an entire book to the claim that these state instructions to the Congress were the real declarations of independence, not only more important but better argued than Jefferson's later document.[3]

But the three points can be answered thus: (1) Most colonial assemblies did not set up governments before the Declaration of Independence—revolutionary committees did it, *on the instructions of the Continental Congress*. (2) The delegates sent by the committees were instructed to consider relations with England in a *joint* way for *joint* action. (3) Their votes did not declare any one colony, or all of them, independent prior to the joint vote of the "*United* Colonies." Most instructions referred to the United Colonies. But Connecticut called them "the United American Colonies," and Delaware recommended independence "for promoting the liberty, safety, and interests of America."[4] The colonies did not act, so far as independence was concerned, singly but in concert. The entity that was declared independent was the united body of states, as we learn from the most careful study of the historical sequence, prepared by Richard Morris. He concludes that the states "were created by the Continental Congress, which preceded them in time and brought them into being."[5] Lincoln was right, after all, not Reagan.

This is how Congress declared independence for the entire set of colonies: "We therefore the representatives of the *United* States of America in *General* Congress assembled . . . declare that these *united* colonies are and of right ought to be free and independent states . . ." (emphasis added). Those who believe in the states' sovereignty would make "free and independent states" mean that they are independent *of each other*. But Lincoln rightly said that "the object plainly was not to declare their independence of *one another*, or of the *Union*; but directly the contrary, as their mutual pledge, and their mutual action, before, at the time, and afterwards, abundantly show" (L 2.225–26). Benjamin Rush had said the same thing in 1786: "No individual state as such has any claim to independence; she is independent only in a union with her sister states in Congress."[6] The Declaration ends with the words "we mutually pledge *to each other* our lives, our fortunes, and our sacred honor." And in declaring their rights, as freed and independent states, they specified the "full power to levy war, conclude peace, contract alliances, establish commerce, and to do all other acts and things which independent states may of right do." This did not mean that each state, taken singly, had such powers, as their actions demonstrated. The states did not sign thirteen different treaties with France for the waging of the war or thirteen different treaties with England for ending the war.

Well, it might be answered, perhaps the confusions of plunging into and through a revolution led to acts that were not legally tidy; but the states made clear their own legal status when they began joining the Confederation drawn up under a set of Articles in 1777. The mere fact that they took separate votes to *enter* the Confederation shows that they were not already *in* it. The full thirteen states did not ratify till 1781. In that interval, therefore, some states were in the Confederation and some out of it, refuting Lincoln's point that none of them ever had a separate existence. Those outside the Confederation certainly *look* like separate entities.

On the other hand, they did not *act* as if they were. While they debated the terms of their union, they acted in conjunction with the other states. They were, after all, waging a war, with members of all the states (including those that had not ratified the Articles) serving in the Continental Army, with delegates voting in the Congress, submitting to the measures taken by the Congress. They did not lead separate lives. The disagreement was over the conditions spelled out in the Articles—more specifically, about the claims of some states to certain western lands. The debate over ratification was a way of negotiating those disputes within the Union, not a bid for separate existence outside the Union.

But the Articles themselves give what looks like a definitive answer to the question of the states' sovereignty. The document did not set up a single government. It says at the outset that it is no more than "a firm league of friendship" (Article III), in which "each state retains its sovereignty" (Article II). People might talk about divided sovereignty in the later Constitution, but sovereignty in the Articles is single and undivided, and it resides wholly, solely, in the states—or so the document claims. But were the states in the Confederation actually sovereign?

There are many theories of sovereignty, with much of the dispute involving the source of sovereignty (God under some old theories, the people in most modern ones), its indivisibility, its delegation in leagues or confederations. But in practical terms the sovereign is the *supremus* (the word's Latin root), the highest, the authority subordinated to no other authority. Lincoln, as usual, puts the matter succinctly and indisputably: "What is a 'sovereignty' in the political sense of the term? Would it be far wrong to define it 'a political community without a political superior'?" (L 2.256).

That definition makes our task easy in determining whether the states under the Articles were sovereign. Did they in fact have a political superior? Could they do all the things we think of as appertaining to an independent nation? Could they make war? Could they make treaties? Could they coin money? Could their justice system cover all crimes committed in their territory? Could they create a navy? Could they create their own armies? Could they create their own postal system? Could they subordinate the military to their own civil officers? Could they refuse to recognize other jurisdictions' rulings? Could they set their own qualifications for citizenship? The answer to all of those questions is no. If you went to the citizens of a sovereign nation and said that they were going to be deprived of any *one* of these powers, they would rightly complain that they had lost independent authority as a nation. To take them *all* away at one swoop would, one must feel, make a mockery of any claims to sovereignty.

Yet this is not the worst of it, this saying what the states could *not* do. An even greater affront was the list of things they *must* do, whether they wished to or not. They *must* go to war if seven states told them to. They *must* contribute to that war, or to any peacetime costs, in the proportion set by others. They *must* honor other nations' claims if seven states accepted them under treaty. They *must* submit their border claims to binding arbitration controlled by others. They *must* stay in the Union unless all twelve other states gave them permission to change the Union or dissolve it. They *must* accept new members into the Union if nine of the other states told them to. All these compelled actions could be thrust upon them if they were in a dissenting minority. For most actions, a simple majority of the states, each given one vote, could bind the whole Union. That meant that huge New York could be forced to actions it opposed if small states like Delaware and Rhode Island were part of a seven-state majority requiring the actions.

Then what did Article II mean when it asserted that the states were sovereign? Not much. The proof is that the man who drafted Article II and worked for its inclusion in the draft, Thomas Burke of North Carolina, went back to his state and urged it not to ratify the Articles, since they denied sovereignty to North Carolina *even though the document contained his own article in his own words*. Merrill Jensen, in what used to be the standard work on its subject, *The Articles of Confederation*, makes Burke the hero of the "radicals" who thwarted conservatives like John Dickinson in the Congress that drew up the Articles.[7] But Burke's principal opponent on Article II was the "radical" Richard Henry Lee, and Jensen does not examine the grounds on which Burke asked that North Carolina reject the Confederacy.[8]

In a letter preceding his return to his home state, Burke ticked off the ways the Confederacy denies sovereignty to North Carolina—by denying it the right to set the norms of citizenship, to make election rules, to coin money, to collect duties, to enter into treaties, to raise a navy, to form partial alliances, to deal with Indian nations (CC 2.552–58). Though Burke was willing to enter an alliance with other sovereigns for mutual defense, he did not think that should mean the entire surrender of independent judgment on matters of war and peace: "wherever a war should be declared before actual invasion, or commencement or threatening of some actual hostilities, any state ought to be at liberty to renounce the war and become a neutral power" (CC 2.554). Nor could he acquiesce in the denial of each state's right to form its own commercial treaties with other sovereigns: "I can perceive no reason for a power in any common council which can restrain the commercial or other peaceful intercourse of the states, among themselves or separately with foreign powers" (CC 2.554). Although the

Articles said—five times, no less—that the Union shall be perpetual, Burke opposed "all pretence for a continuance of Congress after the war is concluded" (CC 2.557).

Burke initially persuaded the North Carolina assembly to reject the Articles as a whole—the state consented to only five of the articles proposed, and parts of another two, while rejecting six articles entirely and two partially, in order to protect its "sovereign independence."[9] Nine months later, under the pressures of war and of other states' action, the assembly surrendered its objections (R 1.124–25). Burke himself, when elected governor of North Carolina, became convinced of the need for greater central authority—we met him in the first chapter wielding dictatorial powers and cooperating closely with the Continental Army. His experience as a governor destroyed his sense of the virtue of the people, and he ended his life as "a hopeless reactionary" advocating a hereditary nobility.[10] But that does not mean that he was not the best interpreter of his own amendment at the time when he drew it up and rejected the bulk of the surrounding document as inconsistent with it. That it was his own conception emerges from the fact that he at first had trouble getting anyone to second it, and he never did persuade Virginia or New Hampshire to vote for it (CC 2.346). Thus Jensen's argument that Burke's second article effectively guaranteed sovereignty to the states goes against Burke's own judgment of its effect.

Given all the powers invested in the Confederacy, powers essential to any independent state, one naturally wonders why the states were willing to maintain union on such terms. If they had a prickly desire to remain sovereign, why didn't they? There are two answers to that question. First of all, they knew that union was a necessity forced upon them by war. They had no chance of defying England one by one. After they declared their independence as united states, they had to sink or swim together, and management of the war called for central decision-making powers over strategy, the fielding and provisioning of armies, and the maintenance of consistent policy. The marks of war are all over the Articles. In fact, as the war progressed, the Articles were read in such a way that wider and wider powers over the war were given to Congress and its agents (committees, generals, and supply officers).

The second answer to the question of the states' willingness to abide in the Confederacy is that they felt they had provided sufficient checks on any abuse of power by the Congress—unicameralism, the omission of a separate executive or judiciary, short terms of office, rotation, recall, and the requirement of super majorities or unanimity for drastic decisions. It may seem strange to us, conditioned as we are by misunderstandings of the later Constitution, to think of unicameralism as a check. We have been taught that a great check on our Congress is the separation of the Senate from the House. But the framers of the Articles did not think of constitutional machinery as checking itself. For them, the only real check was provided by the people. Their control of the single-chamber Congress came from the fact that delegates to it were still tied so closely to the states they represented. Their terms were short, they were issued instructions from the state assembly, and they could be recalled at any moment. To provide another chamber, based on some other principle of representation, would be to remove it in some degree from this instant and constant control. Some states had upper houses based on property representation, or on election by the lower house. This was considered too aristocratic for a national body outside the traditions of the local governments. So even those who were worried by the "democratic" legislature of Pennsylvania, which had a single chamber, were happy to have only one accountable legislature above the states.

The same logic led to the elimination of a separate executive body. John Dickinson's first draft of the Articles contained a Council of State, with one member for each state, chosen by the delegates at the Congress, whose principal function would be to handle interim business when the Congress was not in session or could not maintain a quorum. The fact that the state assembly would not directly appoint these delegates told against this measure, and so did the fear of a "runaway" executive wielding power in the absence of the Congress. The final draft of the Articles dealt with the problem of intersession activity by appointing ad hoc committees to serve as the information nexus till Congress could reconvene. The fecklessness of the committees forced Congress into the attempt to stay, as much as possible, in year-round session, with all the problems of maintaining quorums that this entailed.

An independent judiciary had to be rejected on the same grounds that excluded the executive. A body of judges removed from control by the state assemblies, sitting at periods when Congress might not be able to muster a quorum, could be dangerous, especially since the states had not yet formed a body of law to replace the Crown procedures. A court would, in effect, be making laws as well as applying them. It was better to keep judicial proceedings to a minimum, at least at the outset, and commit them, as well as executive tasks, to the Congress. Thus Article IX gave Congress the power to decide on boundary disputes between the states and to set up arbitration procedures for other contested matters between them. The Congress could set up special courts to adjudicate prize claims from ships captured in war, but these were ad hoc courts, not an independent body. They were little more than committees exercising Congress's legislative right to judge.

Short terms and rotation, at a time when these were about to prove impractical at the state level, were felt to be a necessity for controlling delegates far from the local scene. No term of office under the Articles exceeded a year, and delegates could serve only three years in any six. Thus, though seven states could commit the whole union to war, second thoughts at home, or the suspicion that a delegate had exceeded his instructions, could lead to the instant recall and replacement of a delegation in the majority, defeating the war measure. The president of the Congress was literally the presider over it, more like our Speaker of the House than like a president under the Constitution. Though he had to be elected by the delegates in the Congress, this presider's power was strictly controlled by rotation, limiting him to one year in office followed by two years out of it.

That all these checks were powerful is clear from their operation once the Articles were ratified. The states could and did hamstring the Congress, by their inaction as well as by their action, by inadvertence as well as by intent. This led to the seizure of irregular powers in the war, and to frustrations in peacetime that led to the overthrow of the Articles by the entirely illegal proceedings of the Constitutional Convention. The Articles had sealed off any realistic possibility of their own reformation.

How, it may be asked, can so weak a body as the Confederacy be called sovereign? The question confuses de jure sovereignty with de facto strength. There are weak sovereign states; there are strong nonsovereign bodies. The states had the ability to hamper the Confederacy in its exercise of sovereign activities, but they had no right to assume those sovereign activities themselves.

Preventing the exercise of a right of sovereignty does not *remove* the right. For instance: the requisite number of states could prevent the Confederacy from declaring a new war, but that right remained intact for other cases, and no one state could assume the right for itself. War-making, a sovereign activity, resided in the Congress and nowhere else. Its nonexercise did not create a right elsewhere, in a minority of Congress, or in the states (singly or in some ad hoc combination). The right was absolutely denied the states, and—as Lincoln said—that denied them sovereignty, the freedom from having any superior legal entity above them. The same was true of all the other sovereign rights lodged in the Confederacy and denied the states—the coinage of money, the maintenance of treaties and diplomacy, the setting of terms for citizenship, for elections, for postal communication.

In much of the discussion of the Articles, a rather simple-minded equation is assumed: sovereignty = power. We shall find the same confusion darkening discussion of the Constitution. Sovereignty gives the body it is invested with the authority, in Locke's terms, to "conclude" the whole—to make determinations for the entire political body.[11] The idea that sovereignty is indivisible is not vague or mystical, but practical and observable. There cannot be two powers to conclude the whole. If one has done that, there is no room for another to do it in a contrary way. Other powers are powers to conclude the part, not the whole—and that is not sovereignty. It is just power. Sovereign power is not absolute power. It can submit to conditions, but the conditions are not imposed by some higher government. If that were the case, the higher body would be the sovereign. It is conditioned by the consent of the components within the state, established by its frame of government. (In a divine-right monarchy, the government is conditioned by the consent of the citizens to God's will.) Such limitation is not a removal of sovereignty. The British monarchy was, at the time of the Revolution, a sovereign body (king-in-Parliament), even though it was a constitutional and not an absolute monarchy. And the United States is "a state" in a way that no state is—an independent body with the right to do all the things a sovereign state can do.

If we look back to the list of values mentioned in my introduction, it is clear that the Confederation sponsored the governmental, not the anti-governmental attitude. By many measures, the Confederation was not efficient. But it was *on the side of* efficiency, and it was certainly at odds with the counter-value (spontaneity). It justified its actions in the name of efficiency, and expanded its powers in the process. In the same way, it was regulatory, not voluntary. It had the right to exact contributions of men, provisions, and money, in the proportions it set up, no matter how hard it was to enforce that right (mainly from the lack of an executive). But this great flaw in the Articles did not mean that the Confederacy was not a sovereign body. Nations have good or bad constitutions, workable or clumsy ones, just or unjust ones—yet they are all sovereign. Constitutional monarchy may improve on absolute monarchy in all those terms, and many others, yet both forms of government are sovereign forms.

Why has it been so difficult for Americans to accept the obvious fact that the states in the Union are not sovereign? They may answer that Article II in the first constitution, like the Tenth Amendment in our second one, reserves certain powers to the state. But neither of these reserve *sovereign* powers—powers to make war or peace, to form commercial treaties with other nations, to raise armies or navies, to control the rules of citizenship, to coin money, and so on. Benjamin Rush wrote in 1786: "The people of America have mistaken the meaning of the word sovereignty; hence each state pretends to be sovereign. In Europe it is applied only to those states which possess the power of making war or peace."[12] Lois Schwoerer, the historian of English militia law, writes, "That military authority expresses sovereignty as no other function of government is axiomatic."[13] This makes Article VI emphatic on the point of sovereignty:

> No vessels of war shall be kept up in time of peace by any state, except such number only as shall be deemed necessary *by the United States in Congress assembled* for the defense of such state or its trade. Nor shall any body of forces be kept up by any state in time of peace, except such number only as, in *the judgment of the United States in Congress* assembled, shall be deemed requisite to garrison the forts necessary for the defense of such state . . . (emphasis added).

Whether a state could keep up a military force did not lie within its authority. Though this article forbids a standing army to each state, it goes on to permit—nay, require—a militia, and to set the standard for its maintenance:

> But every state shall always keep up a well regulated and disciplined militia, sufficiently armed and accoutered, and shall provide and constantly have ready for use, in public stores, a due number of field pieces and tents and a proper quantity of arms, ammunition and camp equipage.

The language is prescriptive—"shall always . . . shall . . . constantly." The states are not free to decide they may *not* want a militia. Sovereign control of military policy is thus denied them.

Some seem to confuse the idea of sovereignty with absolute power, irresistible in all areas. But every just sovereignty recognizes human rights. There are democratic sovereigns, aristocratic ones, monarchical ones. They arrange for different distributions of power in the working of society. The question is: who has the last word in deciding on that arrangement of power? Not necessarily the first word, or the most frequent word, but the binding final word that "concludes the whole." The individual state was not the final arbiter of its own right, even under the Articles—much less under the Constitution. I shall be returning to this question when we look at Madison's views on sovereignty, but here it is enough to note that people are as reluctant to admit that states were not sovereign as they are to admit that minutemen did not win the Revolution, or that rotation of office was a Revolutionary ideal that failed. It is the whole cluster of values in the anti-governmental pattern that makes them unwilling to accept the fact that the larger government is sovereign, not the smaller units. But Thomas Burke knew better.

So far I have considered the question of state sovereignty under the Articles. If it was lacking there, then—*a fortiori*—it should be even less discoverable under the Constitution, which set up a stronger federal apparatus. But so nimble are the minds of those who cannot give up their dream of state sovereignty that they manage to find an item that languished under the laxer Articles somehow staging a comeback under the increased authority of the Constitution. The new powers of the federal government could not cancel state sovereignty since its authority was cleverly designed to be deliberately inefficient. Or was it? It is time to address that dogma.

4.

Checking Efficiency

Americans are proud of their government's ingenious system of checks and balances, which keeps it from being despotically efficient. Contriving such inefficiency is taken as a marvel of political engineering. But one wonders why it took such effort to accomplish fecklessness. That was what the framers began with, and they did not like what they had. The complaint about the Articles system was that *it* was inefficient. How could one cure that problem by creating more inefficiency? Jefferson made it clear that the Articles would, if continued, be "terminating in anarchy, as necessarily consequent to *inefficiency*" (J 16.492, emphasis added). Washington said that a new government was needed, one with energy and dispatch to oppose the states' "thirst for power and the bantling [bastard]—I had like to have said monster—sovereignty which have taken such fast hold of the states individually."[1]

Actually, we do not have to go further than the Constitution's first words to see that it was not set up to attain inefficiency: "We the people, in order to form *a more perfect* union. . . ." In the eighteenth century, "perfect" still had its root sense of "completed." A perfect law was one whose enactment had run the full authorizing course (which was referred to as "perfecting the bill"). A perfect baby had all its parts. A perfect man had completed his maturing. A perfect report covered all of its subject. Jefferson said that the Confederation was like an incomplete man, one without legs that would support him:

> Our new constitution, of which you speak, has succeeded beyond what I apprehended it would have done. I did not at first believe that eleven

states out of thirteen [the number that had ratified as he wrote] would have consented to a plan consolidating them so much into one. A change in their disposition, which had taken place since I left them [for Paris], had rendered this consolidation necessary—that is to say, had called for a federal government which could walk upon its own legs, without leaning for support on the state legislatures (J 14.420).

As a minister in France, negotiating trade under the Articles, Jefferson was sensible of the Confederation's failings in foreign policy:

You see that my primary object in the formation of treaties is to take the commerce of the states out of the hands of the states, and to place it under the superintendence of Congress, so far as the imperfect provisions of our constitution will admit, and until the states shall by new compact make them *more perfect* (J 8.231, emphasis added).

In 1785, two years before the Constitutional Convention met in Philadelphia, Jefferson was already saying: "The want of power in the federal head was early perceived, and foreseen to be the flaw in our constitution which might endanger [risk] its destruction" (J 7.630).

A perfect state had, from the time of Aristotle, been one that had all its necessary parts and could be self-sustaining.[2] The task the drafters of the Constitution took up was the addition of necessary parts that had been lacking, especially a separate executive branch. Jefferson, remembering his own service in the Continental Congress, deplored the way Congress was crippled by involvement in all the executive details of running a war. It had to attend to the clothing of the army, the storing of provisions, and other petty matters that impeded devotion to its properly legislative tasks:

Nothing is so embarrassing [hampering] nor so mischievous in a great assembly as the details of execution. The smallest trifle of that kind occupies as long as the most important act of legislation, and takes place of everything else. Let any man recollect, or look over the files of Congress, he will observe the most important propositions hanging over from week to week and month to month, till the occasions have past them, and the thing never done (J 11.679).

The Articles had merely perpetuated the nature of the Congress that drew them up. Thomas Burke, serving in the wartime Congress from North Carolina, complained of "the *imperfect* constitution of Congress which cannot reject any business addressed to them," so that "much time is spent on unimportant business" (CC 4.367–68, emphasis added). Robert Morris wrote: "No man living can attend the daily deliberations of Congress and do executive parts of business at the same time" (CC 2.178). John Adams told his wife (July 11, 1776) that he, like many other representatives, lacked executive skills in "military or commercial branches of knowledge," yet they were expected to perform well in all those branches.

Clearly what was needed, both for domestic and for foreign affairs, was a separate executive. Madison used an efficiency argument for creating "separate departments" of government: "The limited powers now vested in Congress are frequently mismanaged from the want of such a distribution of them" (M 9.319). We have been taught that the separation of powers was meant to provide mutual checks, with consequent inefficiency in operation. But the primary need, for those observing the Confederation's feebleness, was for a separation in order to *achieve* efficiency. That is why the executive was recommended for its "energy," as a tool for getting things *done*. Madison described the separated powers as complementary, not conflicting, "to unite a proper energy in the executive with a proper stability in the legislative departments" (M 10.207).

A separate judiciary was called for as well, again in the name of efficiency. For Congress to set up ad hoc arbitration boards, courts that came and went, was a clumsy process. Having a stable and continuing body of expert judges was far more effective. The eighteenth century was learning again from Adam Smith a dictum that was as old as Plato, that the best way to organize human endeavor is by a division of labor. James Madison certainly did not think he was framing a government to be ineffectual: "Energy in government is essential to that security against external and internal danger, and to that prompt and salutary execution of the laws, which enter into the very definition of good government" (F 37.233).

The concept of separate powers as mutual checks rested on the existence of different sectors of European society (estates), each of which needed its distinct representatives—in England, for instance, the Crown, the lords (spiritual and temporal), and commoners. But America does not have different orders in that sense. The same class of voters and the same class of candidates deal with every part of our government. Our separate departments do not exist by having different origins in the community, but by a distinction in their *functions*, in what they *do*. The executive is designed to show energy by "secrecy and dispatch." The legislature is to provide deliberation. And the bicameral internal division of the legislature is also called for to achieve different goals. Madison said that the Senate, the stable "anchor" of Congress, has the institutional memory and continual membership needed to handle relations with other nations, where long-term agreements are desired. For this purpose, the Senate has a higher age requirement than the House, six-year terms for its members, and a staggered election rate that turns out no more than a third of the body in any election. That is why treaty ratification and consent to diplomatic appointments are assigned to the Senate, whose role Madison described in *Federalist* No. 63:

> Without a select and stable member of the government, the esteem of foreign powers will not only be forfeited by an unenlightened and variable policy, proceeding from the causes already mentioned, but the national councils will not possess that sensibility to the opinion of the world which is perhaps not less necessary in order to merit than it is to obtain its respect and confidence (F 63.422).

The House, by contrast, was designed with lower age requirements and shorter terms to reflect domestic concerns, especially over the economy. It was given budgetary priority. Jefferson recognized the usefulness of this division of labor:

> I like much the general idea of framing a government which should go on of itself peaceably without needing continual recurrence to the state legislatures. I like the organization of the government into Legislative, Judiciary and Executive. I like the power given the Legislature to levy taxes; and for that reason solely approve of the greater house being chosen by the people directly. For though I think a house chosen by them will be very illy qualified for the union, for foreign nations, etc., yet this evil does not weigh against the good of preserving invio-

late the fundamental principle that the people are not to be taxed but by representatives chosen immediately by themselves (J 12.439–40).

Once their separate functions are assigned them, the departments of government may, *precisely in the name of efficiency*, have to fight off encroachment on those functions. Should the executive try to legislate, or the legislature try to execute, they would be returning to the inefficient confusion of functions that the Articles created. They check each other in that sense. But opposition is not encouraged for its own sake. If the separate departments' interaction slows any process, it is not because stalling is a virtue. If the executive vetoes a bill, for instance, he is not in theory making law himself, but suggesting that the execution of the proposed law may pose problems, which the Congress should reconsider (and, if it still thinks well of the bill, pass it by an override). If the Congress refuses consent on a treaty or an ambassadorial appointment, it is justified on the supposition that deliberation may contribute something that executive "energy" overlooked. The rationale for the arrangements is functional. To meet the objection that the checks in his system were, as Patrick Henry put it, mere "paper checks," since different estates were not represented in the different departments, Madison said that pride of office, of the assigned *function*, will keep the spheres separate: "Ambition must be made to counteract ambition. The interest of the man must be connected with the constitutional rights of the place" (F 51.349). Keeping the boundaries clear will maintain the proper functions.

The modern cult of checks as the primary virtue of the Constitution was not shared by its framers. In fact, Hamilton said that checks were a fatal characteristic of the Articles, in which the states checked each other's action (F 11.68). The term "check" does not occur in the Constitution itself, either as noun or verb, and Madison uses it only nine times in *The Federalist*. Of these uses, only five refer to governmental machinery—two to an interdepartmental check (F 48.335, 51.349), three to a bicameral check (F 62.417, 419, 63.425). Once Madison refers to the *voters'* check on House members by biennial election (F 53.365), and once to the federal government's check *on the states'* trading powers (F 44.302).

That last use of a check to control the states should give pause to those who equate modern "federalism" with states' rights. The modern (and decentralizing) Federalist Society uses Madison's silhouette as its identifying symbol, but Madison did not go to the Constitutional Convention to defend the states—more nearly to destroy them. From the minute he entered the Continental Congress, he had resented and resisted the ability of the states to stymie general action. In 1781 he tried to amend the Articles so that Congress could use the army and navy against states not meeting their financial requisitions, a cause he was still promoting six years later on the way to the Constitutional Convention (M 3.19). As long as the nation tried to operate under the Articles, he was convinced, "the states will continue to invade the national jurisdiction, to violate treaties and the law of nations, and to harass each other with rival and spiteful measures dictated by mistaken views of interest" (M 9.384). He pushed with fervor for the extra-legal activities of the Constitutional Convention, which evaded the Articles themselves and the instructions of the states sending delegates to it. He prepared for the convention a "Virginia plan" that rained blow after blow on the states. He explained to friends how the states would be curbed:

1. They would not have equal representation as states, even in the Senate.

2. Their legislatures would not elect senators.

3. Their legislatures would not ratify the Constitution (as they had the Articles). Separate conventions would be drawn up, since "a ratification must be obtained from the people, and not merely from the ordinary authority of the legislatures" (M 9.385).

4. They would not control delegates by paying them from state funds.

5. They would have over them "a government which, instead of operating on the states, should operate without their intervention on the individuals composing them" (M 10.207).

6. They would not have the veto given them in the Articles by a requirement of unanimity to change basic law.

7. They could no longer claim sovereignty, however fancifully, under a structure that "will at once support a due *supremacy* of the national authority and leave in force the local authorities, so far as they can be *subordinately* useful" (M 9.369, emphasis added).

8. The federal government would have a "negative in all cases whatsoever on the local legislatures" (M 9.318).

9. For enforcing federal laws within a state, "the right of coercion should be expressly declared" (M 9.385).

Madison did not get his way on all these points. The small states refused to accept a new government unless at least one chamber gave them an equal vote with the large states. The legislatures retained their right to elect delegates to that chamber. But the measure Madison argued for vigorously to the end, with regard to which he was most bitterly disappointed when it failed, was number 6 in the original Virginia plan: "to negative all laws passed by the several states contravening, in the opinion of the national legislature, the articles of Union, and to call forth the force of the Union against any member of the Union failing to fulfill its duty under the articles thereof" (M 10.16). This is not an incidental part of his plan, but vital to it. Without such a "defensive power," Madison feared the states would reassert themselves and cause the same havoc they had under the Articles. They "will be continually sensible of the abridgement of their power, and be stimulated by ambition to resume the surrendered portion of it" (M 10.211).

The doggedness with which Madison fought for the veto as a sine qua non of his plan has embarrassed most of his biographers, as Charles Hobson established in the best treatment of the matter.[3] Madison even risked offending some by comparing his absolute veto with the royal veto that Jefferson had complained of in the Declaration of Independence (M 9.370). Madison said that the only difference between the two vetoes would be the democratic nature of the federal Congress exercising it in America (M 10.214). His comprehensive study of confederacies throughout history had convinced him that they failed when they did not have this veto power at their center (M 10.209–10). At the convention he described his veto as the binding principle of the whole system, comparing it to the force of gravity in the universe: "To recur to the illustrations borrowed from the planetary system, this prerogative of the general government is the great pervading principle that must control the centrifugal tendency of the states, which without it will continually fly out of their proper orbits and destroy the whole harmony of the political system" (M 10.41).

At the start of the Constitutional Convention, Madison had let his Virginia colleagues soften his call for a veto on all state laws to one that would cancel *unconstitutional* laws, but at the earliest possible moment he strengthened his position again. When Charles Pinckney moved for a veto on all "improper" state laws, Madison seconded, praising "an *indefinite* power to negative legislative acts of the states as absolutely necessary to a *perfect* system" (M 10.41, emphasis added). For a while the concept of the veto was supported by the convention, but then smaller states objected to the power this would give to more populous states (the states' equal votes had not yet been established). Others disliked the veto's resemblance to the Crown negative. And some were put off by the sheer volume of work it would require from Congress. To reconsider every state law would place an intolerable burden on the congressional calendar. Furthermore, it was felt that the supremacy clause would allow the Supreme Court to void unconstitutional state laws. Madison was not happy with what he considered this halfway attitude (M 10.211). He left Philadelphia fearful that the new Constitution would be doomed by its lack of the veto, and he wrote a long letter to Jefferson arguing that the veto was the real center of his plan (M 10.209–14). He gave in this letter a sketch of what would become his most famous *Federalist*, No. 10, on the extent of territory in a republic. That essential part of his thought is contained in the section arguing for the veto—a point that is not often enough remembered in analyses of that Number (see Chapter 6). Despite the opposition the Constitution had aroused, even in what he considered its weakened form, he returned to the effort at giving Congress the oversight of state laws when he introduced the first amendments to the Constitution (see Chapter 7).

Madison at this stage intended to deprive the states of any claim to sovereignty. After all, a body that cannot make its own laws except at the sufferance of a higher body, and which can be coerced by that body, is not the master of its own domain. He used the classic argument that sovereignty is single since there can be no paramountcies under a paramountcy, no *imperia in imperio*. Speaking of the veto on state law, he said "without such a check in the whole over the parts, our system involves the evil of *imperia in imperio*" (M 10.209). And his veto would involve no *mutual* check, would leave no room for the states to check the federal power. His federal veto would work in only one direction.

But the convention did not give Madison his much-desired veto. Does that mean that the states, under the Constitution as it was finally drafted and then ratified, retained some form of sovereignty? The critics of the document, who were able to persuade themselves (against the evidence) that the states had been sovereign under the Articles, did not think they could retain that sovereignty under the Constitution. The Antifederalist pamphleteering was one long cry that the states were being asked to give up their sovereignty. When James Wilson suggested that the states would retain some kind of diminished sovereignty, his opponents answered that they were being bamboozled. There is no such thing as a diminished sovereignty. If it is reduced, it is not sovereignty. If you give away some of it, you lose all of it. This did not occur to most of them when the Confederation exercised exclusive power over war, diplomacy, and coinage. But they rediscovered the indivisibility of sovereignty as a way of staving off the Constitution:

> For the idea of two sovereignties existing within the same community is a perfect solecism.
> —"Impartial Examiner" (AF 5.178)

> It is a solecism in politics for two co-ordinate sovereignties to exist together.
> —"Centinel" (Samuel Bryan) (AF 2.131)

> I never heard of two supreme co-ordinate powers in one and the same country before.
> —William Grayson (R 9.1170)

In his private writings, Madison too said that the Constitution did not allow the states to retain sovereignty. The lack of a veto made it hard for the Congress to enforce the subordination—but that had been true of the Articles, which also deprived the states of sovereign powers. Reporting to Jefferson after the draft was completed, Madison said of the convention: "It was generally agreed that the objects of the Union would not be secured by any system founded on the principle of a confederation of sovereign states" (M 10.207). Antifederalists, who had only the draft to go by and not Madison's efforts in the convention, thought that even so the Constitution aimed at destroying the states. That had never been Madison's goal. He knew the states were "subordinately useful" as administrative districts—he compared them to counties within the states (M 10.82). The very principle of efficiency through division of labor would lead him to that conclusion. But a sovereign power of self-determination for the separate states would destroy the Union, he thought, as surely as it had destroyed every confederacy where it had existed.

Writing anonymously in *The Federalist,* Madison hid his southern origins and suggested that he was a New Yorker in order to make the most convincing case he could for ratification of the Constitution without amendments.[4] There he soothed the states with the assurance that they retained a "residual" sovereignty. He could argue in good conscience that states will have functions separate from those of the federal government— that is just good division-of-labor principle. But even in *The Federalist,* where he is being most accommodating to those fearful of the states' extinction, he does not surrender his criticism of all leagues that tried to keep their components sovereign.[5] And on the key question—who shall decide where authority resides?—he is firm:

> It is true that in controversies relating to the boundary between the two jurisdictions, the tribunal which is ultimately to decide, is to be established under the general government. But this does not change the principle of the case. The decision is to be impartially made, according to the rules of the Constitution; and all the usual and most effectual precautions are taken to secure this impartiality. Some such tribunal is clearly essential to prevent an appeal to the sword, and a dissolution of the compact; and that it ought to be established under the general

rather than the local governments, or (to speak more properly) that it could be safely established under the first *alone,* is a position not likely to be combated (F 39.256–57, emphasis added).

It was Madison's whole case against the states that they were "parties in their own cause," and could not be impartial, while the neutral features of the federal government made that possible. So the general government gets the last say on what authority is and where it resides. This is the very definition of sovereignty—not omnipotence or omnicompetence, not the power to do everything or anything, but the right to have the final decision that binds the entire body. And this, like most of Madison's case for the Constitution, was a matter of efficiency. The whole body cannot act decisively without some authority to speak definitively for it:

> Experience is the oracle of truth; and where its responses are unequivocal, they ought to be conclusive and sacred. The important truth which it unequivocally pronounces in the present case is that a sovereignty over sovereigns, a government over governments, a legislation for communities as contradistinguished from individuals, as it is a solecism in theory, so in practice it is subversive of the order and ends of civil polity, by substituting *violence* in place of *law,* or the destructive *coercion* of the *sword* in place of the mild and salutary *coercion* of the *magistracy* (F 20.128–29, emphasis in the original).

Though Madison is discussing civil not military enforcement, he does not disguise the fact that coercion is to be exercised. In any government worthy of the name, some such power of enforcement over all the parts is necessary, or

> the world would have seen, for the first time, a system of government founded on an inversion of the fundamental principles of all government; it would have seen the authority of the whole society everywhere subordinate to the authority of the parts; it would have seen a monster in which the head was under the direction of the members (F 44.306).

Hamilton, too, argued from the need for governmental *energy* that there could not be "sovereignty in the union and complete independence in the members," which would produce "the political monster of an *imperium in imperio*" (F 15.93).

That Madison meant for the supremacy clause to substitute for his preferred state veto, giving the Supreme Court power to review state laws, is proved by a little-noticed episode. In 1818, the journals of the Constitutional Convention were finally published (to Madison's regret), and the radical Virginia republican John Taylor of Caroline found that they confirmed his own disapproving estimate of *The Federalist*. He saw proof in the June 8 proceedings that Madison had intended a veto on the states, and on June 13 that he settled instead for the supremacy clause. On this basis Madison had construed a broad federal power: "Mr. Madison, under a decided preference for some supreme national power, has constructively bestowed it upon the Supreme Court."[6] Madison wrote to Jefferson that he did hold the views attributed to him by Taylor, and always had: "I have never yielded my original opinion, indicated in *The Federalist* No. 39, to the ingenious reasonings of Col. Taylor against this construction of the Constitution."[7] Taylor, though often a political ally of Madison in the early days of the Republican party, had always maintained that *The Federalist*, under cover of some sweet phrases thrown to the states, argued in fact for national sovereignty. The modern enthusiasts for what they take to be federalism cannot bring themselves to admit this. Instead, they have taken Madison's position (Federalist) and Taylor's position (Antifederalist) and tried to make them out to be the same thing. This leaves them with what they obviously consider the best of both worlds—a government adopted for anti-government reasons, what *The Federalist* itself calls a "monster."

5.

Co-equal Branches

When I argue before students that the Constitution was written to make the nation's government more efficient, their response is almost always the same: "If that is so, then why were the branches made co-equal?" Clearly that is to make them check each other more easily, slowing the wheels of government. If I ask, "Where is it written that the branches are co-equal?" they are quick to respond, "In *The Federalist*." Where in it? A search turns up a surprising (to them) fact: "Publius," the author of *The Federalist*, never says that the departments (his word for the branches) are equal. He uses "equal" in one or other of its forms 187 times, but it is applied to the three departments only once, and that is to *deny* them equality: "But it is not possible to give to each department an equal power of self defense" (F 51.350). When components of government are described as equal, Publius is condemning a *flaw*.[1] Madison, one of the three men using the pen name of Publius, says six times that the *Confederation* under the Articles— or the ancient confederations which it resembles—was deadlocked by the equal votes of *its* component parts (the states). Hamilton, who shared in the identity of Publius, says the same thing five times. The three uses of "co-equal" also described this deplorable condition. Here is Madison's only use of "co-equal," in his description of the faulty Dutch confederacy, which was as weak as the American confederation under the Articles:

> The union is composed of seven co-equal and sovereign states, and each state or province is a composition of equal and independent cities. In all important cases, not only the provinces but the cities must be unanimous (F 20.124).[2]

What is the result of this Dutch co-equality? "Imbecility in the government; discord among the provinces; foreign influence and indignities; a precarious existence in peace, and peculiar calamities from war" (F 20.126). So co-equality is just what Madison does *not* want to find in the new government he is constructing.

Where did this extraordinary misperception come from, that the departments are supposed to be co-equal? It may have arisen in part from another term, one that Publius does apply to the departments—balance. In modern Constitutionspeak, checks and balances are like love and marriage in the song, "you can't have one without the other." But Publius (Madison) uses the terms in conjunction only once, to describe interdepartmental relations—and there he is simply quoting Jefferson's description of the *lack* of balance in Virginia's state constitution, where the legislature had absorbed the activities of the executive and judiciary (F 48.335, quoting JW 245–46). Hamilton's only joint use of checks and balances is not to describe the relations of the departments but of chambers in the legislature (bicameralism), at F 9.51.

So there is only one use of checks and balances to describe the relations of the three branches, and that one is secondhand from Jefferson's work on Virginia. Balance, all by itself, is used of the departments only once, by Hamilton at F 71.484. More often we hear of a balance of interests or motives (three times), of society or government in general (two times), of trade (two times).[3] That last usage, like any description of a balance of power between nations (F 11.68), shows that balance does not mean equality of all the parts to each other. In a balance of trade, not all partners are equal in revenue. In the balance of power, not all nations are equal in strength. Rather there is a distribution of different forces in play that leads to an "equilibrium of power" (F 15.94). Hamilton says there will be an equilibrium (not an equality) in the financial burdens of the states (F 21.134), or between the legislature's two chambers (F 66.448). The "constitutional equilibrium" Madison speaks of (F 49.341) is like that of the planetary system, in which bodies hold to their own spheres despite the fact that they are not of equal size. The constitutional system does not resemble a horizontal seesaw on the playground, but a Calder mobile, its different parts delicately counterpoised.

Madison's favorite terms for the relations of the three departments, in

The Federalist as well as in his correspondence, are the *organization* of its functions and the *distribution* of its powers.[4] A well-organized government has three distinct departments. Organization does not imply equality of the parts, as we can see from the fact that a militia must also be well organized, though it (like all military bodies) will have a hierarchical structure (F 4.22, 29.181).

It was a high Enlightenment ideal to apply the mind to social arrangements that had been taken for granted as simple givens. To make society *bien organisée*, as the French Encyclopedists put it, was to define functions and distribute powers according to a "well-digested plan." That is what Madison aspires to do, and the task is not simply one of creating equal bodies and letting them fight things out. There is a hierarchy of function, stated unequivocally: "In republican government, the legislative authority necessarily predominates" (F 51.350). Where two are dominated by a *predominating* third, there can be no co-equality.

Lawmaking is a society's highest function; it sets the rules by which all things are to be done or judged. It precedes in time and dignity the execution or adjudication of the laws. Without prior legislation, there is nothing to be executed or adjudicated. The other two functions necessarily serve the first. That fact is implied or asserted in every part of the Constitution. The Congress can remove officers from the other two branches—President, agency heads, judges in district or supreme courts. Neither of the other two branches can touch a member of the Congress. Congress sets the pay for the other two and also for itself. It decides on the structure of the other two departments, creating or abolishing agencies and courts. It decides on the number of judges to serve on each court.

With regard to treaties and diplomats, the President proposes. Congress disposes. Only its ratification makes the treaty, or anything else, law. In domestic legislation, the President can object to a law's implementation by a veto; but if the Congress wants the law anyway, it can override the veto, and there is no recourse left to the President but to enforce the law he objected to. If the Supreme Court declares a law that Congress has passed unconstitutional, it is not asserting judicial supremacy, but upholding a legislative act, that of the Constitution, whose creature the judges are. If Congress disagrees with the Court's reading, it can initiate the amending process, or impeach one or more judges, or expand the number of judges. If it does any or all of these things, the judges have no recourse but to sit by and watch the predominate branch exercise its rights.

No matter what the sequence of action among the three departments, if the process is played out to the end, Congress always gets the last say (if it wants it). It may not want to exercise that right, for any of a number of reasons—ignorance, indifference, division in its members, the unpopularity of the move. But that does not deprive it of the right, or deposit it elsewhere, in the order of law. For many years, the Congress did not exercise the right to impeach a president. It seemed a dead letter in the law. But when it decided to assert the right against President Nixon, the right was still there (and would have been exercised if Nixon had not pre-empted congressional action by his resignation). The right had not evaporated or traveled anywhere else; it had not become the right of a president or judge to impeach a congressman. For a period in the middle of this century, Congress failed to assert its right to declare war, letting the President exercise it. The Supreme Court refused to consider any case brought against this diverting of the war-making power. But the power was still there, held in abeyance but held.

The hierarchy of functions in the Constitution is legible on the document's face. Article I is devoted to the legislature, beginning with the more representative chamber, closer to the people as the source of lawmaking power. Article II, less than half the length of the first one, is devoted to the application of the laws provided for in the first article. Article III, about a third the length of the preceding one, is about the adjudication of applied laws. *The Federalist* observes the same order and proportion in its treatment of the Constitution. After sections describing the weakness of the Articles and the principles for a new government, it deals with the legislature in fifteen Numbers (ten for the House, five for the Senate), with the executive in nine Numbers, and the judiciary in six.

What has happened to obscure this clear order or priority in functions? Often people have confused the appearance of power with the legal possession of it, or they confuse practice with theory. In certain periods, especially in wartime, the executive power is so extensive and dramatic that it seems to be the only organ of government. Even in peacetime, the President speaks with one voice, more easily attended to (and usually more interesting) than a single congressman's views or than the babble of a multitude of legislators. But dramaturgy is not constitutional order. A simple but illustrative example of the transition from legal subordination to the appearance of superiority is the use that has grown up, over the years, of the President's annual message to Congress. That has become a way for the President to state his own legislative agenda, so much that he might berate the Congress for lassitude or recalcitrance if it does not pass the laws he asked for. But in the Constitution the order for the President to appear before Congress was a duty imposed on him, to give an account of his executive activity and tell the legislators what he feels he needs ("recommend to *their* consideration," emphasis added) in order to perform the executive tasks entrusted to him by the Constitution. Reporting on "the state of the Union" looks to the order of fact, not of law. The Constitution does not ask the President what legislation should be passed but what executive problems Congress should be aware of as *it* legislates.

That this was the intent of the order is clear from its internal structure. Superiors summon inferiors, not vice versa. That this is an obligation is evident from the use of the phrase "from time to time" (that is, as part of a continuing record), which was used of other factual reports *required* in the Constitution—of moneys expended or legislation debated.[5] The intent is also confirmed by the practice of early presidents. Though President Washington's was such an imposing presence that he might awe the Congress, he was summoned to the legislators' domain, and he was careful to show deference. His first address, which Madison helped draft (and he surely knew what the Constitution was demanding), reported the need for a basic organization of the military. Despite the fact that he was clearly the country's first expert on this subject, Washington left it to Congress to form a "well-digested plan."[6] One of the reasons for creating a separate executive branch was the need to relieve Congress of following in detail the diplomatic or economic details of administration. Washington gave an account of his dealings with the Indian nations, and noted the need for increased scientific work on national improvement. Though he favored a national university himself, he did not set the terms of law for lawmakers:

> Whether this desirable object will be best promoted by affording aids to seminaries of learning already established, by the institution of a national university, or by any other expedients, will be well worthy of a place in the deliberations of the legislature.

Thomas Jefferson was famously diffident about directing Congress to legislate, relying on indirect hints relayed through others. In his first annual message he reported on his dealings with Barbary pirates in order to give Congress the information it needed to exercise its war-making powers:

> I communicate all material information on this subject, that in the exercise of the important function considered by the Constitution to the legislature *exclusively,* their judgment may form itself on a knowledge and consideration of every circumstance of weight (JW 502, emphasis added).

Though, unlike Washington, Jefferson reports no need for national "improvements," he does not present his view as precluding their consideration of the matter on their own: "If in the course of your observations or inquiries they [improvements] should appear to need any aid within the limits of our constitutional powers, your sense of their importance is a sufficient assurance they will occupy your attention" (JW 507). His military cuts and expenditures "will be a more proper subject for legislation" (JW 507). The difference in tone and expectations between these communications and the legislative agenda issued by modern presidents shows what those who passed the Constitution considered the properly subordinate attitude of the President.

Those who think of the three departments of government as co-equal are also convinced that they should be entirely separate from each other, as a way of maintaining their equality. But the critics of the Constitution urged, at high volume, that it should not be ratified because it did *not* guarantee a separation of powers. This might seem an odd position to be taken by those who defended the condition of government under the Articles. In that system there was no separation of powers at all. The Continental Congress was the whole of government, engrossing legislative, executive, and judicial tasks. Then why complain about another scheme that *it* did not separate powers? The answer, of course, is that the Continental Congress was directly checked by the state assemblies who sent delegates hampered by short terms, rotation, instruction, recall, and pay from their home base. Asked what would replace such "real" checks, Federalist friends of the Constitution said that the government would have an internal checking apparatus, its parts pitting office against office to prevent any over-reaching. The Antifederalists refused to be assured, noting that there was not a clear separation of powers after all. The executive gets into the legislative business when the President calls Congress into session or settles disagreements about adjournment, or when the Vice President chairs Senate sessions, or when the State Department drafts treaties. The legislature gets into the executive business when it ratifies treaties or appointments, and it gets into the judicial business when it tries impeachments.

The Senate's cooperation with the President on treaties and appointments was especially feared, since it would set up an alliance making the Senate loath to impeach a president for whose administration it was jointly responsible. This was the "unholy combination" frequently denounced in the ratifying conventions. Patrick Henry called the supposed separations and counterbalances "paper checks," not real ones.

> There will be no checks, no real balances, in this government. What can avail your specious imaginary balances, your rope-dancing, chain-rattling, ridiculous ideal checks and contrivances? (R 9.959).

In the British system, which Henry frequently praises in the ratification debate, the different estates provided real checks on each other because they were based on self-love, a solid play of opposite interests, not ideal or theoretical functions (R 9.1062).

How did Madison respond to such accusations? He calmly admitted them. There is no perfect separation of the departments, and—given his functional defense of separation—there could not be. In order to work, the gears of government must mesh, giving the departments a "partial agency in" one another's activities (F 47.325). They could not control each other for the common tasks without some engagement. That bothers him less than it would others because he believed freedom would be preserved by his own theory of representation (see Chapter 6). Besides, as he says, the despotic power others feared would occur only with "the accumulation of *all* powers legislative, executive, and judiciary in the same hands" (F 47.324, emphasis added). Madison also points out that no government has had a perfect separation of functions, including those of the states themselves. And the British Constitution, the very institution on which

Montesquieu based his theory of separated powers, has a decided mixture of its powers (F 47.324–31). In fact, a perfect isolation would mean that each department spins its gears in the air, going nowhere, affecting nothing but itself, defeating the system's efficiency.

Madison's lack of concern about entirely separating the departments came out in the very first State of the Union message President Washington delivered. Though he was a leader in the House of Representatives, Madison helped draft the President's message. Then, as spokesman for the House, he wrote the congressional letter of thanks for the President's appearance. And, to complete the triangle, he then drafted the President's reply to his own reply (M 12.120–24, 132–33, 141–42), thoroughly mingling executive and legislative activities in his own person. He also confirmed one of Patrick Henry's predictions by his own acts. Henry had said that the separate diplomatic function of the Senate would be invaded by the House—"the House of Representatives will break through their balances and checks, and break into the business of treaties" (R 10.1247). And sure enough, when Madison's fellows in the House of Representatives objected to John Jay's treaty with England in 1794, Madison went along with a House demand that the President furnish that body with the negotiating record, arguing that the treaty would involve some expenditures that only the House could initiate, so it should have a voice in the approval of the document. Though that motion was ignored, similar House requirements have become customary. Madison was undoubtedly less concerned about this nicety because it was the legislature that was making the demand, and "in republican government the legislature authority necessarily predominates" (F 51.350).

Here as elsewhere, only a fierce desire to believe can make anyone think that co-equal departments exist in the Constitution, or were ever meant to. Both friends and foes of the Constitution *denied* that in the debate over ratification. But the anti-governmental attitude that suspects any organization of power for the sake of efficiency makes people prefer to believe that our government is divided against itself.

6.

The Uses of Faction

Representation was the central issue in debates over ratifying the Constitution. The critics of the new government, the Antifederalists, said that it would have too small a number of representatives, meeting too far from their constituents, considering policy in isolation from the actual problems it would affect. In *Federalist* No. 10, the most famous and influential work of political theory in American history, Madison cleverly turned all these objections on their head, making them *recommendations* of the Constitution. This essay was an abomination to the "small government" Antifederalists—which makes all the more wondrous the effort of later "small government" theorists to claim *Federalist* No. 10 for themselves.

The Antifederalists recognized at once that Madison's theory went against every principle they had acted on in forming America's first government, that of the Articles of Confederation. That charter perfectly expressed the values this book calls anti-governmental—localism, amateurism, intense citizen participation, official candor. Its system trammeled representatives in a net of fine meshes that held them close to their constituents. Strands in the net included these:

- short terms of office
- rotation in office
- instruction how to vote
- open proceedings to make sure instruction was followed
- recall of any representative not following instruction
- refusal to give authority to an independent executive or judiciary (i.e., to *un*instructed *non*representatives)

- refusal to create a source of pay for representatives separate from their home base
- refusal to allow plural officeholding (where the representative might acquire an interest other than his constituents')

Madison seemed deliberately to reject these tenets' entire basis, in effect calling everything Americans had done up to this time, in the way of self-government, a profound mistake. No wonder his approach to the Constitution released a flood of objections to his treatment of representatives' number, terms and length of tenure, freedom from instruction or recall, pay at the federal level, and elite superiority to the play of local bias.

The first thing the Antifederalists noticed, when the Constitution was made public, was what they called a fatal lack of "a numerous representation." With only one congressman for every thirty thousand people, the great diversity in any group of thirty thousand individuals could not be represented. This would, among other things, make instruction of the representative difficult if not impossible—a point Antifederalists suspected, with good reason, that the framers had in mind. It is just this high ratio of delegates to their electors that made critics hold that an extended republic was impossible. A small group of people, gathered from a large general population, could not possibly reflect the number and range of attitudes in those being governed. It could not meet the standard set, on behalf of the Antifederalists, by the antifederalist writer known as "the Federal Farmer":

> A full and equal representation is that which possesses the same interests, feelings, opinions, and views the people themselves would, were they all assembled. A fair representation, therefore, should be so regulated that every order of men in the community, according to the common course of elections, can have a share in it. In order to allow professional men, merchants, traders, farmers, mechanics, etc. to bring a just proportion of their best informed men respectively into the legislature, the representation must be considerably numerous (AF 2.238).

The Farmer goes on to say that representation of all the states would have to have as many legislators, at least, as the sum of those in each of the states—that is, over two hundred rather than the eighty-five proposed. When Federalists said that this would result in too unwieldy and expensive a body to assemble from all parts of the country, their opponents answered, in effect, that this is what makes an extended republic a "solecism."

After objections to the number of representatives came those over the length of their terms. Under the Articles, *every* continental officeholder had a one-year term, and *every* one was subject to term limits. In the new structure, *no* officer had so short a term as one year, and *every* one could be reelected indefinitely. This seemed outrageous to the Antifederalists, and it gave pause even to some who favored the Constitution. George Will, in his book on term limits, claims that the framers favored rotation in office but omitted it from the Constitution because of the mere rush of business.[1] But so important a point could not have been left out absentmindedly. It was clear that this would be one of the major sticking points for those considering ratification—and so it proved. Even Thomas Jefferson, reacting favorably to the reports on the draft that Madison sent him in France, was instantly, emphatically opposed to "the perpetual re-eligibility of the President" (J 14.188). Patrick Henry said that a president who could remain in office, and who as commander in chief could build up a loyalty in the army, would be a de facto monarch: "The army is in his hands, and if he be a man of address it will be attached to him" (R 9.964).

But, contrary to what we often assume, it was not an overweening executive that was most feared by the Antifederalists. As their best student, Herbert Storing, notes, the Senate was the most dreaded feature of the document (AF 1.49). The senators' long and overlapping terms, their small number, their partnership with the executive in diplomacy and appointments, their extensive powers to try impeachment cases, the possibility of continual reelection, made men fear that they would become an aristocratic clique running the government almost entirely. If the representation in the House was not "numerous," that in the Senate was nonexistent. Fourteen men could, as a majority of the quorum in the original Senate, wield all its ordinary powers. George Mason spoke the fears of many:

> The Senate have the power of altering all money bills, and of originating appropriations of money and the salaries of the officers of their own appointment, in conjunction with the President of the United States,

although they are not the representatives of the people or amenable to them. These with their other great powers (viz., their power in the appointment of ambassadors and all public officers, in making treaties, and in trying all impeachments), their influence upon and connection with the supreme executive from these causes, their duration of office, and their being a constant-existing body almost continually sitting, joined with their being one complete branch of the legislature, will destroy any balance in the government and enable them to accomplish what usurpations they please upon the rights and liberties of the people (AF 2.11).

The mere proposal of such a body was an affront to the Antifederalists' dearest beliefs about government. But the justification offered by James Madison sounded even more heretical, if not actually harebrained. He said that the extent of the country was the solution, not the problem, and that a high ratio between represented and representing (made necessary by the geographical and demographic extent of the country) was a blessing. Patrick Henry attacked the absurdity of such a claim when he said:

> This Constitution reflects in the most degrading and mortifying manner on the virtue, integrity, and wisdom of the state legislatures [which have "numerous representation"]. It presupposes that the chosen few who go to Congress will have more upright hearts, and more enlightened minds, than those who are members of the individual legislatures. To suppose that 10 gentlemen shall have more substantial merit than 170 is humiliating to the last degree. If, sir, the diminution of numbers be an augmentation of merit, perfection must center in one. If you have the faculty of discerning spirits, it is better to point out at once the man who has the most illumined qualities. If 10 men be better than 170, it follows of necessity that one is better than 10—the choice is more "refined" (R 9.1064).

Though Madison explained his paradox in many places—most famously in *Federalist* No. 10—there has been continual disagreement on the real point of his argument. Perhaps one place to begin is with a less theoretical reason offered for the Constitution's ratification, one voiced by

John Jay (the third sharer in the identity of Publius) in *Federalist* No. 3. Jay, whose expertise was in diplomacy, argued that the Confederation made it hard to draw up and maintain equitable treaties with the Indians because local regions, with grievances along their borders, defied congressional efforts to maintain order:

> Not a single Indian war has yet been occasioned by aggressions of the present federal government [the Confederation], feeble as it is, but there are several instances of Indian hostilities having been provoked by the improper conduct of individual states who, either unable or unwilling to restrain or punish offences, have given occasion to the slaughter of many innocent inhabitants (F 3.16–17).

Jay is here challenging the idea, frequently expressed by Ronald Reagan and other defenders of states' rights, that local government is always best, since it is closest to what the people want. But when local passions have been inflamed against others, it is hard to get a reasonable hearing for all sides. That is the story of every lynching. If a larger arena is engaged in the sifting of such matters, local bias will not be the only force involved:

> The bordering states, if any, will be those who, under the impulse of sudden irritation and a quick sense of apparent interest or injury, will be most likely by direct violence to excite war with those nations; and nothing can so effectually obviate that danger as a national government, whose wisdom and prudence will not be diminished by the passions which actuate the parties immediately interested (F 3.17).

There *in nuce* is the Madison argument for an extended republic—only Madison would add that the injury done in the case Jay imagines is not only to the wronged Indians, but also to that part of the local community that favors restraint and fairness, which is overborne by the impassioned majority. This is exactly the situation for which he tailored his plan for a national veto on unjust state laws. He felt that such laws wronged people in the state *and* outside it. A favorite example was the issuing of paper money in a state to favor a majority of debtors. This not only wronged the creditors in the state, but also all those outside the state whose financial claims were met with payment in the debased currency. Individual states could destabilize the whole Confederation's economy.

A direct and local democracy, according to Madison, invites injustice because it makes the parties to any dispute the judges of it, a basic violation of fair adjudication (F 10.59). If all a government can do is react to the pressure of the largest group, there is no way for others, outside that group, to get a fair hearing. For that, they must appeal to a larger sphere, where local passion will not be the only factor in play. Some have treated this argument as if Madison were saying that the more factions there are at play, the more they will check each other, automatically, in a political version of the free market. But free markets are meant to make one product prevail by better manufacture or marketing, not to *prevent* any one from prevailing because of some mutual check. Madison is saying that the representatives who are not totally immersed in the local strife can achieve, together, a more disinterested view on the merits of any legislation.

What would prevent a larger passion from taking over the national council as a smaller one does the local assembly? Madison's partial answer to this problem has often been misread because key words in his famous statement have been ignored, or have been interpreted amiss. I underline the crucial words:

> Extend the sphere, and you take in a greater variety of parties and interests; you make it less probable that a majority of the whole will have a common motive *to invade the rights of other citizens*; or, if such a common motive exists, it will be more difficult for all who feel it to *discover* their own strength, and to act in unison with each other. Besides other impediments, it may be remarked that where there is a consciousness of *unjust or dishonorable* purposes, communication is always checked by *distrust* in proportion to the number whose concurrence is necessary (F 10.64).

Madison wants to check not interest in a neutral sense, or majorities of any sort, but majorities that are factious—ones that have the unjust purpose of wronging others. On the local scene, passion may run so high that the wrongdoers need not explain themselves. But before a large and less engaged audience, they will be inhibited from revealing their naked aggression. Otherwise, they will betray the fact that they are not simply a majority but a factious majority:

> By a faction I understand a number of citizens, whether amounting to a majority or minority of the whole, who are united and actuated by some common impulse of passion or of interest, adverse to the rights of other citizens or to the permanent and aggregate interests of the community (F 10.57).

Some take "discover" to mean that factious people will not be able to *find* each other in the extended community—raising the problem that good majorities will not be able to find themselves, either. The factious group would not be distinguished by that note. Besides, the committees of correspondence had demonstrated how rapid could be communication between like-minded people in the American colonies. "Find" cannot be the meaning here, and the original audience would not have understood it in this context. In the eighteenth century, "discovery" still had the meaning preserved in old legal terms like "pretrial discovery"—that is, "revelation." That is why Publius can speak of a flaw or error that "discovers [reveals] itself" at F 38.242 or 73.494.

Another word not carefully scrutinized in this key passage is "distrust." Who is being distrusted—the co-factioneers? But they are already called united in their intent to do wrong. Why would they distrust each other? The rest of the community? But they are already defined as a majority. Why should they care about the rest of the community? But "distrust" can, in the eighteenth century, mean "a diffidence or lack of confidence." At F 10.57, Madison speaks of "distrust of public engagements" (lack of confidence in them). We are told that the evil group's confidence will falter the more they have to reveal their strength. Why?

Let us go back to the case John Jay proposed and see how Madison's theory might explain that. Borderers wronging Indians will rely less, at the immediate site of hostilities, on arguments about justice than on shared memories of grievances, real or imagined, and a rush to avenge them. They are too inflamed to need explanations among themselves. But if they must speak through representatives to a council that has not experienced the same conflict, one that can get above the particulars of evils traded, away from a fear running out of control, then locals' representatives would have to make a calmer argument, would have to address queries they did not allow themselves to entertain in the immediate situation. They would not "discover" their mere thirst for revenge and expect that to carry the day before this less-engaged body. Already, they have been inhibited from revealing themselves, in conjunction with any others, as intent on wrong. They must explain why they are *right*.

There might be other representatives at the national level who are biased about Indians, who have their own feelings of revenge to nurse. But their experience will not be *exactly* the same as that of the aggressors now making their case, and the language of passion will not be self-explanatory. Those in agreement will not simply "discover" their hate but will argue even for faction in disguised (nonfactious) terms, modifying their own position in the process (at least on the surface). And if they cannot convince a majority of the national delegates of the justice of their position, they will lose even the moderate ground they are staking out. It is unlikely that most of the delegates from an *extended* republic will have the same experience with Indians, judged the same way, reaching the same degree of animus, and willing to express itself as mere passion and not reasoned pleading.

Madison makes another point. Those sending delegates to a national congress—one where they cannot represent every single interest in their state (so they cannot be instructed in detail), and where they will have to address a broad range of issues dealing with foreign nations as well as with other states—will find it serves them to choose men capable of weighing many different views in order to protect the genuine and long-term interests of their own states as well as the general good of the Union. In the Jay example, a state would not send *all* its representatives to express *just* the passion against Indians. It would recognize that other matters could be brought up by other states, or by foreign crises, where shrewd acquaintance with non-Indian affairs might be required of their delegate. The state's own interest, as well as its pride, would pressure it to send a qualified person as its spokesman. Since Madison thinks of the legislative process as partly adjudicative, where one is not to be a judge in one's own case, the choosing of a good representative is like sending an experienced and resourceful lawyer, one who will know the persons and things he is dealing with and be able to command a respectful hearing. Such a man will represent the best interests of his clients, but those clients are foolish if they try to "instruct" him on all that he can do to accomplish that goal. The result of such considerations, according to Madison, will be "to refine and enlarge the public views by passing them through the medium of a chosen body of citizens whose wisdom may best discern the true interest of their country, and whose patriotism and love of justice will be least likely to sacrifice it to temporary or partial considerations" (F 10.62).

This passage has been mocked as if Madison were expecting a race of superhuman legislators. (So much for the idea that Madison is a pessimist, with a low view of human nature.) But he is simply asking, in the first place, whether such men are more likely to be found at the national level or in the state assemblies. And the men he describes are not likely to take the larger and longer view simply from nobility of nature. They will be *educated* to such concerns by the experience of meeting other minds and issues on a larger scene, with less insistent pressures from parochial views. We see this when he speaks of the Senate as having its mind broadened by consideration of other nations' views:

> An attention to the judgment of other nations is important to every government, for two reasons—the one is that, independently of the merits of any particular plan or measure, it is desirable on various accounts that it should appear to other nations as the offspring of a wise and honorable policy; the second is that, in doubtful cases, particularly where the national councils may be warped by some strong passion or momentary interest, the presumed or known opinion of the impartial world may be the best guide that can be followed (F 63.423).

The first reason given suggests the representatives' lawyerly role—they will be equipped to make a convincing defense of their country's position before other nations. The second looks to the senators' *education* by exposure to other views. At this level, the international community serves to "refine and enlarge" men's views just as the national council "refines and enlarges" those of the state assemblies. The articulation of society lets in light from broader horizons. In terms of the values discussed in this book,

Madison, a man of the Enlightenment, seeks a cosmopolitan, not a provincial form of rule. Once we grasp his theory of representation, a number of common misconceptions crumble, among them these:

1. *That Madison's system is built on self-interest.* Patrick Henry, you remember, attacked the system because it was not selfish. But the *opinio vulgaris* is that voiced by George Will: "Madison's attention is exclusively on controlling passions with countervailing passions; he is not concerned with the amelioration or reform of passions."[2] We have just read Madison's words about the Senate rising above passion to recognize views of justice, even from other nations. John Jay devoted *Federalist* No. 3 to ways of keeping the nation out of unjust wars. The republican view was that a virtuous people would be reflected in a virtuous government. Wanting their representatives to deal with others justly, they would be more likely to choose men able to accomplish that. It was the Antifederalists who took the low view of human nature, who thought that any grant of power was bound to be abused. It was to answer them that Madison rose in the Virginia ratifying convention with this plea:

> I have observed that gentlemen suppose that the general legislature will do every mischief they possibly can, and that they will omit to do every good which they are authorized to do. If this were a reasonable supposition, their objections would be good. I consider it reasonable to conclude that they will as readily do their duty as deviate from it. Nor do I go on the grounds mentioned by gentlemen on the other side, that we are to place unlimited confidence in them, and expect nothing but the most exalted integrity and sublime virtue. But I go on this great republican principle, that the people will have virtue and intelligence to select men of virtue and wisdom. Is there no virtue among us? If there be not, we are in a wretched situation. No theoretical checks, no form of government, can render us secure. To suppose that any form of government will secure liberty or happiness without any virtue in the people is a chimerical idea. If there be sufficient virtue and intelligence in the community, it will be exercised in the selection of these men, so that we do not depend on their virtue, or put confidence in our rulers, but in the people who are to choose them (R 10.1417).

2. *That Madison wanted to cure faction by multiplying factions.* George Will again: "There must be a plenitude of passions among the multiplicity of factions to prevent the existence of a stable and tyrannical majority."[3] Since Madison defines "faction" as "a group intent on wronging others," it is hard to believe that he would think the cure for evil is much *more* evil. People are misled here by an analogy Madison uses in No. 51: "In a free government, the security for civil rights must be the same as for religious rights. It consists, in the one case, in the multiplicity of interests, and, in the other, in the multiplicity of sects" (F 51.351–52). "Interests" is the term used here, not "faction." Interests are not necessarily factious. Sects, though they "may degenerate into a political faction" (F 10.64), do so only when they threaten the religious liberties of others. *That* is what is unlikely to succeed, for the same reason that Jay's Indian haters will have a hard time making their case outside their provincial region—because the delegates are more enlightened and reasonable at the national than at the local council.

Some have read Madison's reference to sects as if he were defending here the separation of church and state. That is another argument, which he urges elsewhere on other grounds (freedom of conscience). Here, there is nothing to prevent the play of interests at the national level, or the play of sects; only the invasion of "religious rights" is being discussed.

3. *That Madison thought his system would work automatically.* His was a system, in Will's words, that "would work well even if no one had good motives."[4] Extent of territory and articulated government would combine so that "society itself will be broken into so many parts, interests, and classes of citizens that the rights of individuals, or of the minority, will be in little danger from interested combinations of the majority" (F 51.351). If every interest, view, or policy were checked by this automatic "breaking," then nothing would be enacted, there would be no laws to be executed or adjudicated. Even nonfactious views would be paralyzed. For Madison, on the contrary, the play of *nonfactious* views ventilates the atmosphere, as it were, allows the national legislators to see more sides of things, more elements to be taken into consideration—and this equips them to cope with the *factious* views they must reject (no machinery does it for them).

Madison's whole system resembles in spirit one activity that the Confederation engaged in under the Articles. In Article IX an arbitration procedure is established for disputes between the states. Each state sends spokesmen, who agree on neutral arbitrators. If they cannot agree, then Congress names a pool of three men from each of the thirteen states, from which both litigants can strike one person per state, leaving a final board of thirteen arbiters, whose verdict is binding (R 1.90). Considered as a representative system, this takes the matter away from the local scene and commits the fate of the states involved to outsiders. By the Reagan rule, of virtue lying at the local level, this does not allow those most concerned to determine for themselves. But of course others are concerned, and who is to speak for them? Resolution of such conflict can come about peacefully only if some fair and disinterested parties can be agreed on. Getting the matter into their hands is the whole trick of the intricate process.

The ad hoc nature of the Article IX procedure made it clumsy, nonauthoritative in appearance, and time-consuming. But some of its positive features are echoed, in a more efficient and continuing way, in Madison's effort to make Congress resemble a body of disinterested umpires. One reason *Federalist* No. 10 has so often been misunderstood is that Madison, writing as Publius, was not defending his system as he had conceived it, but the Constitution that departed from his system in two major respects (equal representation of the states in the Senate, and no veto over state laws). His purposes are better understood if we read his defenses of it in its original form (especially in the letter to Jefferson at M 10.207–15). But even in *The Federalist* he could not pass by the opportunity to show how much better off the states would be with a national adjudicator settling their internal disputes when a minority was being mistreated:

> In cases where it may be doubtful on which side justice lies, what better umpires could be desired by two violent factions, flying to arms and tearing a state to pieces, than the representatives of confederate states not heated by the local flame? To the impartiality of judges they would unite the affection of friends. Happy would it be if such a remedy for its infirmities could be enjoyed by all free governments; if a project equally effectual could be established for the universal peace of mankind (F 43.294–95).

There speaks the Enlightenment optimist who did so much to craft our Constitution. And in time, because of developments like the extension of the "due process" rights of the Fourteenth Amendment, something like what Madison was hoping for came about. Look back over the passage just quoted and see if it is not a very accurate picture of what happened during the civil rights movement, when states were tearing themselves apart over the oppression of black majorities, until the federal government stepped in, "not heated by the local flame," to act as judge and friend.

For advocates of local government, Madison's attempt to open people up to cosmopolitan horizons will look elitist, taking government away from the people, giving it to their betters. He believed, on the contrary, that only virtuous people will have faith enough in their cause to commit it to arbiters, rather than stay imprisoned in the local passions Jay described. It is understandable that there should be continuing conflict between those championing parochial values and those who side with cosmopolitan ones. The weird thing is that Madison, of all people, has been represented in our history as standing on the parochial side, as a *praiser* of division and sects and faction. His system was fashioned to be an *escape* from faction, local interest, and judgment in one's own cause.

7.

Bill of Rights

If it is true that Madison opposed localism and distrust of government in the body of the Constitution as it was originally passed, then he seems to have retreated from that position when he drafted and pushed through the first amendments to the Constitution, the so-called Bill of Rights. In fact, it has often been claimed that the Antifederalists lost the battle with ratification of the Constitution in 1788 but won the war when their objections were embodied in the Bill of Rights, that package of ten amendments ratified in 1791. Is *this*, then, what makes ours an anti-government government after all?

The Antifederalists had demanded that certain individual rights—most notably, of religious practice and free speech—be declared exempt from federal jurisdiction and remain the states' concern. (The individual states, for instance, decided whether to have an established religion.) Madison's first position, maintained during the ratification struggle, was that the federal government offered no threat to those rights, and that the Antifederalists were using this as a weapon to rewrite the draft Constitution, as a way of impeding its progress or preventing its passage altogether. But as soon as he was elected to the House of Representatives in the new government, Madison became the most ardent proponent of amendments concerned with these rights, and pushed their passage through a Congress more interested in immediate tasks of structuring the new government for action. Why did Madison insist on returning to issues raised during the ratification struggle, as if he had not won that battle?

Madison's change in attitude toward the Bill of Rights has been a persistent mystery of our founding period. In the drafting period, as we have seen, he felt that the Constitution did not go far enough in granting power to the central government. Why would he now cut back on what power was left in the document? Some, like Leonard Levy, believe that Jefferson's warm advocacy of a bill of rights finally convinced Madison, but Paul Finkelman shows that Madison's switch came before he received Jefferson's letter on the matter.[1] Others say that Madison was forced to promise voters a bill in order to get elected to the first Congress. His rival in that race, James Monroe, was calling for a second constitutional convention to re-draft the entire Constitution, and Madison had to head that off at all costs. A third group believes what Madison had always said, that the Constitution never did claim for the federal government the powers formally (but superfluously) renounced in the Bill of Rights.

These explanations miss the real point of what Madison was up to. He thought he could quiet Antifederalist objections to the Constitution *and* sneak back into the document the veto on state laws that he had fought for from the outset. If amendments were supposed to improve the original document, we know what improvement he considered essential. After sifting the states' various suggestions for things to be included in a bill of rights, he proposed a list of seventeen amendments, one of which was not on anybody's list but his own, the fourteenth item on his list—"No *state* shall violate the equal rights of conscience, or the freedom of the press, or the trial by jury in criminal cases" (emphasis added). The first eight amendments, as finally ratified, would forbid such violations to the federal government. Now Madison wanted to give the federal government power to forbid these incursions to *the states*. This amounted to the kind of veto on unjust state laws that had been rejected by the drafters of the Constitution.

Madison was as persistent over this amendment as he had been over his proposed federal veto on state laws. He did not treat item fourteen as subsidiary to the other amendments, but as more important. He argued more vigorously for this than for any other amendment, even the one guaranteeing his cherished freedom of religion.

> I wish, also, in revising the Constitution we may throw, into that section [Article I, Section 10] which interdicts the abuse of certain powers in the state legislatures, some other provisions of equal if not greater importance than those already made. The words "No states shall pass any bill of attainder, ex post facto law, etc." were

wise and proper restrictions in the Constitution. I think there is more danger of those powers being abused by the state governments than by the government of the United States. The same may be said of other powers which they possess, if not controlled by the general principle that laws are unconstitutional which infringe the rights of the community. I should therefore wish to extend this interdiction and add, as I have stated in the fifth resolution, that no state shall violate the equal right of conscience, freedom of the press, or trial by jury in criminal cases, because it is proper that every government should be disarmed of powers which trench upon those particular rights. I know, in some of the state constitutions, the power of the government is controlled by such a declaration; but others are not.[2]

Then Madison appealed to the Antifederalists' claimed concern for basic rights, saying that they must protect them even from the states:

I cannot see any reason against obtaining even a double security on those points, and nothing can give a more sincere proof of the attachment of those who opposed this Constitution to these great and important rights than to see them join in obtaining the security I have now proposed; because it must be admitted on all hands that the state governments are as liable to attack the invaluable privileges as the general government is, and therefore ought to be as cautiously guarded against.[3]

Later in the record of the debates, it was reported that he returned to this amendment with all the emphasis he could lend to its importance:

Mr. Madison conceived this to be the most valuable amendment in the whole list. If there was any reason to restrain the government of the United States from infringing upon these essential rights, it was equally necessary that they should be secured against the state governments. He thought that if they provided against the one, it was as necessary to provide against the other, and was satisfied that it would be equally grateful to the people.[4]

Just as in the Constitutional Convention, Madison had an initial success with his measure. His veto on state laws had been provisionally accepted in the convention before it was finally defeated. Now, the House of Representatives voted for his amendment, but the power of the small states in the Senate defeated Madison's effort to break the states' independence of the federal government. If he had won on this point, all the other parts of the Bill of Rights would have been read in a different way. Take, for instance, the First Amendment. That denies Congress the right to establish a church or interfere with freedom of speech, but it leaves intact the states' power to do both things. The First Amendment was given emphatic support by the New England states because it would block the federal government from *disestablishing* its state religion.[5] In the same way, federal authority would not reach to state restrictions on free speech. As Jefferson wrote in 1804, "While we deny that Congress have a right to control the freedom of the press, we have ever asserted the right of the states, and their exclusive right, to do so."[6] Even in cases where states "do not admit even the truth of allegations to protect the printer," and have therefore "gone too far," Jefferson said, the federal government could do nothing about the matter precisely *because of* the First Amendment, which says Congress shall "make no law" in this area.

The situation would have been drastically different if Madison's suggested fourteenth item had been passed. Although that amendment mentioned only three things on which the states could be called to account, they were very inclusive—"equal rights of conscience, or the freedom of the press, or the trial by jury in criminal cases." Under the rights of conscience, the federal government would have had the ability to disestablish a state religion that infringed on the freedom of others' consciences. It would have been given authority over a vast range of issues—oath taking, compulsory patriotic exercises, conscientious objection, school curricula, and on and on. The same broad issues of free speech would have been opened by the federal government's power to protect freedom of the press. Even that evil the southern states were desperate to keep clear of federal reach—slavery—would someday prove vulnerable on the grounds of conscience and free speech. (Southern secession, as we shall see, was preceded by years of struggle over denial of the freedom to print anti-slavery material in the South.) The national government would have had, by virtue of

Madison's rejected amendment, the powers not won for the federal government until this century, when a series of Supreme Court decisions extended the right of due process to include action against the states. If Madison had been successful, this long wait would not have occurred.

Madison's amendment would have affected even the so-called states' rights amendments, the Ninth and Tenth, which say that powers not enumerated or delegated are retained by the states or the people. Some treat these amendments as tautological, but there are important differences of phrasing. The Ninth Amendment talks of "rights" enumerated, and says "the people" retain unenumerated ones. The Tenth mentions "powers" as delegated. The rights in the Ninth are not rights *of the state*, which can, strictly speaking, not have rights. Governments have prerogatives; people have rights—so Hamilton speaks of "abridgments of prerogative" in the state to protect rights in the citizens (F 84.578). What the Ninth says is that rights enumerated *as protected* by the Constitution do not exhaust all the rights inherent in a people. The Tenth talks of powers delegated (not, it should be remembered, of sovereignty). The states can retain powers, though not rights. So "states' rights" is something of a misnomer, no matter how common its use. The states have no natural rights. Their powers are artificial, not natural—they are things *made* by contract. The equation "states are to the federal government as people are to the states" mixes apples and oranges. Citizens alone have rights, in relation to both the states and the federal government.

Madison's proposed amendment would have made *both* the states and the federal government accountable for the protection of those rights. If the states infringed the rights of conscience or free speech, *even in areas not enumerated or expressly delegated,* the federal government would have had the authority to intervene. It will be said that this renders the "states' rights" amendments nugatory. Well, Madison thought of them that way. Even at the moment of proposing them, he trivialized them:

> I find, from looking into the amendments proposed by the state conventions, that several are particularly anxious that it should be declared in the Constitution that the powers not therein delegated should be reserved to the several states. Perhaps words which may de-

fine this more precisely than the whole of the instrument now does, may be considered as superfluous. I admit they may be deemed unnecessary, but there can be no harm in making such a declaration, if gentlemen will allow that the fact is as stated. I am sure I understand it so, and do therefore propose it.[7]

So there was no change in Madison's position between 1787 and 1789. He was still trying to *cut back* on states' rights, offering palliatives to the Antifederalists as a way of bringing back his own favorite plan of federal power.

Hamilton had warned the Antifederalists that if they wanted the federal government to have a bill of rights, that would draw the government into the arena of rights, even while limiting its activity there:

> I will not contend that such a provision would confer a regulating power; but it is evident that it would furnish, to men disposed to usurp, a plausible pretence for claiming that power. They might urge with a semblance of reason, that the Constitution ought not to be charged with the absurdity of providing against the abuse of an authority which was not given, and that the provision against restraining the liberty of the press afforded a clear implication that a power to prescribe proper regulations concerning it was intended to be vested in the national government (F 84.579).

Hamilton proved a good prophet on this point. Though the nineteenth-century interpretation of the Bill of Rights—established by John Marshall's ruling in *Barron* v. *Baltimore* (1833)—was that it did not limit local governments (in this case, to seize property by eminent domain), Akhil Amar has shown that judges kept slipping into an assumption that it did. These "Barron contrarians," as Amar calls them, were constantly tugged into defending rights mentioned in the bill against all comers.[8] But this was not done in a systematic and fully advertent way until the modern extension of due process. Now the federal government does exactly what Madison was calling for, both at the convention and in the first Congress—it blocks states from making law violative of individual rights. If Federalists won a battle with the Constitution but lost a campaign with the Bill of Rights, they are the final winners of the war. What Madison considered the great flaw in the Constitution has been remedied.

With what result? Have Antifederalist fears been realized? Some of them have. Patrick Henry's fear that a national government would interfere in the racial relations within a state has certainly come true. But has this destroyed human freedom or increased it? Henry and others spoke of states as the only shield against despotic control from a central authority. But the real despotism that had to be broken up by (for instance) the civil rights movement in this century was what Madison had identified in 1787—the power of a political majority to impose a conformity with local custom. (Southern blacks were a political minority even in locales where they were a numerical majority, since they were denied the vote.) This is not simply a matter of racial despotism. The importance on the local scene of certain industries can lead to the sacrifice of workers' rights, of safety, of environmental safeguards, where the need to favor the industry takes precedence over other factors. The only remedy in such a case is appeal to the federal government. The competition between states for natural resources or commercial advantage cannot be adjudicated in one or the other state. For that Madison's neutral umpire is needed. In fact, the federal government now plays (however imperfectly) the very role Madison wanted for it.

It is his optimism that some "realists" distrust in Madison. They want to talk of nothing but selfish interests at play. And these interests are judged in purely quantitative terms. A preponderance of any power will be, by definition, an oppressive power, since all power is at the service of selfishness. This leads to a crudely hydraulic approach to government. What flows to one part is taken from some other part—federal power must drain power from both the states and the citizens. This does not distinguish different kinds of power. An increase of power does not necessarily entail a corresponding loss of rights. Sometimes greater power is precisely what leads to greater rights. The citizens are freer because the federal government can protect their rights from the nearer and more biased authority. In certain kinds of war, the most basic right of all—the right to live—can be protected only by the state's assumption of vast war-making powers. In the time of unfettered capitalism, the rights of workers and consumers could be protected only by the assumption of large-scale federal authority. The ability to protect people from contaminated food, air, and water must transcend the sphere of any one state. Madison argued that a state's power to issue paper money contaminated the whole currency of the nation. If the old packinghouses in Chicago could ship meat anywhere without the kinds of regulation that were lacking in 1906, the year of Upton Sinclair's attack on them, the contamination spread to other states would be far more deadly than tainted currency.

Madison was not interested in mere amounts of power, but in different kinds of it. The federal government will be in a position to use whatever power it has with less local entanglement, with a broader play of views, than will more limited jurisdictions. Also, though he could not have predicted this, the modern media of communication make the federal government more easily scrutinized than local government. More people know who their United States senator is than can identify their state senator. This very fact makes people aware of other states' interests—an effect that resembles Madison's description of senators as becoming more aware of foreign views and needs. The federal government makes the citizens more cosmopolitan, not just the officeholders. We all discuss things that are good or bad for the country, not just for our own locale. Our opening to the world and to each other is in great part a consequence of our attention to the national government. In that sense even the American who is antigovernment is educated by the government he or she criticizes. It is the forum for expressing discontents as well as agreement. Some people feel frustrated by it precisely because they need it. Their lives would be emptier if they did not have a president or a Congress on hand to vilify.

8.

No Standing Army

One reason for the move from the Articles of Confederation to the Constitution was military. John Jay argued that a central government could avoid war more readily than could individual provinces chafing against hostile neighbors. But if war should come, the joint strength of the states would be needed to sustain it. Military talent could be drawn from a larger pool, and uniform discipline would prevent reduplication of efforts (F 4.20–21). It did not take a militaristic spirit to see that war was likely, since foreign powers loomed on hazy boundaries all around the new nation—Britain to the north and west, in Canada and the territories; Spain in Florida and Louisiana; France and other powers in the entrepot of the Americas, the Caribbean. Forts and garrisons had to be created and manned in the West where Indian conflicts could arise. America had suffered indignities at sea because it lacked a navy.

Defenders of the Articles said that state militias could handle any challenge; but Hamilton, who had fought beside both Regulars and militiamen in the Revolution, remembered what many people were trying to forget about the militia's performance in the Revolution:

> Here I expect we shall be told that the militia of the country is its natural bulwark and would be, at all times, equal to the national defense. This doctrine in substance had like to have lost us our independence. It cost millions to the United States that might have been saved. The facts, which from our own experience forbid a reliance of this kind, are too recent to permit us to be the dupes of such a suggestion. The steady operations of war against a regular and disciplined army can only be successfully conducted by a force of the same kind (F 25.161–62).

The Antifederalists, nonetheless, were very disturbed by the war powers given Congress and the President under the proposed Constitution. They did not object to the power to declare war, since that had been a congressional power in the Confederation. Few objected to the raising of a navy, since that was both needed and was beyond the resources of a single state. But a fear of "standing" armies (those that "stand over" in peacetime, rather than being disbanded at the end of any war) was strong in the liberal British tradition, and that fear was sharply aroused by the new Constitution. The Antifederalists, acting on this fear, singled out four clauses of the Constitution as particularly dangerous:

1. Power to raise an army in peacetime (Article I, Section 8, Clause 12)

2. Power to arm and discipline the militias (Article I, Section 8, Clause 16)

3. Power to call up the militia for national service (Article I, Section 8, Clause 15)

4. Power of the President as commander in chief (Article II, Section 2, Clause 1)

The first made a standing army legal, the next two established a right of that army to absorb the state militias, and the fourth combined civil and military office in a way redolent of monarchism. All four clauses were attacked vigorously and at length in each state's ratifying convention, with the aim of having them eliminated from the Constitution before it was ratified or having the Constitution itself rejected.

It is frequently, indeed generally, said that the Second Amendment, guaranteeing the existence of state militias with a right to bear arms, was meant to address this fear of standing armies as a threat to freedom. This is an astonishing claim, since the Second Amendment did not eliminate, alter, or weaken a single one of these four objectionable clauses. A standing army was just as possible after its passage as before; and the militia guaranteed to the states was still subordinate to Congress for equipment, pay, training, and absorption into the larger force at need. (The source of pay, remember, was a particular concern of Antifederalists, who objected to federal pay even for nonmilitary officers like congressional delegates.) Thus the basic fear of a standing army was not addressed at all by the Second Amendment. Those who cite the many passages on standing armies from the ratification debates as explicating the rationale for the Second Amendment do not notice the first and most obvious thing about that amendment—its total disconnection from the Antifederalists' complaints. They had promoted the state militias as a way of saying that the standing army was not needed, that they could perform the job without any subjection to a federal military structure. Instead, the Second Amendment just more thoroughly incorporated the militias into that structure. We have a standing army today, of a scale and power beyond the imagination of any Antifederalist in the 1780s; but no one—not even the most ardent idolater of the Second Amendment—thinks that the amendment can or should be used to dissolve our army, navy, and air force.

If Madison had wanted to address the Antifederalists' real concerns, he would have done something about the four clauses on which the debates were obsessively focused. The fact that he did not do so means that we should consider his attitude toward those clauses, one by one. Since we know that he was simultaneously trying to pass the fourteenth item on his list of proposed amendments, the one that provided for federal monitoring of state laws, we must suspect beforehand that aggrandizement of the states was not a motive for his drafting of the Second Amendment. A consideration of each clause will confirm that suspicion.

1. *The standing army.* The British opposition to standing armies was stiffened in the seventeenth-century struggle between king and Parliament. The Parliament's hold on the king was his need for its authorization of new taxes. He could not refuse to call a Parliament, or ignore its demands, if he needed money for a war or the raising of armies. If a provision were made for a standing army, then Parliament would have to authorize a standing fund for its upkeep, and he could thenceforth ignore the Parliament on military matters. In order to preclude this, the Whig party advocated an extensive militia equipped to handle all peacetime emergencies, making the standing army otiose. But practice never matched theory—the ideal of arming the whole male citizenry was as little realized in England as in America. The militia's actual use, just as in America, was as a manpower pool sporadically activated, often at the direction of country squires, for

purposes of internal police and the suppression of dissent.[1] The militia was, as an ideological concept, used for rhetoric against monarchy's pretensions.

And this, as Madison and Hamilton pointed out, made the rhetoric pointless in a country without a king. For them, the Antifederalist fear of a standing army was a bugaboo, a misreading of the American Constitution. The fear was based, moreover, on a misreading of the Whig position even in England. The British Bill of Rights (1688), which opponents of standing armies like to invoke, had not really forbidden standing armies. It had declared (in Article 6) "that the raising or keeping a standing army within the kingdom in time of peace, *unless it be with consent of Parliament,* is against law" (emphasis added). The objection was not to a standing army as such. The Parliament had proposed an army *under its control* in the 1641 Militia Bill, but the king (Charles I) vetoed that.[2] Lois Schwoerer writes that the final success of Parliament was not the abolition of standing armies but the establishment of civilian control over the military.[3] Madison (R 9.992–93) and Hamilton (F 24.153) pointed out that this principle was already won in the American Constitution. Here, the executive cannot raise an army. Only the American parliament—Congress—can do that. What the British Whigs feared was an army independent of the Parliament. Under the American Constitution the army has to be reauthorized every two years, and any attempt to defy its congressional master would lead to the instant loss of its funds.

Besides, the situation of America was far different from that of England and its dependent isles in the eighteenth century. The British had no contiguous land with foreign powers on it after the subduing of Ireland and Scotland. Surrounded on all sides by water, the British homeland was generally not threatened with alien invasion. Any invasion across the Channel would require previous preparation, allowing time to raise a defensive force. Thus the British use of armies on its own islands had mainly been for internal purposes, in dynastic struggles of rival houses for the throne, or in religious wars—between Protestants and Catholics, or between Presbyterians and Anglicans. This experience had led to a natural fear of armies as repressive. In America, not only would the army be under legislative control, but there was no Crown to be struggled for, no establishment of national religion in need of repressive power. And the presence of Indian war bands, or of European troops in territory adjacent to American boundaries, made it foolish to wait for an attack before beginning to raise an army. This, Hamilton said, would "exhibit the most extraordinary spectacle which the world has yet seen—that of a nation incapacitated by its constitution to prepare for defense before it was actually invaded" (F 25.161). Madison developed the same argument in *Federalist* No. 41: "How could a readiness for war in time of peace be safely prohibited unless we could prohibit in like manner the preparations and establishments of every hostile nation?" (F 41.270). At the Virginia ratifying convention, he made this argument:

> Ought it to be known to foreign nations that the general government of the United States of America has no power to raise or support an army, even in the utmost danger when attacked by external enemies? Would not their knowledge of such a circumstance stimulate them to fall upon us? If, Sir, Congress be not invested with this power, any powerful nation, prompted by ambition or avarice, will be invited by our weakness to attack us; and such an attack, by disciplined veterans, would certainly be attended with success when only opposed by irregular, undisciplined militia (R 9.993).

Madison made this same argument to Jefferson when Jefferson supported a prohibition on standing armies (RL 1.545): "Should an army in time of peace be gradually established in our neighborhood by Britain or Spain, declarations on paper would have . . . little effect in preventing a standing force for the public safety" (RL 1.566). Only such a standing force on the American side could deter war, or give Americans a fighting chance if war should be launched from so near a vantage point.

2. *Federal use of the militia.* The Constitution states that Congress may summon the militia "to execute the laws of the Union, suppress insurrections, and repel invasions." Since the Confederate Congress had tried to raise troops to send to Massachusetts when Daniel Shays led a rebellion there (in 1786, just a year before the Constitutional Convention), Antifederalists imagined their own people being called over long distances to put down such violence. The federal government, George Mason claimed, would be "harassing them [militias] from one end of the continent to the other" (R 10.1271). Southerners spoke of having to trek up to New Eng-

land, and northerners imagined service on the borders near Florida or New Orleans. The Federalists said that such activities would be expensive and self-defeating, so there was no need to fear that they would happen. Neighbor states would always be called on first, though prescribing that would not allow for truly rare circumstances (F 30.187, R 10.1272).

What was truly feared was not so much going off on other states' business as having others come into one's own state. Some locales would rather deal with Indians or smugglers or internal dissent in their own way, without federal oversight or scrutiny. And the greatest fear was felt in the South, where the militia's one constant use, one that was considered crucial, was to patrol, intimidate, and keep down the slave population. Carl Bogus has argued very plausibly that uneasiness about the militia's use against slaves underlay many of the objections raised to federal control of the militia.[4] Patrick Henry was especially touchy on this point. When he had gone to the Continental Congress in Philadelphia, he learned how ardent could be the feeling of outsiders about his slaves. He carried letters of commendation from Virginia Baptists, whose religious freedom he had defended, for delivery to the famous Quaker philanthropist Anthony Benezet. Henry was asked how he could defend some men's freedom of religion while denying freedom in its entirety to masses of black slaves.[5] He did not want people who thought like that interfering with Virginia's slave policies. He imagined that Congress, given authority over federalized militia companies, might even put blacks in the ranks: "May Congress not say that every black man must fight?" This would be done as an indirect way of freeing the slaves: "They may, if we be engaged in war, liberate every one of your slaves if they please" (R 10.1476). The militia was a bastion of safety in a very pressing and concrete sense for whites in the South. It was what stood, near at hand, as the protective wall between masters and their slaves. "Internal police" had a sinister meaning there, one necessarily connected with the next point of Antifederalist concern, the federal provision of arms.

3. *Federal discipline of militia.* Henry entertained opposite fantasies on this head. On the one hand, he said that Congress, empowered to arm the militia, could disarm it by not providing arms at all, or not in sufficient numbers (R 9.958). On the other hand, he felt that federal arsenals, magazines, and garrisons on Virginia soil might put arms near the slave population. Guarding their arms caches was a matter of high priority with

southerners. In 1736, rebellious slaves had broken into an arms depot near Stono, South Carolina, and waged a little war. Placing such magazines where slaves could not get at them was a matter of life and death. Yet the federal government would have control of these, since arming the militias was a federal responsibility under the Constitution. Henry's apprehensions on this head were dire:

> They are also to have magazines in each state. These depositories for arms, though within the state, will be free from the control of its legislature. . . . If our legislature be unworthy of legislating for every foot in this state, they are unworthy of saying another word (R 9.1065–66).

•   •   •

> Their garrisons, magazines, arsenals, and forts, which will be situated in the strongest places within the states . . . will reduce the power of the latter to nothing (R 9.961).

•   •   •

> Your strongholds will be in the hands of your enemies (R 9.963).

While openly arguing for militias as the guarantor of Whig freedoms, what Henry and others had in mind was making sure the militias could continue to deny freedom to their slaves.

4. *The power of the commander in chief*. The eighteenth century feared charismatic military leaders. So menacing was the picture of an ambitious man at the head of troops that the dissidents in the Maryland ratifying convention demanded this amendment: "That the President shall not command the army in person without the consent of Congress" (AF 5.97). Patrick Henry thought a monarch would be safer than the president being foisted on the states:

> If we make a king, we may prescribe the rules by which he shall rule his people, and interpose such checks as shall prevent him from infringing

them. But the President, in the field, at the head of his army, can pre-
scribe the terms on which he shall reign master, so far that it will puz-
zle any American ever to get his neck from under the galling
yoke. . . . Can he not, at the head of his army, beat down any opposition? (R 9.964).

But this objection ignored the nonmonarchical nature of the President en-
visioned in the United States Constitution. There is a careless modern usage that refers to the President as "our commander in chief," or simply to
"the commander in chief." When Al Haig was chief of staff in Richard
Nixon's White House, he even told a civilian, "Your commander in chief
has given you an order." But the President is not "our" commander in chief.
His constitutional title is a full but limiting one—"Commander in Chief of
the Army and Navy of the United States, and of the militia of the several
states when called into the actual service of the United States." He is not
even the commander in chief of the militia except when it is actually federalized for a specific task. As soon as that is completed, he is no longer the
commander in chief of those troops.

The American President cannot declare war, or fund it, or ratify a
treaty ending it. If he tries to, he can be impeached. When, in modern
times, he has initiated war activities without authorization, it was because
Congress and the courts were not intent upon restraining him. The fault
was legislative and judicial, not executive. The President is, by his very office, a champion of civilian control of the military, not of military aggression against civilian leadership. As President Truman proved when he
dismissed General MacArthur for insubordination in the Korean War, the
American ethos is supportive of a commander in chief who is *not* a military
lord himself.

So Madison had every reason to support the four clauses that the Antifederalists were objecting to when they said militias must be used to preclude a standing army. But if Madison was not supporting the militias for
that purpose, what made him propose the Second Amendment at all? Why
even take up this widely discussed matter unless he meant to ease some of
the discontent expressed in the debates? Some think he just changed the
subject, not dealing with the militias but with a private right to possess and
use firearms. But that was not a subject on which great concern had been

expressed. In fact, it was raised only once, and even then not discussed, in all the ratifying debates—and if he was not dealing with militias, why did he mention them in the Second Amendment? If he was talking about both a private right and the militias, the militia part must still have to make *some* sense, even if it could not satisfy those who objected to a standing army.

Since the private right to own guns would later be connected with the Second Amendment, I shall be addressing that claim later on (see Chapter 20). The more immediate task is to recognize the overwhelming mass of attacks on the four military clauses in the Constitution. Another later claim would be that the amendment recognizes a right to insurrection against the government (an unlikely thing for Madison to espouse at a time when he was trying to strengthen the federal government, not promote attacks on it). Whatever the merits of that argument—and it, too, must be addressed later (see Chapter 18), since it has become part of Second Amendment lore—it was not what the Antifederalists were trying to assert. Their whole point was that resistance to the government, whether by insurrection or other means, would be doomed if the government were given the crushing power of a standing army.

Why, then, did Madison think he was assuaging Antifederalist anxieties when he proposed the Second Amendment yet retained the standing army clauses? There is a clue to be found in the amendment as he proposed it. Before changes were made by Congress in his draft, it read like this:

> The right of the people to keep and bear arms shall not be infringed, *a well armed and* well regulated militia being the best security of a free country; but no person religiously scrupulous of bearing arms shall be compelled to render military service in person (emphasis added).[6]

Congress, when it rewrote the amendment, omitted the words "well armed and." Yet that was a clear signal of Madison's purpose. The Antifederalists had feared that federal control of the militia's arms would mean that arsenals might go unstocked, that arms not be kept in supply, or not be updated, or not be kept in repair. We have seen Patrick Henry's worry on this score, connected with the use of the militia for slave control. Madison's guarantee of a well-armed militia to the states met this fear.

The whole amendment affirmed the way militias could continue their past role, but now with federal support. Madison was implying that the militias are "subordinately useful," as he said the states would be.

Congress, though it removed one comforting phrase from the Madison draft, seemed nonetheless to grasp what he was trying to accomplish, since it changed his "security of a free country" to "a free state"—indicating the intrastate functions Henry wanted to protect. It also showed great delicacy when it rejected the suggestion that "for the common defense" be added to the draft. That would have limited militia use only to joint efforts by several states, not the individual states' employment of it for internal police. What Madison and the Congress did was underline the independent action of the militias when they were not federalized, pledging that the new government would keep them equipped for that local purpose. The right to demand this service is the first and foremost meaning of "Second Amendment rights."

Whether there are other Second Amendment rights must, as I said, be considered later. But something can be said here about those later discussions. Modern commentators like to quote extensively from the Antifederalist attacks on standing armies in the ratification debates, as if they still applied to the Second Amendment when it became law. But the issue of a standing army was a dead one by then. The Antifederalists had lost. They wanted the militias as an *alternative* to a standing army. When they got militias *and* a standing army, they were not satisfied. Their main object had been defeated. The proof of that is their refusal to support the Second Amendment. Not only did they fail to support ratification, they actively opposed it, saying this was a diversion from the real issue. Patrick Henry tried to block Virginia's ratification of the whole Bill of Rights, suggesting that a new convention be called to redraft the Constitution from scratch. When that ploy did not work, he tried to table the Bill of Rights indefinitely (M 12.463–65). He was joined in his opposition by other Antifederalists, Richard Henry Lee and William Grayson.[7]

Henry's younger ally in Virginia, John Taylor of Caroline, never stopped calling for a *real* militia amendment, one that would take away Congress's power to fund a peacetime army. He proposed this amendment while serving in the United States Senate during Washington's presidency, and he begged Jefferson to sponsor it when *he* became president.[8] It is entirely mistaken, then, to suppose that the Second Amendment prevented the creation of a standing army. And it is futile to look for anti-governmental views in a piece of legislation Madison framed in order to *protect* the powers of government—in this case, the power to have a peacetime army. His actions were taken, in fact, to disarm opposition to the four military clauses in the Constitution, as the Antifederalists well understood. They would be astounded if they could hear modern commentators claim that the Second Amendment actually expressed their views.

III.

Nullifiers

Criminals break laws, and most often recognize that they do. Others act contrary to law without breaking the law. For them, there is no law to be broken. The apparent law is in fact a nullity, a void. The most common way to recognize a null law is to look past it to a higher law, which takes precedence over the voided law. That is the way of Antigone in Sophocles' play. She follows the law of the gods with regard to family burial rights, not the law of her city, Thebes. Christian martyrs followed God's law when they refused to offer sacrifice to the Roman Empire's idols. Dr. King disobeyed segregation laws because God wants his children to live together.

But there is another way of finding a law null and void, an especially American way. That is by obedience to what might be called the lower law. The higher law is transcendent and general. All people in Antigone's situation, no matter what their city, might recognize the law of the gods protecting family rights. She appeals upward, from a particular spot on earth to an overarching principle. The rule of the lower law is an appeal downward, from some large social arrangement to the specifics of a regional code that is deeper in people's lives than the law they break. The response to the higher law is heaven-piercing. That to the lower law is ground-hugging.

The administrators of the law being broken do not, usually, recognize the validity of a higher law. If they did, they would not have passed a lower law at odds with it. Nor does Antigone take any position with regard to the city's laws in general. Thebes might be right in every other way, wrong only where the higher law nullifies its decree. But in America, at least, those who appeal downward to the lower law expect the larger society to recognize its validity. That is because the American government is federal, made up of components that (in the myth of our founding) precede it and have greater authenticity than it does. These components hug the ground.

So we have matching (or inverted) paradoxes. Antigone appeals to the higher law, which seems general, but otherwise accepts the validity of the Theban government—which we might call a *governmental* government, enclosed in its self-sufficiency. The American nullifier appeals downward to a law that seems local and specific, and therefore not a challenge to the whole structure of government above it. But in fact the lower law subtly delegitimates any government above it. Nullifiers invoke what we have seen Carol Rose call the "ancient [local] constitution" against the "plain vanilla [fits all sizes] constitution." Here the whole cluster of anti-governmental attitudes listed at the outset of this book comes into play—amateur and provincial and participatory values are more legitimate than the expert and the cosmopolitan and the delegated. The latter qualities should be willing to yield to the former ones. That, after all, is what gives us an *anti-governmental* government, one that checks itself, defers to state and local authority, questions its own authority, and denies itself efficiency. The authority of Thebes *might* at times be overridden by the higher law, but our federal authority must *expect* to be "underridden" by the lower law.

America's nullifiers believe, therefore, that they are following the Constitution, which is a self-doubting document, a perpetual twitch of nervous checks and abjured efficiency. The lower law actually comes to the rescue of this poor constipated thing, stepping in with a more genuine and assured form of authority, which is just another form of the word "authenticity." The larger government will always be artificial, nonauthentic, when compared with the expression of the people's will in the one domain where it is clearest and least filtered—the idealized small towns and farm communities of Reagan's America. The nullifiers just put into practice what the myths of the Constitution taught them—the myths of sovereign states, of a government denied efficiency so that people can follow their own ways, of branches made co-equal so they can gridlock, of extra-governmental factions authorized to be self-correcting by their interplay.

Some of the greatest men in our history have been nullifiers. Jefferson was one. So, briefly, was Madison—despite his past as the great centralizer of government during the founding period. The appeal of nullification is bound to be great with Americans, expressing as it does so many of their attitudes. It arises most naturally where local traditions are strong and outside interference is most resented. It is resistance on principle—which separates it from mere lawbreaking, whether by bootleggers during Prohibition or traffic violators in our time. The nullifiers are law-abiding—but the law they abide by is the lower law.

9.

John Taylor of Caroline:
Father of Nullification

John Taylor of Caroline (1753–1824) is not considered one of our nation's founders, though he was their contemporary—he fought in the Revolution, served in the first Senate under the Constitution, and wrote influential books on the Constitution. For many of his contemporaries, service in the Continental Army created a continental vision, to match that of the army's leader, George Washington. But Taylor was always decidedly local in his views, a man of his own acres and of neighboring fields. It is appropriate, though an accident, that he is named for his county in Virginia, Caroline County. (He received that appellation when he served in the state legislature, to distinguish him from another delegate named John Taylor.) The Constitution as he expounded it not only allowed for nullification, but was almost built on it. For him, no constitution could be valid that did *not* recognize the primacy of local rule. So deeply was this principle embedded in his thought that other nullifiers, like Jefferson, drew on it extensively, making Taylor the principal theorist of nullification. His appeal has been a quiet but broad one. In this century, he could be admired by a socialist like Charles Beard, a libertarian like H. L. Mencken, and a conservative like Russell Kirk.

After his father's death, Taylor was brought up by the great Virginia lawyer Edmund Pendleton, who sent him to the same Latin school that the young James Madison was attending. Unlike Madison, Taylor went on to study law, and was the opponent in several court cases of the Virginia lawyer whose principles he most detested, the nationalist John Marshall. That was an antipathy he shared, among other things, with Thomas Jefferson. The two even looked somewhat alike—tall, thin, redheaded men. As soon as possible, Taylor used his legal earnings to buy land, the real source of value in his view. He became an expansive plantation owner, acquiring acre after acre, along with the only thing that made such land productive—slaves.

Taylor was an important figure in the nascent Republican party, formed by Madison and Jefferson to oppose the financial credit system of Alexander Hamilton, Washington's secretary of the Treasury. Taylor was the most systematic opponent of Hamilton, since he considered all banking systems unnatural.[1] His views on what was natural, what artificial, resemble mediaeval notions that money cannot "breed." Money that makes money without labor, without creating an extra-monetary product, undermined (in his view) the value of labor. The "paper feudalism" of the money traders made it possible for the commercial few to prey upon the agrarian many.

Robert Shalhope, Taylor's best biographer, noticed that he thinks in antinomies, with the basic conflict between the natural and the artificial behind them all.[2] These antinomies track very closely with the cluster of opposed values I drew up in the introduction to this book. For Taylor, the natural order was personal, direct, organic, religious, candid, productive, simple. The artificial order was impersonal, indirect, mechanical, secular, manipulative, unproductive, intricate—a system, as he repeatedly called it, of "force and fraud." In his works, government fell under the same strictures as commerce.

The way he could use this bipolar method is seen in his defense of southern slavery. He was one of the first to make a claim that would become popular in the 1830s, as the South steeled itself against the abolitionists—that plantation slaves were better off than "wage slaves" in the North. The wage slaves were subject to an impersonal system, not to a personal master, where human contact is softened by affection, compassion, and the duties of religion:

> Did a hierarchy of a paper system ever shed tears over its oppression, or feel compunction for its extractions? . . . It is otherwise with the personal owner of slaves. Religion assails him both with her blandishments and terrors. It indissolvably binds him and his slave's happiness and misery together.[3]

Taylor admits that slaves are not treated perfectly by some masters. But that is because of the intrusion of artificial forces into the natural (paternal) relationship of master to slave. There are three such artificial invaders. First, commercial interests place the owner under the economic duress of earning credit, making him more exigent with his workers. (Like Jefferson, Taylor was deeply indebted to the banks he denounced.) Second, the same commercial pressure leads to the introduction of overseers to maximize production. In Taylor's eyes, the overseer stands to the owner in the same relation as a mercenary does to a militiaman. Third, the presence of black freedmen creates slave unrest that forces the master to be harsher than he wants to be. Freedmen are artificial in the sense that they do not organically belong to either of the "natural" classes in the South, free white men or black slaves. They disturb the natural order and must be removed. Like Jefferson and other southerners, Taylor wanted all freedmen colonized elsewhere, either isolated in western territories or shipped back to Africa. Despite his opposition to the federal government, he called for it to supply the money for this colonization and supported federal jurisdiction in the territories for the sake of it.

Taylor's conviction that only the South had a natural order of society was strengthened when he served in the Continental Army during the Revolution. The northerners he met were a rabble, they were not gentlemen. Pawns of war profiteers, they had no sense of honor: "I wish from my soul we had more Virginias than one, but as we have not, the honor of preserving America must be acquired by one alone."[4] This antipathy was renewed when Taylor went to Philadelphia as a senator in 1792. He saw all the North in thrall to Hamilton. After Taylor heatedly denounced John Jay's 1794 treaty with England for favoring northern shipping, Senators Rufus King of New York and Oliver Ellsworth of Connecticut took him aside and said that if regional differences were so great perhaps it would be better to dissolve the Union. Taylor took this as a scheme to make the North secede and rejoin monarchical Britain, but Madison assured him that it was said only to make *Taylor* less intransigently sectional.[5]

Taylor said that he did not want to dissolve the Union—he was not a secessionist—but he did feel that Virginia must protect itself from a Congress subservient to commercial interests. On his return home from the Senate in 1793, he wrote a pamphlet called *An Enquiry into the Principles and Tendency of Certain Public Measures.* Here Taylor first argued that each state has the power to decide for itself which laws are valid, and to nullify the invalid ones. He sent a copy of the manuscript to Madison, who forwarded it to Vice President Jefferson. Much taken with the argument, Jefferson had excerpts from it printed in the *National Gazette* (RL 2.759–60). Five years later Jefferson would be making similar arguments when he became a nullifier.

The *Enquiry* argues that state legislatures have "at least as good a right to judge of every infraction of the Constitution as Congress itself," since they were "annual conventions of the people."[6] The people continually make and remake all law, since they never surrender their sovereignty to any government. Taylor would be inconsistent in his treatment of state sovereignty. Sometimes he denied sovereignty to any government. At other times he called state legislatures sovereign since they were interim conventions of the people. He disliked using the term "sovereign," since only God is truly competent to all his purposes—sovereignty, "sacrilegiously stolen from God," was bound to be "equivocal and illimitable" when applied to human life.

Despite these reservations over the word, Taylor admitted it into his language, applying it only to the people, not to their agents. He argued, then, for the indivisibility of sovereignty, and mocked claims that the federal government and the states can both have sovereignty: "Is there not an obvious inconsistency between the admission of two distinct governments, constituting different provinces or departments of power, and the assertion that one possesses sovereignty or supremacy over the other?"

Since, for Taylor, the interpersonal level of society is natural, and therefore good, it is to be trusted as absolutely as government is to be distrusted. On this issue, Taylor differed from his old schoolmate Madison. Though Taylor's principal work, *Inquiry into Principles and Policy*, is mainly an attack on John Adams's concept of balanced government, Taylor also mounts an assault on Madison's views about factious majorities. The direct expression of majority will is always bound to have more good in it than evil. If it errs, it is by an error unlikely to be corrected by anything but itself. Since it is the majority, it does not have to fear other forces, whereas a minority, feeling oppressed, will take desperate measures to gain unfair advantage:

> The force of self-love is as strong in majorities as in an individual, but its effect is precisely contrary. It excites one man to do wrong because he is surrounded with objects of oppression, and majorities to do right because he can find none.[7]

The relation of majority to minority is like that of master to slave. The dominant partner, assured of his dominance, is free to express a *natural* goodness. In a speech to the Senate in 1803, Taylor argued that *only* minorities can be factious.

The people are always sovereign in Taylor's system, and the majority are the people—but only when they are speaking directly. Representation dilutes the natural voice of the people, and is only a conduit of its virtuous decisions if tied directly to the people by instruction. Here, too, he differed from Madison. The people's agents cannot *be* agents if they are not carrying out the people's instructions. Freeing a delegate from that responsibility "would divest the representative of the character of agent and transform him into a despot, at liberty to pursue his own ambition, interests, caprice or vanity, without regard to any principal." The people's sovereign will is best expressed in a *convention* of all the people. State assemblies, so long as they have rotation, instruction, and short terms, can be considered provisional conventions for ordinary purposes. More distant agencies—like the federal government—are hard to control, and their enactments are null if they escape the control of state conventions.

Since the states are close to the source of all authority, the people, they obviously have a greater right to decide what is binding than do more distant bodies. If a majority in one state raises an objection to a federal law, the naturally good majorities in other states are likely to agree with it. Taylor imagined a kind of solidarity among state majorities like the solidarity of slave owners in Virginia. If other states failed to respond to a call for nullification of an unjust law, it could only be because they had been corrupted by commercial interests.

For his followers in the South, the purity of Taylor's system was very attractive. He was praised for his uncompromising attitude. But in fact his scheme was too pure to be followed, even by him. Nothing was more important for him than rotation in office, especially at the remote level of the federal government; but when Jefferson was finishing his second term, Taylor, fearing that the anti-majoritarian Madison would succeed him, urged Jefferson to stay on for a third term. When Taylor was serving in the Senate, his purist conception of the separation of powers made him stop corresponding with his friend James Monroe—since Monroe was serving as an ambassador, part of the executive branch, it would be an improper mingling of the branches for a legislator to communicate with him. Yet Taylor urged Jefferson, while he was president, to assume some legislative powers.

Taylor's belief in the goodness of nature—in the soil, as in those who owned it—showed up in his well-known agricultural reforms. He refused to use mineral fertilizer since it had to be taken from below the earth, and God provided all the natural nutrients above the earth. His famous "living fences" (close-planted trees) were treasured because they were not "artificial" fences made by man. (Planting the trees did not count as "manufacturing," like making rails for a conventional fence.) Taylor considered the essential agreement of Virginia voters to be the product of a natural rationality in men close to the soil, not as the solidarity of a white population that had to maintain a common front against its black slaves.

Taylor knew little of the rest of the country—his misreading of King's and Ellsworth's comments in Philadelphia was typical of his provincialism. He was uncomfortable away from his plantations, and rushed back to them after his few brief journeys. He claimed to know Virginia well—but he idealized the state, despite the blots on it formed by bankers, overseers, and freemen (*not* by slaves, whom he considered an ornament, not a blot). In this, as in so many other cases, the man who thinks he knows only one thing does not know even that. Taylor thought that only commercial interests could be avaricious. He found nothing greedy about adding acres to acres. One reason he was in such deep debt was that he tried to acquire ever more plantations. This man who grew up fatherless wanted to leave each son a plantation, and he even had one left over, by the end, for a grandson.

Taylor is important because he first put Virginia's values in a deceptively theoretical and "objective" framework. He gave a purer metaphysical air to Jefferson's hunch that virtue was innate in the "yeomanry" (the agricultural class). Above all, he was successful in passing off the paradox of class solidarity as a form of individualism. His rigor was rhetorical rather than logical. He pretended to be reasoning his way to the laws of nature when he was just spinning a shiny cocoon around the shared values of his province. He was right to distrust Madison, who felt that men's prejudices need airing in cosmopolitan forums.

10.

Jefferson:
Prophet of Nullification

Thomas Jefferson became a secret nullifier in 1798, when John Adams was president and he was vice president. A war with France seemed in the offing, because of French violation of American shipping rights on the high seas. In the frenzied atmosphere of impending war, the Federalist-dominated Congress passed four laws—the Alien and Sedition Acts—meant to exclude or expel or silence sympathizers with the French. Jefferson, a French sympathizer himself, was put in a very delicate situation. As vice president, he had actually chaired the Senate when some of the obnoxious laws were passed. To oppose the laws openly would not only have led to accusations that he was undermining his own president's administration but could have exposed him to the very laws whose passage through debate he had presided over.[1] Yet he believed that the acts undid the entire American Revolution. He could not sit by and do nothing. So he worked clandestinely, with Madison and others, to coordinate attacks on the laws by various state legislatures, beginning with those of Virginia and Kentucky. In an almost hysterical reaction to the laws, Jefferson privately went beyond urging nullification and talked recklessly of secession or insurrection (JW 454–55, M 17.258).

The 1798 acts, bad as they were, cannot explain this extreme response by Jefferson. He saw them as only one sign of a vast conspiracy by the Federalists, under the evil inspiration of Alexander Hamilton, to impose a monarchy on the American people. His panic over the conspiracy was later neglected or downplayed by Jefferson's admirers, who had to explain his own secret plot solely in terms of the Alien and Sedition Acts. The acts became not only the harbingers of despotism but its full-blown advent. More than a dark moment in our early history, they would be read as the prototype and forerunner of all later acts of repression. This status was confirmed when James Morton Smith published, in 1956, what became the standard book on the Alien and Sedition Acts, *Freedom's Fetters*. The book had been composed during the McCarthy period, and it was taken as a commentary on the witch-hunts of the early 1950s. Part II of Smith's book was called "The Time of the Witches," a phrase coined by Jefferson.

Since Jefferson's response to the laws of 1798 gave nullification the warrant of his great name, he is the prophet to whom later nullifiers have traced their ancestry. This makes it important to see what justification he had for mounting so desperate an effort against Congress's legislation when he was vice president. Were the laws explicable only in conspiratorial terms, as a coup against the Republic, or can they be understood in a less extreme context? Before that question is considered, the laws themselves should be listed.

1. *The Naturalization Act.* This was meant to discourage immigrants, mainly from France. It extended the period that must precede naturalization from five to fourteen years.

2. *The Alien Enemies Act.* This gave the President authority, in time of actual war, to detain or expel citizens of the country with which we are at war.

3. *The Alien Act.* This gave the President power, even in peacetime, to expel any alien on mere suspicion that he is dangerous. The measure was only for the duration of the crisis (defined as two years), and no one was expelled in that time.

4. *The Sedition Act.* Another temporary measure, to expire on March 3, 1801, this was the only one of the four laws actively enforced. The law made it a crime to speak or publish "any false, scandalous, and malicious writing" against the government. All three adjectives had to be proved (they are linked by "and," not "or"), so truth would be a defense—an improvement on the common law of sedition that had recently been

passed in England as the Libel Act of 1792. But this advance was canceled in some of the trials, presided over by Federalist Supreme Court Justice Samuel Chase. In circuit court, he just declared certain things false, brooking no argument on the matter.

It must be admitted that the laws look bad enough, on their face, to make one wonder if a Congress willing to pass them was not becoming despotic. But an explanation short of the conspiratorial is available, if we consider public opinion at the time on four matters related to the acts: (1) the country's early misgivings about foreigners, (2) the problem of citizen loyalty, (3) the rise of political parties, and (4) the freedom of the press. The acts have these four things as their matrix, and they must be considered within that matrix if they are to be understood properly.

1. *Foreigners.* America had not been a country populated at the outset, except by its natives. Arriving British settlers had to compete with French and Spanish settlers on the same continent. It seemed important, in frontier conditions, to retain the ethos of what petitioners in the early 1770s would call "the rights of Englishmen." This was not so much "nativism"— exclusion of new arrivals from a settled society—as the solidarity of people who were themselves comparative newcomers. Their attitude was expressed in 1753 by so liberal a thinker as Benjamin Franklin. He feared that a heavy influx of Germans into Pennsylvania, where a difference in language made it hard to convey the attitudes of British law to the immigrants, would undermine that law: "In short, unless the stream of their importation could be turned from this to other colonies, as you very judiciously propose, they will so outnumber us that all the advantages we have will not, in my opinion, be able to preserve our language and even our government."[2]

During the Revolution, Jefferson was still voicing such fears. When he drafted a bill for naturalizing foreigners in Virginia, he considered at first excluding Catholics and Jews, restricting immigration to "foreign Protestants" (J 1.558). And in his *Notes on the State of Virginia*, written in 1781, after telling his French correspondent that America's constitution (at that time, the Articles) is "a composition of the freest principles of the English constitution with others derived from natural right and natural reason," he said that immigrants would now be coming from the lands of "absolute monarchy," used to living with a corrupt system of politics and religion. He pictured the results of such immigration in apocalyptic terms:

> They will bring with them the principles of the governments they leave, imbibed in their early youth; or, if able to throw them off, it will be in exchange for an unbounded licentiousness, passing as is usual from one extreme to another. It would be a miracle were they to stop precisely at the point of temperate liberty. These principles, with their language, they will transmit to their children. In proportion to their numbers, they will share with us the legislation. They will infuse into it their spirit, warp and bias its direction, and render it a heterogeneous, incoherent, distracted mass (JW 211).

What he feared during the war with England in the 1780s, Federalists feared at the prospect of war with France in the 1790s—though they felt that French visitors would not be bringing the principles of absolute monarchy but of Jacobin regicide. Both attitudes seem almost paranoid to us, but both were connected then to longer-standing concerns voiced by Franklin in the 1750s.

2. *Loyalty.* This, too, was a subject with a history. Leonard Levy, in his famous assault on Jefferson's failings as a liberal, condemns him for administering loyalty oaths as the wartime governor of Virginia, for signing into law a treason bill that punished the expression of opinion, for drawing up a bill of attainder against an individual, and for sequestering Loyalists (in a "precursor of modern internment camps").[3] Levy wrote in the aftermath of McCarthyism, and all the sins he imputes to Jefferson would be outrages in our modern democracy. But Jefferson's loyalty oaths were administered in the midst of a revolution, when separating the supporters of the Revolution from Loyalists who still adhered to the Crown was necessary. After all, the American people had in the past taken an oath of loyalty to their king, and the governor of Virginia, Lord Dunmore, had asked for a renewal of that oath at the beginning of the Revolution. The Revolutionaries broke that old oath and took a new one to the United

States. They demanded the same of people suspected of retaining the old allegiance.

Jefferson's Revolutionary bill of attainder punished expressions of loyalty to the king, assertions of his right to rule the colonies, or efforts to persuade others to share that British allegiance. This was a milder position than that taken in most of our wars—and the Revolution was in some measure a civil war, fought within the larger war of separation from the Crown. Certainly the Revolutionary "internment" of Loyalists was more understandable than our treatment of Japanese Americans in the 1940s. In our Revolution, the British were fighting on our soil, in close association with the Loyalists scattered through society—as opposed to the situation in World War II, when combat was on distant continents and Japanese Americans had not taken a prior oath to the emperor of Japan. The attainder (outlawry) against an individual, Josiah Philips, was less justifiable, though Jefferson always defended it as a war measure, since Philips led a band of Tory bandits who were "standing out in arms" against the state (J 2.189–93). Whatever one thinks of these measures in themselves, they supply a background of agreement on the need for loyalty that was still with the Americans in the 1790s.

3. *Party.* For republicans of the eighteenth century, the very word "party" was in bad odor. It meant that one was partisan, looking to the good of one part of society and not to the common good. It was connected with the British creation of partial loyalties by the bribery of government appointments ("places"), cutting across the constitutional building blocks of Ministry, Lords Spiritual, Lords Temporal, and Commons with adventitious loyalties spanning them all. When America's government was set up, the first Federalist administrations thought they were not a party but the government, and party was only what opposed government. The opposition that would become known as Republicans thought their own organization was a temporary expedient made necessary by Federalist usurpation. Jefferson sincerely believed he could bring partisanship to an end when he became president. The agreement that there was something wrong with partisanship was reflected in the secrecy with which Jefferson organized the opposition, financed its organs, used cat's-paws and "cut-outs" to disguise the coordinated nature of the

criticism being directed at Adams and Hamilton. This does not excuse the criminalizing of opinion in the sedition laws; but it shows that party organization could still be considered an enemy of freedom, not its expression.

4. *The press.* Insofar as newspapers were seen as secretly funded expressions of partisanship, they were subject to the same odium as parties themselves. Also, at a time of suspect loyalties, they were thought (with some justification) to be taking part of their direction and support from foreign powers. Men like Hamilton and the Federalist politician Timothy Pickering did coordinate their propaganda with the British, as Jefferson had supported for a time the propaganda of Edmond Genet, a French visitor who tried to arouse Americans' resistance to President Washington's neutrality policy. When senators asked for and got the French communications on which President Adams was basing his policy hostile to France, they were embarrassed to find that the French had boasted of their ability to influence a part of the American community, dividing the nation (M 17.108–10).

None of this is said to defend the sedition laws—they were clearly unconstitutional. But all these factors undermine Jefferson's suspicion that the *only* explanation for the laws was a plot to create an American monarch. They make it clear that people could support the laws for less horrendous purposes. That fact would be confirmed when, as Levy points out, Jefferson replicated the worst aspects of the sedition law during his own presidency—proving that such legislation need not come from a plot to overthrow the government and install a monarch. Jefferson took measures to punish newspapers that disagreed with him. By an ironic twist he tried to unseat Justice Chase for his views—after criticizing Chase for outlawing opinion under the Sedition Act. Worst of all, he asked for and used powers to enforce his embargo on British trade by what "remains the most repressive and unconstitutional legislation ever enacted by Congress in time of peace." By his own lights, this should have justified nullification at the least, but those who tried to resist his embargo were imprisoned at presidential discretion (see Chapter 12).

It is legitimate to wonder if Jefferson's reaction to the acts was proportionate, wise, or even justified. The bad laws of that year were not monstrous, by comparison with many abuses in our history. About two dozen men were tried under the Sedition Act, and of those convicted all but one served under one year in prison.[4] They became heroes to the country—one, Matthew Lyon of Vermont, was reelected to Congress during his four-month term in jail, others were pardoned. A journalist, Thomas Cooper, was given a pardon during his six-month term but refused to take it, since jail made the ideal pulpit for preaching against the sedition law. The Federalists were ridiculed for their comic zeal—laughter was one weapon that never occurred to Jefferson—and that unpopular zealotry lost them the presidency when Adams was defeated in 1800.[5] Contrast that with the hundreds of lives ruined by McCarthyism, or with the thousands of arrests and six hundred deportations in 1919, when Attorney General A. Mitchell Palmer conducted "Red Raids" to arrest and deport suspected anarchists without due process.[6]

One indication that Jefferson overreacted to the Alien and Sedition Acts can be found in the later work of James Morton Smith himself. When he published *Freedom's Fetters* in 1956, presenting the acts as a great attack on civil liberties, he said he would follow it up with a book on Jefferson's response to the acts, which promised to be a celebration of Jefferson's regard for civil liberties. That book never appeared. Smith was obviously having second thoughts. When, forty years later, he published *The Republic of Letters,* a magisterial three-volume edition of the Jefferson-Madison correspondence, with a lengthy running commentary, he was highly critical of Jefferson's nullification campaign.

What was that campaign? As Jefferson sat in the Senate and watched the progress of the Alien Acts, he became deeply frightened and angry. Just two weeks before debate on the bills, when he received a letter from John Taylor of Caroline calling for secession of the South, Jefferson tried to calm him: "A little patience, and we shall see the reign of the witches pass over" (JW 1050). But he could not take his own advice. Before the Sedition Act reached a final vote, he broke off his attendance in the Senate, left for Virginia, and went straight to Madison's plantation. There he proposed the anonymous introduction of resolutions into southern legislatures calling for opposition to the acts. The result of this was the Virginia Resolutions (secretly drafted by Madison) and the Kentucky

Resolutions (even more secretly drafted by Jefferson). These were meant to provoke similar action in other states, in a chain reaction that John Taylor had once imagined as the proper course of nullification. But the Kentucky and Virginia Resolutions had no immediate effect—though, as we shall see in Chapter 13, they had an undesired impact years later, when their authorship became known. The nation had a better way than nullification to punish the sponsors of the acts—at the polls. Jefferson was the beneficiary of that approach. His covert scheming in 1798 did nothing to carry him into the White House in 1800—in fact, it might have prevented his victory if his part in it had been known. The real lesson of the episode is the utility of elections as a corrective to governmental excess.

Even Madison, Jefferson's closest associate in the undercover campaign, thought that Jefferson was going too far. They had decided to draw up separate documents, to make the effort look more spontaneous, as if it were breaking out in various places, not arranged by a single group. Jefferson originally planned to have friends in North Carolina introduce his paper there (which would have made them the North Carolina Resolutions), but a visitor to Monticello asked to take the document to his native Kentucky and promote it there, and Jefferson acceded. The paper he turned over reflected the indignation that was consuming Jefferson—a fact reflected in its clumsy prose. His admirer Dumas Malone admits that "the draft was prolix and repetitious—a thing which could not often be said of his important papers."[7] The fact that he was not going to be known as the author seems to have licensed a kind of maximum rhetoric. Even Madison was alarmed by passages like this, and, as soon as he had a chance to see it, urged its removal:

> these and successive acts of the same character, unless arrested at the threshold, necessarily drive these states into revolution and blood, and will furnish new calumnies against republican government and new pretexts for those who wish it to be believed that man cannot be governed but by a rod of iron (JW 454–55).

Arguing that the Constitution is a compact between sovereign states, Jefferson said that no one but the partners to the compact can interpret it, and any state can therefore nullify a law. Over and over he sounds the nul-lification formula, like the tolling of a plangent bell:

are altogether void, and of no force . . .
is not law, but is altogether void, and of no force . . .
is therefore not law, but utterly void, and of no force . . .
declaring these acts void, and of no force . . .

He even suggests the setting up of committees of correspondence in the states, to coordinate the nullification campaign—an ominous proposal for people who remembered that the Revolution was hatched from state com-mittees of correspondence.

Because of the unexpected visitor from Kentucky, Jefferson's resolu-tions left his hands before Madison could see them and urge the removal of nullification language—he would use quite different terms in his own Vir-ginia Resolutions. But the Kentucky legislature removed the language Madison was objecting to on its own. It apparently realized what James Morton Smith finally concluded:

This sweeping claim in the name of states' rights, had it been imple-mented, would have placed Kentucky in open defiance of federal laws; it was an extreme argument that was potentially as dangerous to the Union as the oppressive laws were to individual liberty (RL 2.1070).

Jefferson refused to accept Madison's counsels of temperance—with the result, as Smith notes, that "in no instance since their exchange of views on 'the earth belongs to the living' did the Father of the Constitu-tion differ so fundamentally with the Author of the Declaration of Inde-pendence" (RL 2.1072). Madison did not want to use the term "nullify," but the vaguer word "interpose," in order to suggest a range of peaceful ag-itation against the acts. He sent his own document to John Taylor of Car-oline for introduction into the debates of the Virginia House of Delegates (without revealing the author's identity). But the emissary carrying the message to Taylor in Williamsburg stopped off, on his way, at Monticello. Jefferson, looking over Madison's draft, insisted that his own nullification language be inserted. Then, as in a farce about letters gone astray, Madison got Taylor to take the language out again before the final vote on the resolutions.

Thus "nullification" was removed from both the Kentucky and the Virginia Resolutions as those were passed—it was, as Smith writes, "a word that Madison came to abhor" (RL 2.1070). But the word slipped into the public discourse in two ways. First, John Taylor's copy of Madison's text with Jefferson's addition, not the final text, was printed in the newspapers. Second, both the Kentucky and Virginia legislatures, disappointed that they had not caused a stir, inserted the term when reaffirming their resolutions in the following year (1799). By that time Jefferson was contemplating "scission" (secession), writing to Madison that they should be "determined, were we to be disappointed in this [nullification], to sever ourselves from that union we so much value" (RL 2.118). Smith, though a harsh critic of the Alien and Sedition Acts, to which he devoted his first book, calls this "Jefferson's fateful—perhaps fatal—theory of 'scission' " (RL 2.1109). It would come back to haunt both Jefferson and Madison during their presidencies. It would be referred to by almost all later proponents of nullification or secession. Jefferson's Kentucky Resolutions might be called the basic document of anti-governmentalism in America, much cited and even revered. Despite the generally disconnected prose of the resolutions, their author's passion betrayed itself in some famous rhetorical outbursts:

> confidence is everywhere the parent of despotism—free government is founded in jealousy, and not in confidence; it is jealousy and not confidence which prescribes limited constitutions, to bind down those whom we are obliged to trust with power . . . let no more be heard of confidence in man, but bind him down from mischief by the chains of the Constitution (JW 454–55).

These are noble words, unobjectionable in themselves—but they were said in support of two very dangerous things, things that Madison wanted to steer clear of: nullification and secession. Jefferson's position on both points he had to mute as president, and we all have cause to regret his championship of them against the Alien and Sedition Acts. His Kentucky Resolutions have done far more damage, down through the years, than did the laws he wrote against. They became a sacred text to the South as it took the road toward the Civil War. It was as the prophet of nullification that he became the father of that bloody "scission."

11.

Madison:
Abettor of Nullification

Though Madison removed Jefferson's nullifying terminology from his Virginia Resolutions, that did not save him from later accusations that he had promoted nullification in 1798. In the 1820s and 1830s, to Madison's great discomfort, Robert Hayne and John Calhoun cited his resolutions as the inspiration for their attempts to nullify northern tariff laws (see Chapter 13). This was not entirely unreasonable on their part. Not only was Madison politically allied with the activities of the genuine nullifiers of 1798—with Jefferson and John Taylor and Wilson Cary Nicholas—but he adopted, in this period, the arguments on which the doctrine of nullification was based. He even reversed himself on one of his principal contentions during the drafting and ratifying of the Constitution. Then he had argued that the Constitution is *not* a pact between sovereign states. That was his position at the Constitutional Convention, in *The Federalist,* during the Virginia ratifying convention, and at the first Congress under the new Constitution (where he introduced his amendment for federal oversight of citizens' rights). His own survey of governments, drawn up in preparation for the Constitutional Convention, a work he called *The Vices of Political Systems,* concluded that the compact theory was the cause of all confederations' incapacity:

> As far as the union of the states is to be regarded as a league of sovereign powers, and not as a political constitution, by virtue of which they are become one sovereign power, so far it seems to follow, from the doctrine of compacts, that a breach of any of the articles of the confederation, by which any of the parties to it absolves the other parties

from their respective obligations, and gives them a right, if they choose to exert it, of dissolving the union altogether (M 9.352–53).

The compact theory, in other words, leaves a union no legal protection against secession—a truth that would be confirmed by Calhoun and his followers.

Given his views on a compact between sovereigns, Madison is very careful—more so, I think, than has been noticed—in the way he uses the word "compact" in *The Federalist*. He *never* applies it to the Constitution as properly construed. He uses it mainly (six times in No. 43) to describe and condemn the Articles. One use of the word describes a similar confederation (F 19.118), one refers to social contract theory in general (F 44.301), and one describes the dissolution of the Union that would occur *if* the Constitution had not provided for the supremacy of the federal tribunal. By providing such supremacy, the Constitution avoids the fate of a mere contract between sovereign parties:

> It is true that in controversies relating to the boundary between the two [state and federal] jurisdictions, the tribunal which is ultimately to decide is to be established under the general government. . . . Some such tribunal is clearly essential to prevent an appeal to the sword and a dissolution of the *compact;* and that it ought to be established under the general rather than under the local governments—or, to speak more properly, that it could be safely established under the first alone—is a position not likely to be combated (F 39.256–57, emphasis added).

But ten years later Madison adopts the position he had consistently opposed up to this point. His resolutions "explicitly and peremptorily declare, that it [the Virginia assembly] views the powers of the federal government as resulting from the compact to which the states are parties" (M 17.189). Earlier, he had urged that the Constitution be ratified by conventions of the people so that it would *not* be the states ratifying through their legislatures. Patrick Henry rightly saw this as the force of beginning the Constitution with the words "We the people" (rather than "We the states").

Yielding to the compact theory of the Constitution involved Madison in other admissions he had strenuously resisted before—for example, that the Constitution gives the federal government only "the grants enumerated in that compact" (to quote the Virginia Resolutions). In *The Federalist,* Madison would talk only of enumerated *objects* of government (F 14.86, 39.256). This leaves unenumerated the means to those ends. What he means by this important distinction he spells out in *The Federalist:*

> Had the Convention attempted a positive enumeration of the *powers* necessary and proper for carrying their other *powers* into effect, the attempt would have involved a complete digest of laws on every subject to which the Constitution relates—accommodated, too, not only to the existing state of things but to all the possible changes which futurity may produce. For in every new application of a general *power,* the particular powers which are the means of attaining the *object* of the general power must always, necessarily, vary with that *object,* and be often properly varied whilst the *object* remains the same (F 44.304, emphasis added).

What made Madison change his mind on such fundamental matters? This was the last and most extreme step he would take in reaction to what he saw as the collapse of his theory of a federal government in the Congress of the 1790s. He had maintained that the general government would be more disinterested and virtuous than local bodies, which could be made the captive of particular interests. But now, he felt, the Hamiltonian money interest had gained an early and corrupting power in the national legislature—just the thing he had said would not happen there. His reaction came in three stages. In 1791, to oppose Hamilton's plan for a national bank, Madison construed the Constitution strictly, to say there was no power to do such a thing in the document. This was a complete reversal of his argument for loose construction in *Federalist* No. 37 and for enumerated objects rather than powers in No. 44. As Madison's biographer Irving Brant notes, in the bank argument "Hamilton's basic contention was a paraphrase of Madison's explanation of the 'necessary and proper' clause in *The Federalist* No. 44," so Madison was "arguing against himself."[1] That Madison's objection was not really based on a deeper reading of the Constitution, but on his hatred of the bank, is proved, for Brant, by the fact that Madison was simultaneously pushing for other programs not explicitly provided for in the Constitution.

That was Madison's first step back from his own constitutionalism. Three years later, in reaction to another thing he abominated, John Jay's treaty with England, which meshed with Hamilton's commercial policy, Madison abandoned his division-of-labor view of the relationship between the Senate and the House of Representatives. To oppose the treaty, Madison argued that the House had the right to be consulted, and to look at the negotiating documents, since a grant of money might be called for in its application—this despite the fact that Jefferson had agreed that the lower house would be "illy equipped" for such delicate work in diplomacy.

Four years later Madison was goaded by the Alien and Sedition Acts to the most serious defection from his own careful program of a decade earlier. Not only did he change his views on the compact, on enumerated powers, and on loose construction; he used a word less clear than "nullification," but one that would have an influence just as profound on later deliberations—"interposition": "in case of a deliberate, palpable, and dangerous exercise of other powers not granted by the said compact, the states thereto have the right, and are in duty bound, to interpose for arresting the progress of the evil . . ." (M 17.189). As the editors of his papers note, this had one advantage over nullification—it was vaguer (M 17.305). But it was ominous as well. "Interpose" is a strong word, meaning "to block"—and it is here doing something, "arresting" an evil, that sounds like more than a discussion of the evil.

Madison's own use of the word in *The Federalist* shows that it is more active than he would later claim of it. He uses it of an umpire or judge who *forbids* an action (F 38.243). He uses it five times in *Federalist* No. 43 while arguing that the federal government will not *intrude* in the state's proper activities. It is clear that Madison is claiming some special right for the states, not just the right everyone has to discuss the merits of a law, when he says that interposing will *arrest* an abuse of power. Calhoun later contended that it is mere quibbling to say that interposition is in any important way different from nullification. Those who admire Madison as a champion of states' rights are not admiring (as they think) the Madison of *The Federalist* but the Madison of 1798—even though he would spend the rest of his life trying to back away from the Virginia Resolutions. He did this as president. He did it later in sectional disputes— over Missouri statehood, over tariffs, over Texas statehood. He returned, in opposition to John Taylor, to *The Federalist*'s view of the supremacy clause.

The retreat from "the spirit of '98" began as early as '99, when Madison was obliged to soften his resolutions in the act of explaining them. The call for other states to join Virginia in protesting the sedition laws had elicited only four responses from other legislatures—all of them harshly negative. The next session of Virginia's assembly was scheduled to discuss a response to these criticisms. George Washington, who saw the divisive heritage be- ing created by this new doctrine of interposition, begged Patrick Henry to run for the assembly and prevent any escalation of the defiance (M 17.245–47). Henry was now Washington's firm ally, despite his defense of states' rights a decade earlier. Jeffersonians thought he had been cor- rupted by the credit system that brought him more land, or that he was simply indulging his animosity toward Jefferson, but it is conceivable that, given his predictions of a horrendous despotism that would follow on adop- tion of the Constitution, the performance of the government in its early days had pleasantly surprised him. It is also true that he never shared the Jeffersonians' deep hostility toward Britain. In any event, his determina- tion to oppose the resolutions caused great anxiety in Jefferson and John Taylor, who begged Madison to return to the assembly and struggle once more with the formidable Henry.

The contest shaping up promised to be another example of what we constantly find in these early days of the Republic—a dos à dos reversing of positions. Henry and Madison would each be taking up the other man's ar- guments from their first great encounter of 1788. The nation was deprived of that interesting spectacle—Henry died just before the assembly met. But his ghost, could it have haunted the chamber, must have smiled to hear Madison mouthing his own words, claiming that the federal government "would by degrees consolidate the states into one sovereignty" (M 17.313) and describing a compact between sovereign states with the arguments Henry had used for retaining the Articles. Even earlier (1796) Henry had taken a gloomy satisfaction in the way Madison reversed himself to oppose the Senate's sole right to ratify the Jay Treaty. Writing to Elizabeth Aylet on August 20, 1795, he said:

> What must I think of those men, when I myself warned of the danger of giving the power of making laws by means of treaty to the President and Senate, when I see these same men denying the existence of that power which they insisted, in our convention, ought properly to be exercised by the President and Senate and by none other?

Madison's arguments in the assembly of 1799 were released as a lengthy pamphlet called the *Report of 1800*. Though he held to the basic argument of the resolutions on such matters as the compact and enumerated powers, and spelled out more explicitly the power of the states as the ultimate tribunal to decide on constitutionality, he was notably irenic toward the states that had criticized the resolutions, and he tried to reduce interposition to a mere matter of conversation with them. The resolutions were "expressions of opinion unaccompanied with any other effect than what they may produce on opinion by exciting reflection" (M 17.348). This is a claim he would repeat often against southerners who (quite understandably) claimed that he must have meant something else when he first launched a word so laden with future dooms.

One indicator of Madison's future embarrassment at his overreaction to "the spirit of '98" is his response to Jefferson's planned use of the *Report of 1800* as a textbook in the University of Virginia's law school. Though the report had no effect (other than a negative one) on other states (M 17.306), despite Jefferson's high hopes for its impact, the founder of the University of Virginia had persuaded himself by 1825 that the report "appeared to accord with the predominant sense of the people of the United States" (JW 479)—so he put it with his own Declaration of Independence and *The Federalist* as the three basic documents on American law. Madison had evident misgivings about the use of his own words, but his task in replying to the proposed list of texts was a delicate one—had Jefferson not noticed that *The Federalist* and the report contradicted each other? Madison wanted to distance himself from his contradictory past, and he tactfully hinted at some of the problems:

The "Federalist" may fairly enough be regarded as the most authentic exposition of the text of the federal Constitution as understood by the body which prepared and the authority which accepted it. Yet it did not foresee all the misconstructions which have occurred; nor prevent some that it did foresee. And what equally deserves remark, neither of the great rival parties have acquiesced in all its comments. It may nevertheless be admissible as a school book, if any will be that goes so much into detail (RL 3.1924–25).

That is hardly a ringing endorsement, but the comment on his *Report of 1800* is even chillier:

With respect to the Virginia document of 1799 [the date of its drafting], there may be more room for hesitation. Though corresponding with the predominant sense of the nation [to echo Jefferson's bold claim], being of local origin and having reference to a state of parties not yet extinct, an absolute prescription of it might excite prejudices against the University as under party banners, and induce the more bigoted to withhold from it their sons, even when destined for other than the studies of the law school. It may be added that the document is not on every point satisfactory to all who belong to the same party. Are we sure that to our brethren of the Board it is so? (RL 3.1925).

As gently as possible Madison is reminding Jefferson that this is 1825, after all, and sectional fights are threatening the fabric of the Union—not a safe time to call up again the spirit of '98. It was just five years since Jefferson had called the disputes over slavery in the territories "a fire bell in the night." The tariff fights were shaping up. Calhoun was in the wings with his nullification arguments. Caution was called for (as Madison had vainly urged in 1798).

Madison's reading of the times comes out in the two works that he prefers for inclusion on Jefferson's list:

I have, for your consideration, sketched a modification of the operative passage in your draft, with a view to relax the absoluteness of its injunction, and added to your list of documents the Inaugural Speech and the Farewell Address of President Washington. They may help down what might be less readily swallowed, and contain nothing which is not good, unless it be the laudatory reference in the Address to the treaty of 1795 with Great Britain, which ought not to weigh against the sound sentiments characterizing it (RL 3.1925).

It is a mark of Madison's omnipresence at the launching of our government that he had actually written part of these speeches by Washington. By 1825, he preferred Washington's inaugural speech of 1789 to his own resolutions of 1798. The anti-governmentalism of that fevered summer of '98, a time of suspected Federalist coup and attempted Republican counter-coup, was an aberration in the career of the man whose own presidency would be as energetic as Washington's. Yet what was temporary with him became permanent in the lore of anti-governmentalists. When James Jackson Kilpatrick argued for "massive resistance" to school integration in the 1950s, he called it "interposition," inspired by "Mr. Madison's Report," which teaches us not to be "spineless fellows . . . docile, automaton voices repeating, in deadly unison, 'we must obey, we must be slaves, we must comply.'" Words do have consequences, and it is clear that one word Madison wished he had never committed to paper was "interposition." Though never an outright advocate of nullification, he became and he remains an abettor of it.

12.

Nullification North:
Hartford Convention

Nullification first became a serious matter in 1798, led in the South by Thomas Jefferson, abetted by James Madison, in protest at John Adams's anti-French policies. When next it showed up as a serious matter, it would be in the North, and the administrations under assault would be those of Jefferson in 1807 (over his anti-British embargo) and Madison in 1812 (over his anti-British war). The chickens had truly come home to roost.

The situations were formally symmetrical. Caught up in the Atlantic conflict of the Napoleonic Wars between France and England, Americans tried to trade with England in Adams's time, and found their shipping harassed by the French—leading to the Alien and Sedition Acts as a kind of symbolic war on the French. Then we tried to trade with France in Jefferson's and Madison's time, and found the British boarding our ships to impress sailors—leading to Jefferson's embargo as a kind of symbolic war on England, and then (after further outrages) to Madison's real war of 1812.

In these neatly patterned oppositions, the symbolic war measures—the Sedition Act in 1798 and the Embargo Act in 1807—went too far to be submitted to as peacetime policy and not far enough to recruit wartime loyalties. In both, a single sector of the nation took the brunt of the emergency measures. The nascent (pro-French) Republican party, based mainly in the South, fell under harshest suspicion in the Adams era. The commercial (pro-British) class, based mainly in New England, felt the impact of curtailed trade in Jefferson's time. The targeted sectors decided that the federal government was discriminating against important components of the Union, which were justified in nullifying the repressive measures. Just to complete the parallel, some in the North invoked the Kentucky and Virginia Resolutions to justify their own acts. The circle would be completed when nullification returned to the South in the 1830s and South Carolinians cited *New England's* measures to defend their actions.

The Embargo

After the British fired on the United States warship *Chesapeake* in 1807, then boarded it and removed sailors, national outrage in America made Jefferson search for an alternative to war (for which America was not prepared—Jefferson had adopted Washington's formal neutrality policy). By unlucky chance, Madison, Jefferson's secretary of state, had long championed the unrealistic proposition that England needed America's trade more than we needed England's.[1]

If that was the case, then a total embargo on trade with England would soon make that nation beg for resumed trade on our terms. (Technically the embargo was a neutral one on all trade, but it really struck at England's control of the Atlantic, thus helping France in its struggle with the maritime empire.) Madison's belief, as it turned out, was unfounded. But once Jefferson was committed to the embargo, he became as pigheaded in his refusal to admit his mistake as Americans would be in slogging through year after year in Vietnam. Ironically, by demonstrating our dependence on British trade, the Anglophobe Jefferson ensured that dependence in the future.[2]

The New England merchant communities had not only economic ties to England but cultural and religious associations, still, with the dissenting communities from which they had emigrated. They also had resources for evading the embargo on which Jefferson had not reckoned. Smuggling had been a New England specialty over the years, and if shrewd captains could evade customs agents, they could surely evade Jefferson's exiguous navy of gunboats patrolling to enforce the embargo. Besides, the Canadian border was at hand, by land routes or through water systems like Lake Champlain. How was Jefferson to harden that porous line? He had trouble getting the local militias to police their own, and to haul in other states' militias proved, he said, "expensive, troublesome, and less efficacious" than the use of regular troops being raised in case of war with England.[3] President Washington had put down a tax revolt in Pennsylvania (Shays's Rebellion) with militias, but the unpopularity of Jefferson's embargo made that too risky for him. Thus "the first use of the new army and gunboats was against fellow citizens."[4] Leonard Levy describes the results:

> On a prolonged, widespread, and systematic basis, in some places lasting nearly a year, the armed forces harried and beleaguered the citizenry. Never before or since did American history exhibit such a spectacle of derangement of normal values and perspectives. . . . This was the only time in American history that the President was empowered to use the army for routine or day-by-day execution of the laws.[5]

Since the interruption of external trade deranged the entire internal market of the nation, Jefferson asked for and received the power to redistribute necessary items like foodstuffs on a rationing basis. His sympathetic biographer Merrill Peterson writes: "As the commissar of the nation's economy, Jefferson made decisions on such trifling matters as the flour bakers used, the bread people ate."[6] His interference with the justice system was even more drastic. Whole communities were presumed to be collaborating in trade, so the presumption of innocence in individual cases was suspended. In Jefferson's words: "In such a case we may fairly require positive proof that the individual of a town tainted with a general spirit of disobedience has never said or done anything himself to countenance that spirit" (JL 12.194). Ships in the coasting trade were presumed to be going into external trade, and prohibitive bonds had to be posted before they could sail. Jefferson even wanted to have personal control over who should live and who should die as a smuggler: "If *all* these people are convicted there will be too many to be punished with death. My hope is that they will send me full statements of every man's case, that the *most* guilty may be marked as examples, and the less suffer long imprisonment under reprieves from time to time" (JL 12.160).

To exert such powers, Jefferson had to resort to far looser construction of the Constitution than that he had condemned when Hamilton set up a bank. He had to presume sedition on a basis more widespread than

Adams's Sedition Act did. He had to abandon reliance on the militia. He had to defy the laws of free trade at home and abroad. He had to undo the careful economic planning of his brilliant secretary of the Treasury, Albert Gallatin, and sink the nation in a decline it did not recover from for decades, in a series of actions that, Merrill Peterson says, "mocked every principle Jefferson held" before the embargo.[7] The nightmare snowballing of effects during the fourteen months of the embargo is well described in a virtuoso single sentence of Henry Adams, which moves from grand planning to compulsive spasms combining despotism with impotence:

> The first embargo law of December 22, 1807, was a mere temporary measure of precaution; in order to carry out the policy with effect, a completer system had to be formed, and Mr. Gallatin was obliged himself to draft the bill which was to beggar the Treasury; but no ordinary grant of powers would answer a purpose which consisted in stopping the whole action and industry of all the great cities and much of the rural population; thus the astonishing spectacle was presented of Mr. Jefferson, Mr. Madison, and Mr. Gallatin, the apostles of strict construction, of narrow grants, the men who of all others were the incarnation of that theory which represented mankind as too much governed, and who, according to Mr. Jefferson, would have had government occupy itself exclusively with foreign affairs and leave the individual absolutely alone to manage his own concerns in his own way—of these men demanding, obtaining, and using powers practically unlimited so far as private property was concerned; powers in comparison with which the alien and sedition laws were narrow and jealous in their grants; powers which placed the fortunes of at least half the community directly under their control; which made them no more nor less than despots; which gave Mr. Jefferson the right to say "we may fairly require positive proof that the individual of a town tainted with a general spirit of disobedience has never said or done anything himself to countenance that spirit"; and which dictated his letter to the Governor of Massachusetts, then among the proudest, the wealthiest, and the most populous states in the Union, that the President had permitted her to have six thousand barrels of flour; that this was enough, and she must have no more.[8]

One can imagine what Jefferson would have made of these executive encroachments if they had been undertaken by John Adams—and, sure enough, there were voices in New England that declared Jefferson's laws null and of no force. Levy quotes one remonstrance that, he says, reads like the Kentucky Resolutions revived.[9] Louis Sears finds the spirit of Jefferson's own resolutions in a declaration of the Connecticut General Assembly that they, their governor, and all the state's executive officers are bound in duty "to withhold their aid and cooperation from the execution of the [enforcement] act."[10] A meeting in Boston's Faneuil Hall drafted resolutions asking the Massachusetts legislature "for their interposition to save the people of this Commonwealth," and the Connecticut legislature voted to join with Massachusetts to "interpose" between a despotic government and their people.[11] A committee of the lower house in that state declared the fifth embargo enforcement act "not binding on the citizens of this state."[12] The Delaware legislature declared the enforcement act "an invasion of the liberty of the people and the constitutional sovereignty of the state governments."[13] The Rhode Island assembly felt obliged "to interpose for the purpose of protecting them [the people] from the ruinous inflictions of usurped and unconstitutional power." The New Englanders could not realize how appropriate it was to retort Madison's language upon its author. They were quoting the Kentucky Resolutions without knowing, yet, who wrote them. But Madison knew:

> If Madison was not by that time weary of his own words—if the Resolutions of 1798 and the fatal "interpose" of Virginia had not become hateful to his ears—he might have found some amusement in the irony with which [Governor Jonathan] Trumbull flung the familiar phrases of Virginia back into her face.[14]

Senator Timothy Pickering wrote from Washington an open letter to his governor calling for Massachusetts to join other New England states in blocking enforcement of the embargo. (Just to complete this dance of reversals, Pickering, as Adams's secretary of state, had been the most zealous enforcer of the Alien and Sedition Acts.) Jefferson wrote of Pickering's letter: "The author would merit exemplary punishment for so flagitious a libel, were not the torment of his own abominable temper punishment sufficient for even as base a crime as this" (JL 12.20–21). So now seditious libel is a crime, the very thing he had denied in 1798.

The defense Jefferson offered for his embargo and the acts passed to enforce it was that Congress had made them the law of the land—exactly what the Adams administration said about the Alien and Sedition Acts. This shows what, when put to the real test, Jefferson really thought about the right of a state to declare laws null. The protests against his embargo were more widespread and deeper than the resistance he tried to inspire against the 1798 laws, and the offenses of his government were greater, in principle and in effect, than those of the Adams administration. Yet the anti-government celebrants of Jefferson prefer to remember the year of his opposition to President Adams's "despotism" rather than the year of his own far worse repressiveness. Among the famous sayings of Jefferson we rarely hear this one, written in the midst of the embargo troubles: "Should we ever have gained our Revolution if we had bound our hands by manacles of the law, not only in the beginning but in any part of the revolutionary conflict? There are extreme cases where the laws become inadequate even to their own preservation, and where the universal resource is a dictator or martial law" (JL 12.182). In 1798 the laws were supposed to chain rulers down. Now they are manacles to be shed.

Why are the Alien and Sedition Acts better remembered, for liberal indignation, than Jefferson's embargo? Some dismiss the protest of New England as based less on principle than on a concern for trade profits (as if the slave interest of the South was entirely disinterested). Besides, a troublemaker like Timothy Pickering is a less attractive character than Jefferson or Madison, and Federalists are not credited with sincerity in speaking of freedom—which underscores one problem with the view that states should nullify laws they consider unconstitutional: people generally support this position only for people they like or agree with, not as a principle to be applied neutrally. Working through all these attitudes is an anti-governmental instinct that wants to see founders like Jefferson upholding resistance to federal force. In order to get him on record holding that view, much will be forgiven him or consigned to an Orwellian memory hole. *The oppressive act in our early history remains, for most libertarians, Adams's four alien and sedition laws, not Jefferson's four embargo enforcement laws.*

War of 1812

When Madison succeeded Jefferson as president in 1809, the embargo was a discredited alternative to war. Madison tried less sweeping trade restrictions (selective nonintercourse provisions rather than total embargo) without lessening the British disregard for America's rights on the ocean. With increasing insistence the "war hawks" of his own Republican party were calling for outright war with England. Reluctantly, he went along with them. If America could conquer Canada and deny its timber to the Royal Navy, perhaps England would finally recognize our maritime claims.

But when Madison tried to federalize New England's militias for the invasion of Canada, the governors refused to turn them over.[15] Governor Caleb Strong of Massachusetts said that since invasion was not imminent, the militia was not being called, as the Constitution put it, "to repel invasion," so the law federalizing the militias was null.[16] Connecticut, Vermont, and Rhode Island agreed. What's more, they opposed recruitment for the regular army in their confines—Connecticut suppressed recruitment on the grounds that military bands disturbed the peace.[17] The administration responded by cutting off federal funds for the arming of the militias, which gave the states new grounds for grievance—they said this, too, was unconstitutional. (The ironies are endless—Madison, who framed the Second Amendment to assure southern slaveholders that the militias would be kept armed, was the first to cut off money for arms to northern resisters.)

Given this attitude on the part of the political masters of the militia, one could not expect militia troops actually brought to the field to perform very well—and they did not. The forces that were a disappointment in the Revolution became a disaster in the War of 1812, their least glorious hour. New England did not want this war in the first place. Its militias that responded to the mustering call tended to take recruitment pay and disappear, leading James Monroe, the secretary of state, to report:

> It may be stated with confidence that at least three times the force in militia has been employed at our principal cities, along the coast and on the frontier, in marching to and returning thence, that would have been necessary in regular troops, and that the expense attending it has

been more than proportionately augmented from the difficulty if not the impossibility of preserving the same degree of system in the militia as in the regular service.[18]

Henry Adams drew this conclusion:

The military experience of 1814 satisfied the staunchest war Democrats that the militia must not be their dependence. In Maine the militia allowed themselves with hardly a show of resistance to be made subjects of Great Britain. At Plattsburg volunteers collected in considerable numbers, but the victory was won by the sailors and engineers. At Niagara, Brown never could induce more than a thousand volunteers to support him in his utmost straits. Porter's efforts failed to create a brigade respectable in numbers, and at Chippawa his Indians outnumbered his whites. . . . The militia began by rendering a proper army impossible, and ended by making government a [mere] form.[19]

When the governor of Vermont tried to recall his state's militia from national service, Congress proposed to indict him for treason. Harrison Gray Otis said on the floor of the Massachusetts House that, if such measures were taken against a sister state, Massachusetts would "aid the Governor of Vermont and the people of that state, or any other state, with their whole power." Here again was that cooperation of the states in protest that Madison had called for in 1798. But what did he call it when it was directed at his own government? The same thing Jefferson had called the government itself in 1798—"a reign of witches."[20]

Madison's greatest fear was that nullification would escalate to secession in New England. John Quincy Adams thought that was what men like Timothy Pickering were aiming at. The ideal vehicle for such a radical step was the convention of New England states called to assemble in 1814 at Hartford and consider measures of resistance to Madison's war. When the convention went into secret session, Monroe moved up troops to be ready to crush any rebellion that might emerge from the meeting.[21] Fortunately, Harrison Gray Otis organized his allies in the convention to restrain it. Instead of secession or insurrection, the congregation confined itself to the milder step of nullification, "to interpose its authority for their [the people's] protection." While admitting that the Union might "be destined to dissolution," the members of the convention postponed that issue until it could be "the work of peaceable times, and deliberate consent." Its immediate object was to protest Madison's draft laws, which included the drafting of minors (eighteen-year-olds) without parental consent. Commissioners were sent to Washington to negotiate for New England's self-defense by her own militia, to be funded with part of the federal taxes (collected by the state). Seven amendments to the Constitution were also called for.[22]

The Hartford Convention had an aura of mystery in its time. The radical mood of the period led to disappointment in New England that it had not gone further. But John Quincy Adams, along with many Republicans, felt that it was a first step toward secession, part of a plan aborted only by the sudden end of the war. That is the interpretation southerners would later take of the convention, offering it as a precedent for their own withdrawal from the Union. Robert Hayne of South Carolina tweaked Daniel Webster for having supported the Hartford Convention, but not southern forms of interposition.

Recent historians have dismissed the Hartford Convention as much ado about nothing. Of the five states involved in it, two sent a single delegate, and only at the last minute. The three commissioners sent by the convention to Washington had the bad luck to arrive just as news came that the war had been ended by the Treaty of Ghent, negotiated to return Anglo-American relations to the status quo ante. But Henry Adams notes that the next step planned by Massachusetts, had the war continued, was a "sequestering of the direct and indirect taxes," which would have had the most serious consequences.[23] And even as it stands in history, the Hartford Convention was not meaningless. As James Banner says, "it nationalized the doctrine of interposition" by making the North as well as the South invoke it.[24] In fact, Samuel Eliot Morison describes the outcome of the convention this way: "Thus for the third time within six years New England Federalism advanced Jeffersonian principles of state interposition or nullification, in direct contradiction to the Federalism of Washington and Hamilton."[25] (The other times had been in protest against the admission of Louisiana to the Union and against Jefferson's embargo.) How did the Federalists make such a change in their approach? When they went into opposition, the cluster of anti-government values took on new force for them.

In opposing the southern presidents, they could appeal to their own folk-ways. Jefferson, northerners said, was favoring France with his embargo, and New England divines had long associated him with Jacobin atheists of the French Revolution.[26] Even a folkway like smuggling was favored during the embargo—smuggling was a practice in what Carol Rose calls the "an-cient constitution," as John Hancock's association with it proved. During the War of 1812, preachers found new reasons to oppose the godless Vir-ginians. They attacked Madison for drafting minors. Theodore Dwight wrote:

> The fears of parents were excited to the highest degree by this bold and arbitrary attempt to destroy the moral character and welfare of their children—to take them from under parental care and control and place them in the purlieus of a camp, and in the midst of the contami-nating atmosphere of a regular army.[27]

As we have already seen, even the music of the Regulars' military bands was resented as a foreign intrusion on the decorum of New England towns. The cluster of anti-governmental values puts in its appearance, right on schedule—religion, local codes, the organic community, opposed to secu-lar and cosmopolitan efficiency.

In all this sectional struggle, there was a mounting ease of recourse to Madison's dangerous concept of interposition. New England had shown it was willing to go further than discussions about the constitutionality of a law. In fact, there had been an escalation in the vigor of nullification over the early decades of the Republic's life. Jefferson and Madison secretly drafted resolutions that had no immediate effect. The opponents of the embargo defied the law mainly in clandestine ways, by smuggling or the evasion of regulations. But officials openly defied militia calls dur-ing the War of 1812, and the Hartford Convention toyed with the idea of forcible resistance to tax collection. By the time the North returned the weapon of interposition to the South, it had become a deadlier thing than it was when Madison forged it.

13.

Nullification South:
John C. Calhoun

When interposition returned to the South, it did not go home to Virginia but to South Carolina, where it was tragically linked with slavery. At first, the morality of slavery was not at issue, even in the eyes of most northerners. What they resented as "slave power" did not refer to the mastery of white men over blacks, but to the overrepresentation of the South in Congress and the electoral college. As a concession to the South in the drafting of the Constitution, slaves were included in the census, on which representation is based. Though they were not citizens who voted or paid taxes, each one was counted as three-fifths of a person, giving the South extra weight in the Union. In 1800, for instance, Jefferson won the presidency from Adams by eight votes in the electoral college—but only because he had a margin of fourteen extra votes based on the slaves in states voting for him. Without that "bonus" Adams would have continued into a second term.[1]

The North feared endless increases in this bonus if slavery spread through the West. In fact, any expansion there would allow the agricultural states to outvote the manufacturing North. When the northern states tried to inhibit the admission of western states in 1828, Senator Robert Hayne of South Carolina denounced this as a law intended to freeze the slaveholding South in place, and threatened that South Carolina would, if the law passed, nullify it. Addressing the Senate, he cited as the warrant for such "interposition" Madison's 1800 Report. Senator Daniel Webster responded to Hayne's speech with his most famous oration, the one ending "Liberty *and* Union, now and forever, one and inseparable." Because the national union preceded the states, in time as well as authority (see Chapter 3), no state had the power to nullify a federal law.

Madison was horrified that his Report was being used for what he called a "novel and nullifying doctrine," something "preposterous" and a "colossal heresy" (MH 9.472, 497, 511), conveniently forgetting his own words that prepared the way for this "novelty." His position was complicated by the fact that Robert Yates's notes of the debates in the Constitutional Convention, taken down in 1787, were finally published in 1821, revealing for the first time that Madison had argued in the secrecy of the sessions for a federal veto on state laws.[2] He was now on record as championing (in 1787) a concentrated power in the national government not only to make national law but to override state laws *and* calling (in 1798) for a diffusive power in the states to block federal law (his authorship of the Virginia Resolutions had come out earlier). No matter what he said now, one or the other set of his words could be used against him.

Despite his embarrassment, he had little choice but to stick with his long-term commitment to the national government and play down his momentary surrender to "the spirit of '98." His position became even more difficult in 1832, when it was proved that Jefferson (who had died six years earlier) composed the Kentucky Resolutions and included nullification language in his draft.[3] Madison had argued, just two years before, that the lack of such language in the Resolutions as passed demonstrated that nullification was never contemplated (MH 9.402–403). Since he felt he could not repudiate his dead friend, now that Jefferson could not defend himself, he did his best to palliate the language without denying it. The strain of fighting on so many fronts—of facing, wherever he turned, so many of his past selves—prostrated Madison. Drew McCoy, in a sensitive study of these years in Madison's life, writes:

> During the final six years of his life, amid a sea of personal troubles that threatened to engulf him, Madison could not get the nullifiers out of his mind. At times, mental agitation issued in physical collapse. For the better part of a year in 1831 and 1832, he was bedridden, if not silenced, by a joint attack of severe rheumatism and chronic bilious fevers. Literally sick with anxiety, he began to despair of his ability to make himself understood by his fellow citizens.[4]

The South Carolina argument for nullification had moved, in 1828, from the issue of western expansion to that of protective tariffs, which favored the North and hurt the exporting plantations of the South. South Carolina's leading politician and thinker, John C. Calhoun, found himself in the same position that Jefferson had held in 1798. Calhoun, too, was a vice president serving under a president (Andrew Jackson) he vehemently but silently opposed. As Jefferson had presided over the Senate when it passed the hated Alien Acts, Calhoun had to preside while Daniel Webster defeated Hayne, a fellow South Carolinian, in the debate over the West. In 1828, Calhoun followed Jefferson's earlier course, secretly composing for a committee of the South Carolina legislature a statement of nullifying intent, called the South Carolina Protest. He composed a prefatory essay called the Exposition, which was printed with the Protest. Once more the precedent of Madison's 1800 Report was invoked. Attacking the position of Webster, that the states are not sovereigns in a mere compact, Calhoun wrote:

A position more false and fatal cannot be conceived. Fortunately, it has been so ably refuted by Mr. Madison, in his Report of the Virginia Legislature in 1800, on the Alien and Sedition Acts, as to supersede the necessity of further comment on the part of the committee.[5]

The Exposition and Protest was such an ably argued pamphlet that it became a kind of creed to South Carolinians seething with resentment of the federal government. Calhoun, like John Taylor of Caroline, argued that only a specially called state convention, not a regular session of the legislature, can declare a law null and void. For the next couple of years, calling such a convention became the goal that many pursued. Discontent intensified in 1832 when Calhoun was forced to retire as vice president after his authorship of *The Exposition and Protest* became known. He could no longer be the secret enemy of the President and the second man in his administration (a double role Jefferson got away with only by keeping his responsibility for the Kentucky Resolutions a close secret). Calhoun went home to South Carolina, was elected to the Senate, and returned to Washington in 1832 despite threats by Jackson that he would have him arrested as a traitor. Calhoun had upped the ante in 1831, when he issued from Fort

Hill, his plantation, *The Fort Hill Address: On the Relations of the States and Federal Government*, in which he elevated the Virginia Resolutions to canonical status as the supreme statement of American political theory:

> This right of interposition, thus solemnly asserted by the State of Virginia, be it called what it may—state-right, veto, nullification, or by any other name—I conceive to be the fundamental principle of our system, resting on facts historically as certain as our Revolution itself, and deductions as simple and demonstrative as that of any political or moral truth whatever; and I firmly believe that on its recognition depend the stability and safety of our political institutions.[6]

At last, in 1832, the state convention Calhoun had called for met in South Carolina. It voided the national tariff bill. It ordered state officials not to collect the tariff. The convention declared that attempts by the federal government to collect it would be "inconsistent with the longer continuance of South Carolina in the Union."[7] The authority appealed to was, once again, the Virginia Resolutions. The convention felt sure it knew what that document meant, even though "Mr. Madison himself has been brought forward to give a construction to this Resolution contrary to the most obvious import of the terms."

Loyalty oaths were to be administered, as in the Revolution, to break earlier oaths to the United States. Though the state claimed that nullification is a peaceable power within the constitutional order, this looked more like revolution—as did the hasty raising of an army. President Jackson called the convention treasonous and said that Calhoun should be hanged. But Jackson also placed the blame for the treason on *Madison*. He wrote to his chief adviser, Martin Van Buren:

> The absurdity of the Virginia doctrine is too plain to need much comment. . . . The preservation of the Union is the supreme law. To show the absurdity, the Congress have the right to admit new states. When territories, they are subject to the law of the Union, the day after the admission they have the right to secede and dissolve it. We gave five million for Louisiana, we admitted her into the Union, she too has the right to secede, close the commerce of six states, and levy contribu-

tions both upon exports and imports. A state cannot come into the Union without the consent of Congress, but it can go out when it please. Such a Union as this would be like a bag of sand with both ends open—the least pressure and it runs out at both ends. It is an insult to the sages who formed it to believe that such a Union was ever intended—it could not last a month.[8]

There are some who believe that Jackson did not really hold the views expressed in his public Proclamation of 1832, which condemned the nullifiers. Jackson was, after all, a southerner (born, in fact, in South Carolina), a slaveholder, a proponent of limited government. Despite all these things, his Proclamation agreed with Webster before it, and with Lincoln after it, in declaring the nation prior to the states, and in condemning the compact theory of sovereign states. Since the Proclamation was drafted by Jackson's secretary of state, Edward Livingston, it has been claimed that Jackson was not in accord with it. But he demonstrated his adherence to it when his political adviser, Van Buren, urged him not to be so dogmatic about matters on which his southern support depended.[9] Jackson ignored the advice, willing to pay any penalty for the expression of his own belief. When the Union was at issue, he had said, he would rather "die in the last ditch" than see it imperiled.[10]

Despite his private blustering about "treason," Jackson shrewdly contained and deflated the South Carolina rebellion. He maintained close contact with loyalists within the state, encouraging their efforts to form a counter-militia and keeping informed on the plans of the nullifiers. He thwarted efforts to block collection of the tariff by moving the customs office in Charleston to Fort Moultrie, on an island in Charleston harbor, where it could collect the tariff from ships as they entered the harbor. Short of raising its own navy, the state could not even reach, much less interfere with, customs agents.[11]

The state's efforts to arm itself ran into the continuing problems of local militias. Robert Hayne, Webster's debate opponent in the Senate four years earlier, had now become the governor of South Carolina. He tried to raise an army—which should have been unnecessary according to idealizers of the militia (who think of it as always in existence and fully armed). Though he spent $100,000 on new arms, Hayne admitted that four out of

five men still had no guns, and to arm even half of them would exhaust the
state's treasury. He tried to substitute an elite ("select") band of mounted
warriors—he even called them minutemen—but that just drained the hollow shell of the militia and left it ready to collapse.[12]

Calhoun, who saw the folly of challenging the war hero Andrew Jackson to a military showdown, worked feverishly in Washington to craft a
"compromise" tariff that would let South Carolina back down while saving
face. The state withdrew its nullification of the tariff, but went through the
charade of nullifying the enforcement bill Jackson had passed through
Congress to give him power to put down rebellion. Since that bill was no
longer needed, the empty nullification of it was quietly ignored. Jackson
had won by shrewdly maneuvering for time and letting the extremists damage themselves.[13] The French aristocrat Alexis de Tocqueville, who was in
America at the time to write his classic work *Democracy in America*, had
little sympathy with Jackson's uncouth manner, but he admitted that "in
the question of the tariff he has supported the rights of the Union with energy and skill."[14]

The nullification crisis of 1832 stirred all the sentiments of localism we
have seen at play in other confrontations with government. The romantic
ideal of the militia lured Hayne and others into thinking they might repel
an invasion with it. An attempt was made to use local juries to defeat the
collection of tariffs. The threat to local autonomy was broadly read as an
assault on the entirety of the state's institutions, and especially on that institution "peculiar" to the South. If smuggling was part of the "ancient constitution" of protected practices in New England, slavery was the defining
element of the southern economy—of its plantation style and its ideological exigencies—so much so that Hayne had argued, in his debate with
Webster, that holding slaves builds character. In this period, an even
stronger argument—one that appealed to a whole range of local pieties—
was an appeal to the Bible. Slaveholding was taken for granted in both the
Jewish Scriptures and the New Testament. Could northerners claim to be
superior to the Apostles themselves? In fact, southerners were the ones
who could claim an apostolic role, since one result of the importation of
slaves was their indoctrination in the Christian religion. Their attitude
was expressed by the future president of the Confederacy, Jefferson Davis,
who said of slavery and the blacks: "It benefits them, in removing them

from the bigotry and the heathen darkness which hangs like a cloud over the country in the interior of Africa to the enjoyment of all the blessings of civilization and Christianity."[15]

It is fascinating to observe how effective religion can be as the medium in which all other forms of localism are fused, bathing them in an emotional glow of approval. During the War of 1812, northerners felt they were defending their religion from the deist French philosophers favored by Jefferson. Thirty years later, the South was defending the benefit to slaves of living on Christian family plantations, rather than in the soulless coils of a system of northern "wage slaves." For many southerners, the Bible was even more useful than Madison's Report.

For the present book, the most relevant aspect of the 1832 crisis is the stunning way it endorses Madison's attack on states acting as judges in their own cause. He said that this results in a tyranny of the majority in any state, since the minority has no avenue of appeal. In South Carolina, the unionists—the third of the state that opposed nullification—were deprived of their civil rights in peacetime. They were removed from office for not taking the loyalty oath to the nullifying convention. They could not serve on juries or in the militia. The very rights that states' righters claimed to preserve were taken away from those who disagreed with the nullifiers. Despotism, merely alleged in Washington, was real in Charleston.

One person who expressly tied this episode to Madison's views on majority despotism was Alexis de Tocqueville. He included in his book a brief history of the South Carolina defiance, endorsing Jackson's position that "the object of the Federal Constitution was not to form a league, but to create a national government. The Americans of the United States form one and the same people in all cases which are specified by that Constitution."[16] After quoting Calhoun's claim that the states are sovereigns in a compact, he says: "It is evident that such a doctrine destroys the very basis of the Federal Constitution and brings back the anarchy from which the Americans were delivered by the act of 1789."[17]

But Tocqueville did not confine his reflections on majority despotism to the case of South Carolina. The Jacksonian era was a time of strong state activity with minimal federal interference. Tocqueville thought such an arrangement destroyed the Madisonian principle of federal protection for minorities within the states. Local prejudices were hard to challenge, sealed off as they were from interaction with more cosmopolitan views. Even in places where loyalty was not coerced as in South Carolina, there was a kind of censorship by consensus. This can sometimes be more effective, in its quiet way, than outright condemnation by an Inquisition. The latter takes away the *right* to publish heretical views. Local conformity "takes away any *wish* to publish them."

> I know of no country in which there is so little independence of mind and real freedom of discussion as in America . . . the majority raises formidable barriers around the liberty of opinion; within these barriers an author may write what he pleases but woe to him if he goes beyond them. The majority lives in the perpetual utterance of self-applause.[18]

Tocqueville's words would be spectacularly confirmed within the next few decades with the advent of southern "gag laws" that banned publication of any criticism directed at slavery (see Chapter 15). But even apart from that extreme form of censorship, his book challenges the view that local government is always the best government, or that provincial, authentic, traditional, populist forces are of themselves more liberating than progressive and delegated "umpiring" functions. Nullification of the tariff law did not free citizens in South Carolina. It oppressed them.

14.

Academic Nullifiers

It seems that no bad idea can ever die. Despite the nineteenth-century defeat of nullification in the North and in the South, some twentieth-century advocates of it are pouring out books and articles to say that the power to nullify is implicit in the Constitution. They do not argue that states can nullify, but that other entities can—ad hoc bodies dealing with specific injustices. This might be called the Yale school of nullification, from two of its leading advocates at that university, Bruce Ackerman and Akhil Reed Amar.[1]

For Professor Amar, the most readily deployed form of nullification occurs within the jury system. There are organized groups that tell jurors they can disregard any laws they think unjust and/or unconstitutional. One such group is FIJA—the Fully Informed Jury Association. It praises a Dallas grand jury that threw out charges against Black Muslim security guards at a mall who judged and punished four thieves, beating them up instead of turning them over to the police. On the face of it, the members of this jury resemble southern jurors who refused to convict white men who lynched blacks. But modern nullifiers do not simply indulge racist or other feelings. They argue the *principle* of letting jurors consider the constitutionality of the law, not just whether a defendant broke that law.[2] When David Koresh's followers were on trial after a shoot-out at his Waco religious center, jurors received letters from FIJA informing them that they could disregard the judge's exposition of the law. That is a claim also made by anti-abortion activists, who call on juries to acquit those who disrupt abortion clinics because the laws protecting abortion are unconstitutional (they sanction murder).[3]

The modern nullifiers have a connection with their nineteenth-century forebears, at least in the assertion of a principle that juries should decide on the law as well as the facts of a case. In 1830, two years before South Carolina's state convention declared the tariff null and void, leaders of that state's nullification movement tried to accomplish the same thing by jury trials. Merchants regularly paid customs not with cash but with a promissory bond obliging them to settle within a stated period. At the end of that period, in the nullifiers' clever plan, the merchants would refuse to pay, go on trial, and the jury would find the tariff unconstitutional. The plan failed since there was a considerable minority of loyalists in the state. The only way to exclude them from juries would be by some illegal "packing" scheme—which would defeat the whole aim of proving that nullification is legal.[4]

Even after its proclamation that the tariff was null, the state tried to enforce this view through juries, using the same bond mechanism to withhold payment by jury acquittal, not by forcible resistance to the customs officers. This time the juries would be sure to acquit, since all members of the court had to take a loyalty oath to the state convention's decree. The charade never worked, since the customs offices, now offshore, could refuse anything but payment in cash.[5]

By Amar's standard, South Carolina's form of jury nullification was invalid, since he says that the jury cannot nullify as part of a general ideological statement. It must confine itself to the use of the law in the particular case before it. "The jury should not nullify because it dislikes the law or wishes to achieve some larger purpose such as sending a message to the government."[6] If, as seems likely, the jury that acquitted O. J. Simpson of murdering his wife was affected by defense lawyer Johnnie Cochran's argument that the jury should send the government a message about its treatment of blacks in general, then—says Amar—the jury was acting improperly.

On the other hand, Amar believes that juries may have acted properly in acquitting Oliver North (of violating a law against giving aid to foreign insurgents), or Washington, D.C., mayor Marion Barry (of using illegal drugs), or Bernhard Goetz (of shooting blacks he thought a menace) because these juries were probably nullifying the law on just grounds.[7] In such cases, the jury decided that the law should be null and of no force because of the circumstances: North was being used by others, Barry had been entrapped, Goetz genuinely felt endangered. Amar can only say the juries may have been acting properly, since their motives are hard if not impossible to establish. Lesser motives will not normally be confessed to—white juries in the South said they were not acting out of racism. Did the juries actually vote for North because they admired his anti-communism, or for Barry because he was a black leader in a black city, or for Goetz because his victims were black? Were the jurors here, as in Amar's version of the O. J. case, invalidly sending a message? Who knows?

That is the problem with jury nullification. If the law can be set aside for good reason, then one person's good reason is as good as another's. If some people think Barry was entrapped at the time of the crime, others can think Simpson was framed after the crime—and there goes Amar's example of a "bad" acquittal. And how are we to know whether the jury is thinking, as Amar says it must, only of the law's applicability in a single case? After all, if the jury can "review" a law's constitutionality, it is not thinking only of its being unconstitutional in one instance. Even Amar would limit the jury's right to nullify on constitutional grounds to civil cases, where the possibility of higher appeal exists as a check on a jury's interpretation of the law. In criminal cases, where there is no appeal of an acquittal, he would restrict the nullifying power to nonconstitutional objections to the law—like those he finds (or imagines) in the North and Barry juries.

The Supreme Court decided in 1895 (in *Sparf & Hansen* v. *United States*) that juries should determine facts, not the law. Amar thinks that decision should be overthrown. Why? His own examples of "good" nullification show how ambiguous the outcome can be, and how socially divisive. Many people thought that the juries put North, Barry, and Goetz above the law—and put themselves above the law by placing their respective defendants there. That seems a high social cost to pay for a dubious right. But the jury is crucial to Amar's larger project—to show that the people always retain their sovereignty, and can exercise it around and against the Constitution without overthrowing the Constitution or withdrawing from its authority. Amar puts jury nullification among the three most basic rights that show such sovereignty in action—the other two being amendments to the Constitution by mere majority and the threatened use of a militia against the government (for the latter, see Chapter 17). He calls these the powers of the jury box, the ballot box, and the cartridge box.

The old nullifiers anticipated their modern followers not only in efforts at jury nullification but also in novel ways to amend the Constitution. Andrew Jackson, in his nullification proclamation, had taken the Madisonian position that state nullifiers become judges in their own cause, not allowing for appeal to any larger and more disinterested body:

> There are two appeals from an unconstitutional act passed by Congress—one to the judiciary, the other to the people and the states [in the voting and amending processes]. There is no appeal from the state decision in theory, and the practical illustration shows that the courts are closed against an application to review it, both judges and jurors being sworn to decide in its favor.[8]

Calhoun answered that there *was* an appeals process in his system: if a state's act of nullification were vetoed by three-quarters of the other states (the number needed to make positive amendments), it would be declared invalid. Madison replied that "this preposterous and anarchical pretension" would suspend the law in question until most of the states had assembled to take up the matter (MH 9.472). And if one state more than a quarter of the whole (seven in Madison's time) *failed* to veto, then the law would be voided, even though a clear majority stood by it (MH 9.398–99).

Calhoun was moving toward his theory, published posthumously, that government should be an arena of overlapping bodies given vetoes on each other's action. He was vague about how the bodies would be established, but seems to have hoped that they would arise from the continual negotiation of "concurrences." Calhoun was working from the same premise that modern nullifiers accept—that sovereignty is in the people, not in government; that government should be maximally plastic and reshapeable in the people's hands; that the presumption of legitimacy is with the people, whenever it finds a way to articulate its will, not with the government (which is at best only *yesterday's* expression of the popular will).

Neither Ackerman nor Amar likes the methods of amendment contained in the Constitution. One method—the proposal of an amendment by two-thirds of Congress, followed by ratification in three-fourths of the states—seems undemocratic. Amar says that polls showed a majority supported the Equal Rights Amendment, though it could not pass the three-fourths barrier.[9] The other method—proposal by a convention created by two-thirds of the states, and ratification by three-fourths of the states—is so clumsy that it has not been used. The resulting convention would be amorphous in its mandate (since those calling it could not do its work of proposing specific amendments), and the three-fourths barrier would still exist at the end of the process. Ackerman proposes an alternate plan to involve the President in the amending process (as original proposer of the amendment) and the people at large (with the amendment on a ballot for their vote).[10]

Ackerman's scheme would itself require passage of an amendment in the regular (Article V) way. But he and Amar believe that we can amend the Constitution without going through that roadblock. The proof, says Ackerman, is that we have already amended the Constitution outside Article V three times—in setting up the Constitution, in passing Reconstruction amendments, and in accepting the New Deal. Amar also cites the first one of these as a sample of "creative" amendment, since the Constitution was set up in defiance of the amending procedure in the Articles of Confederation. But that founding was not done under the old constitution—in fact, it abolished that constitution. This was, as Madison said, a revolutionary act, one he expressly compares to the Revolution itself, not to any ordinary governmental process (F 40.265). This cannot be equated with amendments made to the present Constitution *while maintaining this Constitution*.

Ackerman's second example is an odd one because the Reconstruction amendments—those passed after the Civil War to declare the status of blacks' and others' civil rights—were proposed and ratified by the regular Article V procedure. He claims they were not legitimate on the Constitution's own terms because the assent of the southern states was coerced. Amendments so obtained, according to Ackerman, were formally illegitimate, and therefore an *informal* way of amending must have taken place, outside the Article V process though masking itself behind that process. At that time the legal status of the southern states was of an intermediate sort, as they were being returned from a rebellious status to that of full partners. The terms of their return were acceptance of the Union's disposition of the causes of quarrel, based on the federal power under the Constitution to guarantee in each state a republican form of government (see Chapter 17). And the states *did* accept those terms, however unhappily, swearing they were back in the orbit of their former condition. The consent was conditioned by their unique status (not conquered aliens, nor yet fully restored partners)—but it *was* consent, making future constitutional government possible.

The juridical task is not to ascertain the motives for consent—states can have many and mixed motives for ratifying anything. Some said that Rhode Island was coerced when it ratified the Constitution in 1790, because it would have been left out of the Union, in an untenable condition, if it had refused. We often decide by judging that we are better off accepting an unpleasant thing than we would be by rejecting it. That is a valid basis for decision, and the consent is genuine. To invalidate a process by declaring motives imperfect, and then to compare that process with an apple here and an orange there, to make it part of a pattern of informal amending procedures—this is playing games with history. For one thing, the populace in general does not seem to have been aware that they were exercising some new and informal way of amending the Constitution. Can a nation amend without having the intention to amend, without even knowing that it is doing so?

That question applies to Ackerman's last example, the New Deal, whose acceptance, he argues, nullified previous constitutional provisions over the limit of governmental action. The Supreme Court, by a "switch in time," gave in to the will of the people and declared actions constitutional that were up till then considered unconstitutional. But that was an act of judicial review, not of amendment, no matter what one thinks of the New Deal programs themselves. Again, there was no intention to amend. Franklin Roosevelt and his forces thought that their acts were constitutional. That the Court changed its mind does not mean that there was an amorphous amendment (itself unwritten) blessing some social programs. If that were the case, we could say that the Constitution is amended every time the Supreme Court changes its mind.

Why is Ackerman so insistent on a process which, even by his capacious definition, has occurred only twice since the founding of our government? Why devote most of two long books to the matter? This, like Amar's zeal for jury nullification, is just a vehicle for some larger purpose, to find a mode of government the professors consider more authentic, more democratic, than the machinery of normal rule. Ackerman actually says that there are two forms of democracy at work in our nation (what he calls democratic dualism)—one form that acquiesces in ordinary times, when citizens are bribed with "pork" and privileges bestowed on them by uninspired politicians, and another form that rises up in majesty and asserts its will in a time of crisis. In the former case (the normal one), a politician reasons that if the people do not care, then he should not make himself vulnerable by feeling deeply about anything: "Rather than invest heavily in ideological politics, isn't it wiser to appeal to the bread-and-butter interests of constituents: Vote for me, I can do more for Massachusetts!"[11] In the latter case, the skies open to eschatological trumpets and we get "the culminating expression of a generation's critique of the status quo." Ackerman clearly does not believe in Madison's preference for a calm and disinterested judgment rather than one heated by a passionate engagement in one's own cause.

In other words, the modern nullifiers are moved by just those anti-government values listed at the beginning of this book. Ackerman's normal democracy, so ignoble and selfish, is mechanical, delegative, and regulatory. It divides up labor (even the labor of amending the Constitution is parceled out among the houses of Congress and the various states). His creative democracy (on its rare appearances) is authentic, spontaneous, populist, voluntary, participatory. It is an organic wave of culminating judgment. The *genuine* expression of popular will must not be remote and impersonal, carried out by experts in the routines of bureaucracy. Some people subscribe to a theory of charismatic leadership, which places "transformative" leaders above the ordinary rules and everyday legality. Ackerman, who uses the word "transformative" of his creative democracy in action, believes in a charismatic people—even though it shows up only once a century or so.[12]

Only a deep emotional engagement in the anti-government values can explain why intelligent men resort to such skewed history and flawed logic as the modern nullifiers do. And only Americans' share in those same values can explain the accepting audience their work has found in some legal quarters. We shall find the same phenomenon at work when we consider the modern nullifiers' treatment of militias.

IV.

Seceders

Secession differs in one direction from nullification, and in another from revolution. The nullifier blocks one action of the state but does not withdraw from it. The revolutionary does not withdraw from the state and leave it standing. He overthrows it at its base.

The American Revolution was more properly an act of secession than a real revolution. We did not remove King George from his throne or dissolve the Parliament in London. We did not replace them with a new government of our own creation. We simply took our colonies out of the empire—which continued on its course without us—as twentieth-century nations have seceded from colonial powers in Europe.

Seen in this light, secession has a noble ancestry in our country, and one would expect it to be more honored than it has been. The Southern seceders of the Confederacy were aware of their Revolutionary ancestry. They invoked George Washington as the model for their departure from an oppressive government.

But the parallel is not as close as the Confederate States imagined. The American colonies made an argument from weakness. They had never been proper governments, admitted into the Parliament, represented there, with a voice of their own in the councils of the state. In a state of dependence, they had not been able to protect their own rights, and the imperial government had not protected them either. It was time to escape such a weak position of bondage.

The Confederate States, on the contrary, made an argument from strength. Precisely because they had always been sovereign states, with all the authority that implies, they could reassume their only partly delegated powers from the compact that was dependent on *them*.

That argument, from the sovereignty of the states in the American system, received its definitive refutation from Andrew Jackson, Daniel Webster, and Abraham Lincoln.

15.

Civil War

The one great episode of secession in our history was the Civil War, which so discredited the concept that there has been no major attempt at it since. Secessionist efforts now resemble those of a crackpot group in Texas. (I am talking about secession from the Union, not arguments for withdrawing this or that suburb from urban tax areas.) But secession was something that serious people considered in the period before the Civil War. Even under the Articles of Confederation, which was supposed to ensure a "perpetual union," there was talk of withdrawing either the northern or the southern component from the Union, depending on which sector was favored by a treaty with Spain being negotiated in the 1780s.[1] After the Constitution was ratified, the first serious bid for secession came in 1804, when Senator Timothy Pickering of Massachusetts, protesting the Louisiana Purchase as an aggrandizement of southern territory, tried to organize New England for secession.[2] Though Pickering had held important posts in the Union government (he was secretary of state for both Washington and Adams), he could not get others to take his plan seriously. Yet he plowed some of the ground for efforts at nullification by New England in 1812 and 1814—he may even have imparted a nudge to Aaron Burr's 1805 talk of a separate western country to be formed in the territories gained by the Louisiana Purchase.

Secession, like nullification, moved from the North to the South after the War of 1812. The collapse of South Carolina's attempt at nullification in 1832 turned restive southerners' eyes to secession as the only hope for preserving their slave culture. Jefferson Davis, the future president of the secessionist state, typified this reorientation of southern strategy. Though

Davis admired Calhoun as a giant of the preceding generation, he did not believe in the legitimacy of nullification. A graduate of West Point (in 1828, the year of Hayne's defense of nullification against Webster), Davis had taken an oath of allegiance to the Union. He was legalistic about obedience to the Union while one recognized its legitimacy. And the only way to declare the government illegitimate in its hold over a state was to withdraw that state from the compact that had been drawn up by sovereign entities. Nullification, he held, could not be justified. Secession could.

Here was the great flaw in any union of sovereigns by compact. As Madison had put it in his *Vices of the Political System of the United States:*

> As far as the Union of the states is to be regarded as a league of sovereign powers, and not as a political constitution by virtue of which they are become one sovereign power, so far it seems to follow from the doctrine of compacts that a breach of any of the articles of the confederation by any of the parties to it absolves the other parties from their respective obligations and gives them a right, if they choose to exercise it, of dissolving the Union altogether (M 9.352–53).

For Madison, then, secession and the compact theory stood or fell together. That is true even today. People in the South, and not only there, still believe that the Southern states in 1860 had the right to secede, that they failed only because President Lincoln had a mystical (not a legal) attachment to the Union, and that the North had the physical means of preventing the South from following its justifiable decision to secede. I have, over the years, found that many of my students held that view in discussions of Lincoln's war powers.

It was for fear of such consequences that Madison, during the nullification crisis, invented fresh arguments against secession. He said that a state has no more power to withdraw from a national government than does an individual. Any criminal can say that he is not breaking a law that he does not recognize as binding on him. That will not prevent his going to jail. Madison writes: "It is asked whether a state, by resuming the sovereign form in which it entered the union, may not of right withdraw from it at will. As this is a simple question whether a state, more than an individual, has a right to violate its engagements, it would seem that it might safely be left to answer itself" (MH 9.513).

He also argued that a state's right to withdraw would imply a reciprocal right of the national government to expel a state at will—but no one thinks the government has that right (MH 9.489). He contrived a clever reversal of Calhoun's argument that a nullifying state could appeal to the other states and stand vindicated if three-quarters of them (the number needed to amend) did not reject their appeal. This implies (as does the amending power itself) that the minority of nonconcurring states will be bound by the majority—and therefore such states do not, singly, have the right of seceding (MH 9.399, 472). All these arguments show that Madison had abandoned his 1798 argument that the American government is a compact among sovereigns. He was back to his original understanding of 1787—as he had to be, in logic, if he noted the power of three-quarters of the states to bind the other one-quarter in constitutional amendments.

The oddly persistent notion that the South had legality on its side while the North had only force is one that neglects the powerful arguments against secession mounted before and during the Civil War—those of Nathan Dane, Daniel Webster, Andrew Jackson, and Joseph Story. To recall just one of them (which has been called "the ablest and most impressive state paper of the period"), Jackson's Proclamation of 1832 mounted the arguments for national sovereignty cited earlier (see Chapter 13).[3] Here it is sufficient to recall his argument that the Constitution defines treason as making war on the nation, not on a state: "Treason is an offense against *sovereignty*, and sovereignty must reside with the power to punish it" (see Chapter 17).[4]

Lincoln's first inaugural address summed up the case made in these earlier documents under seven headings (L 2.215–24):

1. No constitution provides for its own destruction.

2. It takes all the parties to the Constitution to rescind it (as opposed to simply breaking it, in a criminal way).

3. The Union precedes the states in time as well as authority.

4. Even the Articles provided for a "perpetual union," and the Constitution was meant to provide an even "more perfect union." If unilateral withdrawal were allowed, it would be less rather than more perfect.

5. The majority of the people constitute a binding sovereignty: "Whoever rejects it does, of necessity, fly to anarchy or to despotism."

6. "This country, with its institutions, belongs to the people who inhabit it." In other places Lincoln spells out some of the consequences of this pregnant statement. The people—that is, the nation as a whole—have made institutional commitments, in treaties all must observe with others, in purchasing and maintaining authority over territories, in joint endeavors and expenditures which cannot be selectively honored.

7. Though all people have an extra-constitutional right to revolution, that is to be exercised by the people as a whole, not by a part:

> Whenever they [the people] shall grow weary of the existing government, they can exercise their *constitutional* right of amending it or their *revolutionary* right to dismember or overthrow it (emphasis in original).

Secession can claim neither of those rights.

It was by the force of these arguments—not by mere brute arms or mystical love of union—that Lincoln justified the prevention of secession. The arguments were strong enough that the South had adumbrated them when the Hartford Convention was perceived as a secessionist movement in the North. The South did not abandon those arguments through superior reasoning but out of desperation. The loss of slaves had become literally unthinkable in the South—so literally that any arguments for that loss were forbidden expression. The "gag laws" took away freedom from whites as well as blacks, forbidding the printing or distribution of anti-slavery materials. The South even gagged the federal government, blocking the Senate's reception of constituents' petitions to abolish slavery—a triple violation of the Constitution's protections (of free speech, the right to petition, and the right of free debate in Congress).[5]

Those who think the Civil War was not about slavery but about freedom from the "despotism" of the federal government should reflect that the South was given the choice between slavery and freedom when it came to destroying freedom of speech. It chose slavery. There were three hundred Southern lynchings of *whites* between 1830 and 1860—whites whose crime was a suspected sympathy for abolition, and who were normally whipped or tarred-and-feathered and driven out of town.[6]

Panic, not constitutional theory, drove the South. Anything was preferable to dismantling the slave system. That system, after all, was the entire base of the economy, without which (it was held) the land could not be worked and the South would collapse. The thought of emancipated slaves in any great number was a nightmare for people who believed the freedmen would exact vengeance for all past wrongs. Only an unreasoning dread of that prospect could have led the South into so desperate an endeavor as secession. That frenzy, not Southern chivalry, explains the fierce determination of the war's early stages. General Robert E. Lee felt he had to win fast, since a long war would be a lost war, given the distribution of resources. What he could not face up to was that even a war won by the South would be a lost war.

A victorious Confederacy would have faced, in aggravated form, what it had been straining for decades to stave off. It had opposed high tariffs because it needed free trade to sell staple crops. But for that it needed Northern shipping. It had neither its own merchant fleet nor a military fleet to protect the merchant fleet—and the North had the means to inhibit it from creating one. The South, moreover, could not create an industrial economy, domestically, to reduce dependence on agrarian staples, since the slave system did not provide a consumer market that motivates an industrial work force.[7]

The South had made every effort to expand slavery into the territories, or into Cuba, since it had too much of "a good thing"—slaves were overpopulating the South, where it was more dangerous to free them than to keep them in unproductive numbers. A vent was needed, not only to "diffuse" slavery but to find more unexhausted soil. But any expansion of the nation, westward or in the Caribbean, would be sealed off by secession. The South lost, by secession, the very territories it had struggled for, Kansas and Missouri, along with any future states to be admitted to the Union.

As a final irony, the logic of secession was making national government impossible in the Confederacy even before its military collapse. As if to prove Lincoln's point that no state can be built on the basis of its own dissolution, the Southern states were so jealous of state sovereignty that the Confederate constitution limped badly and courted breakdown. Since the South had opposed judicial review in the federal government, the Confederacy never acquired a supreme court—wrangling over its revisionary power thwarted each attempt to create one.[8] In the absence of a court to interpret constitutional powers, the attorney general's recommendations had to be accepted, in some cases, as binding. Meanwhile the state courts created inconsistent rulings, especially in their opposition to conscription. The Southern legacy of opposition to Hamiltonian systems of credit and banking made it impossible for the Confederacy to establish a sound legal tender.[9]

Jefferson Davis, as president of the Confederacy, was put in a situation where he was alternately accused of lacking authority or exercising too much of it. At times he indulged scruples like those of Governor Jefferson during the Revolution—he vetoed a bill for a veterans home on the grounds that the Confederate constitution did not authorize such action.[10] On the other hand, his own vice president, Alexander Stephens, opposed him—not covertly as Jefferson had opposed Adams, or Calhoun had opposed Jackson—for seizing too much power.[11] At times, Davis's congress refused him the right to suspend habeas corpus in order to fight espionage and subversion. Perhaps, given time in a postwar peace, the Confederacy could have worked some of these problems out. But certain ones pointed to the inherent contradiction in a society trying to form a nation while preserving state sovereignty. The most likely prospect would be a repetition of the experience under the Articles, leading to another convention giving back to government the authority the states tried to wrest from it in the federal system—that or a further cycle of secession from the seceders.

Despite the way the South rigorously suppressed dissent before the war, it has been cast as the freedom-loving underdog fighting off a powerful central government. Southerners are not the only ones who accept this version of history. Despite the modern admiration of Lincoln, General Lee has received an adulation not given to any Northern officer. Even at the site of

Lee's greatest blunder, Gettysburg, vendors who sell boys' uniforms to tourists do a brisker trade in Confederate grays than in Union blues. The North is seen as impersonal, mechanical, efficient—the very things resented in central governments. The South is seen as spontaneous, traditional, organic—it liked to picture its war as a repeat of Washington's war with England, local minutemen up against the disciplined forces of empire. It is an illusion many Americans have, over the years, found themselves unable to resist.

V.

Insurrectionists

Insurrection is an abortive form of revolution. It does not (normally) begin with a plan to replace the government. It is violence used as protest against some specific injustice—a resented tax, for instance. As hostility escalates, insurrection can turn to revolution or secession, but it need not. The Boston Tea Party (1773), which destroyed British tea rather than pay taxes on it, was an insurrection. There was no bloodshed, but there could have been. The "partyers" were armed, prepared to fight resistance if it should occur. Later acts of the British government led to more acts of insurrection, which in 1776 turned into a colonial secession from the British Empire. Without those further provocations by the British Parliament, that insurrection could have ended in 1773.

There is an element of spontaneity, often of accident, at the origin of many insurrections. Even when there is some rough sketch of a long-term plan, as in the case of John Brown's raid at Harpers Ferry (1859), it is rudimentary or provisional. The insurrectionist typically lashes out at an immediate wrong, and has not thought far beyond ending or avenging it.

Some violent eruptions in our history are not clearly insurrections, if we mean by that term an attack upon the government. Labor unrest, for instance, has led to sabotage of the workplace (as with unsafe mines), or violent strikes, or bombing of employers' offices, homes, and sympathetic newspapers. Government was sometimes an indirect target of these episodes, because of policies that favored the companies. But private industry was the primary target, and the armies of detectives, spies, and goons used to oppress the workers were often privately hired.

I confine myself, therefore, to examples of violence directly focused on the government—which consequently exhibit the anti-governmental values so far discussed. Three events caused a major response from the federal government—Shays's Rebellion (1786–87), the Whiskey Rebellion (1794), and John Brown's raid on Harpers Ferry (1859). My fourth example is included because it inflicted major casualties—Timothy McVeigh's bombing of the federal building in Oklahoma City (1995).

16.

From Daniel Shays to Timothy McVeigh

Shays's Rebellion (1786-87)

The rebellion that finally took the name of one of its leaders (Daniel Shays) is now applied to a range of activities in Massachusetts running through the years 1784–87, but it reached its climax when Shays led armed forces against troops rallied by the governor of the state. David Szatmary has divided the rebellion into four stages that could, with only minor adjustments, be applied to some other insurrections in our history. In the Shays example, the stages were these:

1. *Political protest and petition (1784–86).* In the aftermath of the Revolution, the national Congress set up by the Articles of Confederation tried to liquidate war debts and put credit on a sound footing so that foreigners could trade with the new nation on the basis of agreed currencies and financial obligation. Commercial interests in eastern parts of most states tended to support this policy, though we have seen James Madison castigate them for not doing so. The problem was that the hard money and currency redemption policies hurt subsistence farmers in the western parts of the states. Those areas were also subject to Indian conflict and the menace of western British forts not yet removed by postwar diplomacy. They naturally felt that they were shouldering more than their share of the national burden. Lacking hard cash, they needed loose credit for the planting of their future crops. They favored paper money and sliding monetary values, the bane of men like Madison. They protested their plight to the states' legislators, who were forced to balance the need for western electoral support against national demands being made on them. The farmers felt they were being treated as expendable and took measures to prevent their being ignored.

2. *The Regulation (1786)*. The farmers of Massachusetts took the name of Regulators, the eighteenth-century word for "vigilantes" (see Chapter 18). In the name of equity, they declared a determination to close down "usurping" debtors' courts. The choice of what was felt to be a minimizing term for their actions was meant to show that these protesters were *not* revolutionaries. When militia troops were formed to prevent the court closures, the local troops refused to fire on their own.

3. *The clash of armies (January–February 1787)*. Massachusetts governor James Bowdoin, not trusting his own militia to put down the unrest, appealed to Congress for federal troops. Though the Articles of Confederation gave Congress no power to use federal troops for maintaining a state's internal stability, the pretense was made that the troops were being raised for Indian control (M 9.277–78). There was a measure of reality in the pretense, since keeping discipline on the frontiers was considered a prerequisite for Indian relations. With the strong support of Madison and Hamilton, the measure for mobilizing troops was passed. But the states were, as usual, remiss in meeting the requisitions for cash to support the troops—only Virginia passed a new tax on tobacco to foot the military expense (M 9.278).

Governor Bowdoin could not wait for the inefficient Congress to get troops to him. He raised an army in the eastern part of Massachusetts, officered by Revolutionary veterans. The militia of the region was augmented with the kinds of paid volunteers that militias always needed for major tasks. The Shaysites, on their part, had expected such a challenge and done their own large-scale organizing. They planned to seize the state arsenal at Springfield to equip themselves with rifles, cannon, and ammunition. These forces had their own Revolutionary veterans, who planned an assault on the arsenal coordinated from three different directions. As often happens with a complex plan, one of the three forces attacked before the other two and was beaten back.

The rebels regrouped to the north, at Petersham, where they thought themselves beyond the reach of Governor Bowdoin's army, advancing from the east, in difficult conditions of snow and storm, led by General Benjamin Lincoln. Like the Revolutionary militiamen, who thought regular troops could not vanquish yeoman virtue, Daniel Shays said that effete "shopkeepers, lawyers, and doctors" could not prevail against sturdy plow-men.[1] But Lincoln's men made a thirty-mile march through a night of bliz-zard to surprise the rebel force of two thousand with an army of three thousand men, supported by artillery that had been wrestled through the snowdrifts. The military effort of the rebellion was broken, and its leaders fled to other states (Shays to Vermont) or to Canada, where some tried to enlist the aid of the British government. Canada's governor, Lord Dor-chester, promised asylum and assistance to strengthen his government's hand in the negotiations over western forts.[2]

4. *Punitive raids (February–June 1787)*. The scattered rebels left in Massachusetts took out their frustration by raiding merchants' homes until order was fully restored. The raids sputtered out, and new elections seemed to promise hope for redress of grievances when the popular John Hancock replaced Bowdoin as governor. Madison feared that the man he called "an idolator of popularity" (M 9.399) would accommodate the rebels. But Hancock surprised friend and foe by raising money for eight hundred more government soldiers. He was supported by the new president of the Massa-chusetts Senate, Samuel Adams, who had been a radical in the Revolu-tion, but was for harsh reprisals against the western rebels.[3] Though both sides would pull back from the abyss that had opened in Massachusetts, fear of western unrest made other states more favorable to the Continental Congress that was assembling at this very moment. The lasting effect of Shays's Rebellion on American history is to be found in the American Constitution (see Chapter 17).

Whiskey Rebellion (1794)

The next major insurrection occurred after the adoption of the Constitu-tion, during Washington's second term as president—the Whiskey Rebel-lion of 1794 in the backcountry of Pennsylvania. It, too, was the product of western resentment at economic exploitation, an excise tax on the pro-duction of whiskey. Since Alexander Hamilton, as secretary of the Trea-sury, could not under the new Constitution collect direct taxes from individuals, he had to find products of sufficient scale to bring in a national income from excises. Whiskey was produced in the necessary quantity, and—like snuff, sugar, and gentlemen's carriages—could be taxed as a "luxury" (as it still is). But for some western farmers, whiskey was a subsistence product. They could not economically send their wheat across the Alleghenies in any but this distilled form. Their protests against the excise had, with the support of President Washington, brought some moderation in its rate and the means of enforcing it. No longer, for instance, would those in default have to travel to federal court in Philadelphia for their trials (one of the most galling provisions of the original law). But those who had been summoned to trial before relaxation of the law were, foolishly, ordered to meet the old conditions. Some later historians blamed this requirement on Hamilton's desire to stir up trouble and crush resistance. But Thomas Slaughter more plausibly argues that the requirement was a bluff, to enforce readier compliance with the law (the court in Philadelphia was not even sitting at the time when the westerners were supposed to appear before it).[4]

If the writs being served were just a bluff, the bluff backfired. A crowd made up largely of the local militia went to demand that the local tax collector withdraw the writs. If he refused, they would force their way into his house and destroy them themselves. In response to this threat, the collector fired on the crowd, killing a popular leader. This led to rapid mobilization of several township militias, who marched on Pittsburgh with vague aims that were blunted with plentiful supplies of whiskey rolled out by terrified inhabitants of the town. Meetings were called to elect leaders of armed resistance to the law. Moderate westerners—especially Albert Gallatin and Hugh Henry Brackenridge—tried to prevent disobedience, even as they expressed support for the rebels' grievances. They argued that western Massachusetts could not exist, economically, apart from the central government; that armed action would reduce (not increase) their bargaining power with federal authorities in Philadelphia; that help from the British in Canada could not be relied on; that real independence (if that was the thing being sought) could come only later, when the West had geographic and economic self-sufficiency.[5] This placatory talk was later used against Gallatin and Brackenridge, as if they were igniting the resistance instead of extinguishing it. Gallatin was especially suspect for a presumed sympathy with the French Revolution because he was a French-speaking immigrant from Switzerland—though it was Gallatin who reminded the Pennsylvania hotheads that the Shays rebellion had caused an authoritarian reaction in Massachusetts.[6] The moderates made headway against the radical leader David Bradford, who "confidently proclaimed that frontiersmen could disarm and defeat any number of eastern militiamen."[7] The old minuteman myth of untrained virtue dies hard.

At the nation's capital in Philadelphia, the President and Secretary Hamilton were looking at a range of factors involved in western unrest. The Indians' recent defeat of federal soldiers under General Arthur St. Clair made stability in the West imperative. (General Anthony Wayne was about to reverse those Indian defeats, but that was not known in the summer of 1794.) International diplomacy still left the status of western territories in doubt. The rise of Democratic societies in the West made Hamilton fear a union of sentiment with the French Revolution. Pennsylvania's governor, Thomas Mifflin, urged caution on the President, and desired that a peace commission be sent to the rebels. This was a degrading thing for the infant nation—to sue for peace through negotiation with its own citizens—but Washington agreed to the commission, in order to buy time for organizing an army to take over the Alleghenies into the rebel territory. The regular troops were farther west fighting under General Wayne, so Washington federalized militias from four states (Pennsylvania, Maryland, Virginia, and New Jersey) for joint action under the nation's commander in chief.

There was the normal resistance to service in the militia, especially in Maryland, which had its own backcountry grievances. Bounties and the draft had to be used to lure men into service. Hamilton asked that a quarter of the army be mounted, which would have led to use of "the better sort" who owned riding horses, but Washington restricted the mounted troops to 10 percent of the army (necessary mainly for courier and scouting service).[8] The army that finally assembled on the eastern side of the Alleghenies numbered thirteen thousand men, over twice as many as the armed rebels could muster. Washington, wearing again the Revolutionary uniform he thought he had shed forever, reviewed the troops at their two staging areas, and was prepared to lead them over the mountains himself when two pieces of good news made that unnecessary. Word arrived that General Wayne had defeated two thousand Indian troops at the Battle of Fallen Timbers—pressure on the frontier was now eased. And the peace commissioners sent word that much of the rebellious area was now in compliance with the law. Military action was not called for, and Washington could return to the capital in time for the convening of Congress.

The question naturally arises, why did Washington send the troops on without him if the rebellion was, for all purposes, over? Governor Mifflin, leading the Pennsylvania militia himself, was now in favor of the expedition in his native state's disaffected portion. But Washington had national priorities to consult. He realized that the rebels could be temporizing. If he withdrew the troops and the rebellion flared up again (there were still firebrands urging that course), he could not send another army for many months—winter would seal the mountain passes. Besides, as in all his acts, he was considering the precedents being set for this young republic. He did not want it to be understood by future malcontents that they could set up a rival seat of authority and bargain with the government through commissioners. The role of the army would be not only to pacify the land but also to arrest and bring to trial those who had urged treason on their fellows. (Actually, the real leaders fled west and only minor functionaries were caught—both of those convicted of treason were pardoned by the President. But correct principle was affirmed.) Washington also wanted to demonstrate to rival powers on this continent, who had just witnessed two humiliations of national troops by Indian armies, that a large force could be raised by the President and deployed at need. As Thomas Slaughter notes, this part of his plan worked:

> The audience was intended to encompass friends and foes from the East and West, and the President played to an international gallery as well. Long accounts of Washington's presence among the troops appeared in newspapers throughout the nation; and they were dutifully forwarded by European ministers to their home governments. The President wished to communicate to the world that the power and the majesty of this young nation were not to be trifled with, and he was a master of symbolic imagery.[9]

Though the President wanted the majesty of the nation to be asserted, he took steps to emphasize that this was a republican army serving under an elected civil official. When two civilians were killed by troops in barroom-type encounters, he promptly turned the soldiers over to state courts (where they were found not guilty) and issued a public apology to the families of the slain. He not only cut back on Hamilton's call for mounted troops, but also skirted towns where mounted escorts had planned to ride with him in a display of honor for his person. The President traveled back-roads from one staging area to the next so that towns would not assemble official bodies to greet him.[10]

It was feared that the passage of a large army through civilian territory would result in plunder and outrages to the citizenry. The size of the army seemed to warrant such a fear, since its need of provisions would be great. Why did Washington send a larger force than most of those he had led in the Revolution itself? This looks like overkill to some historians. But the number of troops was meant to preclude the killing of civilians, to awe them into compliance. Besides, men in large numbers are less skittish than those in small bands, less fearful for their personal safety, less prone to overreact when challenged.[11] Some have questioned the need for Washington's personal leadership, but it was requested on the grounds that recruiting the militias, and keeping discipline among them, would be facilitated if he took the lead.[12] As it turned out, the inevitable impositions on civilians in western Pennsylvania were comparatively few, and the backcountry, far from suffering economic loss, actually profited by the infusion of specie and goods that the army brought with it. The soldiers were a great boost to the economy, and land prices soared after they left.[13]

The whole operation would have been an unqualified success but for two disastrous mistakes on Washington's part. Though he made Henry ("Light Horse Harry") Lee his replacement as the military commander, he sent Hamilton with Lee to conduct civilian investigations and arrests (it was Hamilton who harassed Gallatin). Hamilton's punitive and authoritarian approach was properly resented. Washington's second mistake, connected with the first, was that he gave too much credit to Hamilton's denunciation of the role of Democratic clubs in the rebellion. Washington criticized those societies (though not by name) in his next annual message to Congress, giving the nascent Democratic-Republican party a rallying issue in their defense of free speech. The topic that would explode in the next administration (over the Alien and Sedition Acts) had been engaged. That is why, though the hand of the federal government was strengthened in the short run, the Whiskey Rebellion did not have the unifying effect that Shays's Rebellion had.

John Brown's Raid (1859)

John Brown's insurrection was a minor skirmish compared to the regional revolt of the Whiskey rebels—only a dozen or so were involved with Brown, as opposed to thousands of Whiskey rebels. But Brown's actions have resonated far more powerfully in our history. I noted earlier that no civic duty can be exacted from slaves who try to regain their freedom by force—they are always in a condition of forced servitude, and there is normally no path out of that condition but counterforce. A problem arises, however, for citizens who must decide whether they should abet such forceful liberation. This was brought home in an excruciating way to those asked to smuggle runaway slaves through the "underground railroad." People were breaking the fugitive slave laws, and doing it in a covert way, if they helped the runaways. But were they using force? This question tortured those who, like the abolitionist William Lloyd Garrison, were pacifists in principle. Harriet Tubman, a runaway herself, who daringly brought slaves out of the South in her midnight raids, carried a pistol and said she would use it if anyone tried to intercept her. Luckily, her cleverness was such that no one ever caught her; but if they had she would have engaged in violence.[14]

The Fugitive Slave Law of 1850, commanding the authorities in northern states to "render back" slaves escaped from the South, forced the issue. Could one stand by and let slaves be captured in free states and taken back to captivity? Bostonians who were in sympathy with the free blacks rushed a courtroom in their city and took back the captured slave Shadrach in 1851, smuggling him off to hiding. Juries refused to convict those indicted for that act, and Garrison could not bring himself to condemn this use of force.[15] When a slave named Anthony Burns was seized in 1854, President Franklin Pierce sent two artillery companies, a cavalry detachment, and a squadron of marines to Boston to make sure that federal law was not defied. The opponents of the law schemed to free Burns, but could not decide on a feasible plan before it was too late.[16] Harriet Tubman had no such hesitancy—in 1860, she led an armed assault on a building in Troy, New York, where a fugitive named Charles Nalle was being held. While her followers struggled with his captors, Tubman, who had acquired her strength working as a field hand, picked up the swooning Nalle and carried him to safety.[17]

While men aired their New England consciences over what they could do directly in the struggle against slavery, they were quick to support proxies who might repeat Tubman's exploits. When the Kansas-Nebraska Act of 1854 declared that Kansas settlers could choose whether to allow slavery in the territory, abolitionists supported drives to populate the land with opponents of the slave system. Armed struggle between the competing settlers led to the formation of the Kansas Aid Society to send money, supplies, and arms to the victims of "border ruffians" raiding out of Missouri to support slaveholders in the territory. In the contest for "bleeding Kansas," John Brown and his six sons took a leading role. One night in 1856, along the Pottawatomie Creek, Brown's small band took three men, presumed slavery supporters, from their homes, along with one man's young son, and hacked all five to pieces with broadswords. Two of Brown's sons, absent from the action, had trouble believing their father could have done this, and two of the sons who were present refrained from the murderous activity. The reaction to the "Pottawatomie Massacre" was so swift and unfavorable that Brown wrote to his wife denying that any killings had occurred.[18] That was still his story when he went to New England seeking support for his broader plan, which was to emulate Harriet Tubman, but on a bigger scale, smuggling slaves into the Allegheny Mountains where they would be armed and allowed to establish their own communities. He even consulted with Tubman on southern routes for reaching slaves and bringing them out.[19] Six prominent New Englanders secretly approved of this plan and raised money for it. They even diverted arms openly collected for Kansas to this covert Alleghenies project.[20]

In order to arm his slaves, Brown meant to capture an arsenal, which had been among the first steps contemplated by the Shays and Whiskey rebels. (As we saw in earlier chapters, the idea that everyone had a gun was not true, even this late in the century.) The arsenal Brown meant to take, at Harpers Ferry, was so vulnerable to counterattack that Frederick Douglass, the most famous escaped slave, refused Brown's heated urgings that he join him. Douglass said that so obviously futile a mission would just "rivet the fetters more firmly than ever on the limbs of the enslaved."[21] But Brown went pigheadedly forward. He took Harpers Ferry, expecting slaves to rally to him there (this was not plantation country, and slaves had not been alerted ahead of time lest they divulge that the seizure would take place). Local militia sealed off Brown in the arsenal, and federal troops under Robert E. Lee shortly arrived and stormed the place. At Brown's trial, his lawyers tried to save his life by arguing that he was insane (who else but a crazy man could have drawn up such a feckless plan?). He dismissed the lawyers and asserted that he was innocent of anything but trying to smuggle slaves out of captivity. He had never shed blood. There were no others involved in his plan but those captured or killed in the arsenal. In fact,

> I never did intend murder, or treason, or the destruction of property, or to excite or incite slaves to rebellion, or to make insurrection. . . . I never had any design against the liberty of any person, nor any disposition to commit treason or incite slaves to rebel, or make any general insurrection. I never encouraged any man to do so, but always discouraged any idea of that kind.[22]

Those words are from the eloquent (and lying) address to the court that Garrison, the committed pacifist, read out loud to his congregation. Ralph Waldo Emerson would later call Brown's speech the equal of Lincoln's Gettysburg Address.[23] It was in the interest of the "secret six" to rely on Brown's protestations of his own innocence and their lack of involvement with him (though incriminating letters from some of them had been found). Others have argued to this day that the manifest injustice of the Fugitive Slave Law and the Kansas-Nebraska Act justified any attacks on them, no matter how violent or random or futile. Brown was made a martyr.

Lincoln had a more balanced reading of Brown's purpose. When some tried to smear the nascent Republican party by saying it indirectly sanctioned Brown's assault on slavery, Lincoln responded (in his Cooper Union speech of 1860):

> That [Brown] affair corresponds with the many attempts, related in history, at the assassination of kings and emperors. An enthusiast broods over the oppression of a people till he fancies himself commissioned by Heaven to liberate them. He ventures the attempt, which ends in little else than his own execution. Orsini's attempt on Louis Napoleon, and John Brown's attempt at Harper's Ferry were, in their philosophy, precisely the same.[24]

The Oklahoma City Bombing (1995)

A frustration born of the union between personal impotence and an omnipotent cause leads to the righteousness that can brook no talk of practicality. Russell Banks uses his novelist's sensitivity to see in John Brown's pointless violence at Pottawatomie Creek a peculiarly modern form of terrorism. Brown tells his son Owen (the narrator of Banks's novel *Cloudsplitter*): "We must strike pure terror into their hearts, Owen. Pure terror. Pure! We must become *terrible!*" And Owen Brown comes to believe that terrorism is the only proper response to a situation where "our entire government and even our nation's destiny itself had been stolen from us, as if we had been invaded and all but conquered by a foreign, tyrannical power."[25]

Those words of Owen could be spoken by most of the terrorist bombers of our time—those on the right who blew up a federal building in

Oklahoma City, or those on the left who planted bombs (like the Weathermen), professed ideological murder (like the Black Panthers), or practiced ideological theft (like the Symbionese Liberation Army). However appalling such acts may be, they are essentially gestures, little dead ends of insurrection. As the military experts John Shy and Thomas Collier note, of the exercises in modern rage, "terrorism has yet to win a victory anywhere."[26] Arthur Marwick, a sympathetic observer of the 1960s, gives this snapshot view of the decade's experiments with terrorism:

> The first public performance by the Weathermen came in what they declared as "Days of Rage," beginning shortly before midnight on Monday 6 October [1969] when they blew up a monument to policemen, situated in Chicago's Haymarket Square. Chunks of masonry were blasted into the surroundings, windows shattered. More ominously, a Chicago police official declared, "We now feel that it is kill or be killed." Between 8 and 11 October, in the same city, the Weathermen smashed up cars and business property. Thereafter, chief resort was had to high explosives, with another group, Revolutionary Force 9, joining in the series of bombings in New York. The damage to property was enormous, but most of the almost fifty deaths were of Weathermen who blew themselves up in error. The most spectacular example was when a bomb factory in a house in Greenwich Village blew up on 6 March 1970, demolishing the house and killing three bomb-makers.[27]

Given this record of fecklessness, what inspires the aborted form of insurrection known as terrorism? Paradoxically, its very lack of effect gives this activity what Banks's John Brown calls its "purity." It is protest for protest's sake, uncompromised by mere tactical likelihoods. It is anti-governmentalism in its most distilled or refined essence. It is beyond success or failure. The hatred of evil, once cleansed of particularity, once made abstract by outsized intensity, becomes both frivolous and fascinating to its agents. The evilness of The Other releases terrorists from responsibility for their acts. There is something giddily liberating about such freedom from consequence which helps explain the exaltation with which John Brown went to his death. It explains as well the furious dedication of a Timothy McVeigh and his supporters.

McVeigh was born in 1968, into a society (and a family) that was subject to upheavals and dislocation. Lockport, New York, where he grew up, took its name from the locks of the Erie Canal on which it stands. He seemed a normal enough child at school, but his parents' unstable and dissolving marriage threw him into the company of his grandfather, whose house had an electrical generator in its basement along with ample supplies of water and food and ammunition. Edward McVeigh was a survivalist, prepared for the disasters from which government cannot protect a man (it may even be abetting the disaster). He was also one who felt that a gun is necessary to one's own preservation. He gave his grandson Tim a .22-caliber gun when he was nine, and helped him learn to use it for target practice (not for hunting, which they never did). From his grandfather Tim acquired an early interest in gun and survival magazines.[28]

When he was sixteen, McVeigh ordered from a mail-order catalogue two 55-gallon plastic drums, for storing water and gunpowder in his own bunker. After he graduated from high school, he supported himself during one year at business school by becoming a security guard for an armored car company. The job allowed him to get a permit, at age nineteen, to carry a concealed weapon. From that time on he was rarely without a gun on his person. Like many people who are anti-authoritarian, McVeigh had a paradoxical admiration for that most authoritarian of institutions, the military. When he grew impatient with business school, he enlisted in the army and was a "super-soldier," rising to the rank of sergeant by the time of the Gulf war, in which he performed so well with a 25-mm cannon mounted on a Bradley armored vehicle that he won the Bronze Star for valor.

Yet even as he fought in the military arm of his government, McVeigh was proselytizing against that government among his fellow soldiers (including his later assistant in bombing preparations, Terry Nichols). He urged others to read William Pierce's novel, *The Turner Diaries*, that tale of insurrection against an oppressive government. He felt that the military was blindly following orders, unaware of the evil purposes it could be turned to. He tried to penetrate the more secret levels of government by applying to join the Special Forces (Green Berets). When he could not meet the strenuous physical tests for that service, he resigned from the military and went back to being a civilian security guard.

McVeigh's knowledge of guns made him gravitate to the gun show circuit, which led to his selling and trading guns. He was part of the gun culture's mixed revulsion and exaltation at the government's 1992 shoot-out with Randy Weaver in Idaho and its 1993 shoot-out with David Koresh in Texas. The revulsion was at the government's aggression, the exaltation at the proof that only citizens' firepower could be relied on in the face of such governmental viciousness. McVeigh made two pilgrimages to the site of Koresh's "martyrdom." At one of these appearances, he was televised passing out pamphlets asking, "Is Your Church ATF-Approved?" (ATF for the Bureau of Alcohol, Tobacco and Firearms, which worked with the FBI at Waco).[29]

The reference to churches is one of the most significant touches in McVeigh's progress toward his definitive act. Both Weaver and Koresh were leaders of religious communities—as was James Ellison, who first planned to blow up the Oklahoma City federal building, in conformity with the fictional directions of *The Turner Diaries*.[30] Believers in such apocalyptic acts are almost obliged—like John Brown himself—to see them in terms of God's ultimate battle with the forces of darkness. As William Pierce has his main character say:

> Everything that has been and everything that is yet to be depends on us. We are truly instruments of God in the fulfillment of His Grand Design. These may seem like strange words to be coming from me, who has [sic] never been religious, but they are utterly sincere words.[31]

McVeigh, who was born into a conventional Catholic family, had by 1995 taken on the messianic afflatus of Weaver, Koresh, or Pierce. The lingua franca of such groups is the paradoxically antisemitic semitism of theologies like "Christian Identity" (founded by James Ellison), which see cosmic struggle in terms of the Jewish Scriptures, but with Jews as the force of darkness—a religious parallel to their anti-authoritarian authoritarianism.

Such religiosity, part of the cluster of anti-governmental values that re-curs in the groups this book is studying, goes with another attitude that might seem unexpected in such a radical friend of violence—tradition-alism. McVeigh had perfectly internalized the view that his opposition to the United States government was in accord with aims of that government's founders. He wore a tee shirt with a favorite saying of his ideological soul mates, Thomas Jefferson's casual praise for the Shays rebels: "The tree of liberty must be refreshed from time to time with the blood of patriots and tyrants" (J 12.356). An expression of the same myth of our anti-govern-mental founding was discovered by the agents who opened McVeigh's car after the bombing.[32] They found this sentence on a note inside the enve-lope of materials left there: "Obey the Constitution of the United States and we will not shoot you." The whole cluster of anti-governmental values listed earlier is implicit there, proving that McVeigh spoke for the authen-tic people, in a voice provincial and amateur, not cosmopolitan and expert (not the voice of "elitist" Jews and officials).

Such ties with the anti-governmental thinking of the militias and the Christian Identity theologians distinguish McVeigh from other violent men with whom he shared some psychological traits—loners like the as-sailants of John Kennedy and George Wallace and Ronald Reagan. Lee Harvey Oswald and Arthur Bremer had no support group like the gun cul-ture's network that McVeigh lived and moved in. These lone agents resem-bled Paul Schrader's fictional Travis Bickle in the movie *Taxi Driver*. Bickle hopes to acquire some order in his chaotic inner life by imposing a harsh order on the external world—an order as arbitrary as it is urgent. He tries to kill a liberal politician first, and kills a pimp only when he cannot get close enough to the politician. In the same way, Oswald first tried to kill a right-wing general (Edwin Walker) before getting his shot at a putatively liberal president. Bremer stalked the archetypically Republican Richard Nixon before getting closer access to the nominally Democratic George Wallace. These men were not insurrectionists, with sympathizers they hoped to rouse against the government. They were sociopaths acting out their hostility against society's celebrities, not against the agents of the government. John Hinckley actually tried to kill President Reagan in order to impress the actress in *Taxi Driver* (Jodie Foster), replicating Travis

Bickle's mad gesture of desperation. McVeigh knew his enemy, government, and he killed appropriately anonymous agents of that impersonal force, not interchangeable celebrities. There was method in his madness, and it was the method of the insurrectionist.

17.

Academic
Insurrectionists

Despite the sorry history of insurrection in America, there is a band of academic lawyers who argue for insurrection as a right guaranteed *within* the United States Constitution—guaranteed, specifically, in the Second Amendment. These scholars exemplify this book's point so well that I suppose I should be grateful to them for that. They hold that anti-governmentalism is such a deep part of the American tradition that any constitution which did not embody *it*, along with the machinery of government, would not be an authentic expression of the American people's ethos. We have seen that others hold this view in a milder form—finding in checks and balances an anti-governmental action *within* government itself. But these men go further and say that the document provides for armed resisters *outside* the government to oppose it with violence. They find this mandate for insurrection in the Second Amendment.

Some of these people we have already met, as academic defenders of a constitutional right to nullify laws (Chapter 14). But there are even more defenders of insurrection as a constitutional right. One of their number, Glenn Harlan Reynolds of the University of Tennessee, calls the muster: "Akhil Amar of Yale Law School, Randy Barnett of Boston University, Raymond T. Diamond of Tulane, Sanford Levinson of Texas, and David Williams of Indiana—all leading figures in constitutional law."[1] How distinguished are the arguments advanced by this distinguished group? They fall into several clusters.

1. There is a "climate of opinion" argument, bolstered with indiscriminate quotations of anti-government expressions from the founding period, or even from the English republican tradition. As Sanford Levinson puts it,

"American thought is significantly anti-statist."[2] Since there was a whole lot of anti-governmental feeling going around, we are to assume, some of it was bound to seep into the Constitution (the alternative is "literally unthinkable" for Levinson): "The American political tradition is, for good or ill, based in large measure on a healthy mistrust of the state."[3] In fact, the feeling of the people was still revolutionary, Akhil Amar tells us, so a revolution had to be embedded in the Constitution: "Fresh from their own revolutionary experience, the last thing the Framers would have done is to deny the People the means of armed insurrection."[4] If this feeling was not universal, these authors are certain, it was clearly regnant among the framers. In fact, Amar can make the astonishing assertion that "In 1789, the Framers worried far more about an abusive federal government than about states and localities."[5] More specifically, he claims that Madison was a celebrant of state governments under the Articles! "If you're James Madison in 1780, you trust your local legislature, but you're somewhat distrustful of the federal government."[6] As we saw in Chapters 3 through 6, state abuses were precisely what drove Madison to argue for a strong central government. Nor was he alone in this apprehension. The need to put down disorder at the state level (future Shays's Rebellions) was one of the principal aims of the body that met in Philadelphia. Washington himself decided to attend that convention—though he had earlier refused those urging him to do so—because of the Shays rebellion, and he thought others were similarly motivated.[7]

Most of the anti-governmental quotations resorted to by the insurrectionists come from the Antifederalists, who were not framers of the Constitution but opponents of it, those who tried to prevent its adoption because it did *not* express their fear of government. There was not a single "climate of opinion" at the time. In fact, the Antifederalists lost the debate over the Constitution to a *different* set of opinions. They had predicted that adoption of the Constitution would eventuate in tyranny, so little did it evidence a proper fear of government. To keep quoting these men as the framers, as authors whose ethos pervades the very Constitution they denounced, is to commit the fundamental interpretive error Jefferson criticized in 1800, when he said that we should ascribe to the Constitution "a meaning to be found in the explanations of those who advocated not those who opposed it."[8] So much for the general assumptions on which the insurrectionists work.

2. How do they argue on the details of the Second Amendment? Here again they go to the Antifederalists, and do so in an anachronistic way. As I pointed out in Chapter 7, the Antifederalist defenders of the militias during the ratification debates were trying to prevent the adoption of the Constitution because it allowed for a standing army and navy. Once the Constitution was adopted, that argument had failed—unless the Second Amendment outlawed the regular army and navy provided for in Article I, Section 8, Clauses 12 and 13. But those clauses were allowed to stand, and—as we saw—the Antifederalists therefore showed no enthusiasm for the Second Amendment when it came time to ratify *it*. This did not meet their demands at all—though the academicians continue to claim that it did. Patrick Henry knew better.

3. Well, the insurrectionists argue, even if there is now a standing army (the nightmare that militias were supposed to fend off), the militias, if they are maintained, may act as a check on the army and navy, they may offer a *threat* of armed resistance that will frighten the regular forces away from any attempted tyranny. But there are five places in the Constitution itself that forbid such armed resistance. The insurrectionists as a rule try to deal with only one of these texts (the treason clause), but another one is more directly involved in the history they pervert when they argue from "climate of opinion." That is the guarantee clause—Article IV, Section 4:

> The United States shall guarantee to every state in this union a republican form of government, and shall protect each of them against invasion; and on application of the legislature, or of the executive (when the legislature cannot be convened) against domestic violence.

John Adams once said that he did not understand what this clause was doing in the Constitution, and he did not think anyone else did either. But the record of the drafting convention is very clear about its purpose. This clause was shaped around a passage Madison put into the Virginia Plan for the convention's consideration, which in its turn grew out of his effort to send troops to put down Shays's Rebellion.[9] Writing down his list of vices in any mere confederation, he listed as the sixth vice "want of a *guaranty* to the states of their constitutions and laws *against internal violence*" (M 9.350, emphasis added). If a state draws up a constitution through its proper representatives, and that legal system is defied by armed resisters, "the hands of the federal authority are tied" under the Articles of Confederation. (We have seen that Madison tried to get around this difficulty, in the Shays instance, by raising troops on the pretense of action against Indians.) Madison wanted to make sure the government's hands would not be similarly tied under the new Constitution.

Preparing to go to the convention, Madison voiced his concern on this matter to Edmund Randolph, who collaborated with him on the Virginia Plan: "An article should be inserted expressly *guaranteeing* the tranquillity of the states against internal as well as external dangers" (M 9.385, emphasis added). This went into the Virginia Plan in this form: "Resolved, that a republican government, and the territory of each state (except in the instance of a voluntary junction of government and territory) ought to be *guaranteed* by the United States to each state" (M 10.17, emphasis added). William Wiecek has demonstrated, in his book *The Guarantee Clause of the U.S. Constitution*, that the primary concern in the convention's debate over this item was with Shays-like rebellions. A secondary concern was the reintroduction of monarchy in any state—which was connected with the Shays case, since some of the rebels tried to form an alliance with the king's government in Canada, and most secession talk at the time involved some kind of reliance on foreign monarchs.

The Virginia Plan's *territorial* guarantee had to do with the threat of French and English disputes over western lands, or Indian claims, or competing states' disputes. This caused disagreement between states with different land claims, so it was omitted in the final form of Article IV, Section 4. What was added to the clause, that the federal power would not act on domestic violence without the request of the state authorities, strengthened the states against their domestic enemies—Governor Bowdoin, for instance, had requested federal assistance to put down the Shaysites.

This was the sense of the clause as Hamilton expounded it in *The Federalist*. It offered a cure for the situation under the Articles, where "without a *guarantee*, the assistance to be derived from the Union in repelling those *domestic dangers* which may sometimes threaten the existence of the state constitutions, must be renounced" (F 21.130–31, emphasis added). The general agreement was that the states had the right to establish their own republics—the federal government could not do that—but that they could call on federal arms to protect that constitution. But what if the state constitution was itself faulty, was not republican? That was the issue in the first great test of the Article IV guarantee—the episode in Rhode Island known as the Dorr War. This episode stemmed from the fact that Rhode Island, always the "rogue state," had not adopted a new constitution at the Revolution, but continued to operate under the terms of its colonial charter, which restricted the suffrage to "freemen," defined as owners of $134 worth of real property and their eldest sons.

In other states, unrest arose in western sectors cut off from seaboard centers of power. In Rhode Island, a heavy influx of immigrants in the East made it the focus of resentment. The rulers of the state opposed these (largely Catholic) newcomers, and resisted petitions to expand the suffrage, letting at least some of them in. This manifest injustice led followers of Thomas Dorr to set up a counter-government in 1842 and call on the President to certify *it* as the republican government that deserved a guarantee. Jacksonian Democrats, especially in New York, supported this new "government" and some hotheads offered it armed assistance. But President John Tyler was a southern slave owner, and southerners always feared that the federal government would someday deny that the slave states were republican systems deserving the constitutional guarantee. Tyler stalled, urging the state governor to seek a compromise on suffrage but promising troops if they were needed to put down armed rebellion. When the state did offer to compromise, Dorr's followers dropped away from him. When he tried to make a stand on the Connecticut border, with the help of some men from New York, the state militia easily put his "army" to flight.[10] The state, when no longer threatened with open defiance, broadened the suffrage.

But the matter did not end there. Dorr and some of his followers wanted to maintain the legitimacy of their short-lived government. They used the case of a man whose house had been searched by a militiaman, claiming that the militia was acting under an illegitimate government's martial law. Supreme Court Justice Joseph Story, riding circuit in Rhode Island, heard the case of the Dorrite (Martin Luther) against the militiaman (Luther Borden) in 1843, and decided that the Dorr War had no more color of law than Shays's Rebellion.[11] Appeal to the Supreme Court was stalled for some years, and when it came up, Daniel Webster argued for the militiaman that Dorr's "People's Constitution" may have been republican but was not a government. It lacked any legal reality or function.[12] The Court agreed with Webster, eight to one, and Chief Justice Roger Taney's opinion (*Luther v. Borden*, 1849) established some key points—that the "United States" (i.e., Congress) is to establish what is and is not a republican government; that the Congress had done that by recognizing senators and representatives from Rhode Island as legitimate representatives of the state in its own body; and that it is not the Court's role to debate republican theory.[13] This proved a momentous decision because it gave Congress the warrant it would use, during Reconstruction, to reshape the southern state constitutions to admit blacks to the suffrage. The Dorr ideals won an indirect and delayed victory in that sense. But in Dorr's own "war," every duly constituted authority said that he did not have the right to *armed* rebellion. He was duly tried for treason, sentenced to life, and pardoned after a year. In that sense, Madison's conception of the guarantee clause was vindicated.

So here we have a clause of the Constitution that was framed and passed precisely to put down domestic insurrections, and vindicated in that meaning by all three branches of the federal government when put to its principal test. Then how can the academicians claim that the Constitution guaranteed precisely the opposite in the Second Amendment, a right to engage in armed insurrection?

I said earlier that there are four places in the Constitution where armed insurrection is forbidden. The most obvious one is Article III, Section 3, Clause 1:

Treason against the United States shall consist only in levying war against them, or in adhering to their enemies, giving them aid and comfort. No person shall be convicted of treason unless on the testimony of two witnesses to the same overt act, or on confession in open court.

This is the only place where the Constitution *defines* a crime. The aim is clearly to limit the power to charge people with "constructive treason," or mere questionable opinion. The act must be overt, a war, seen and sworn to by at least two witnesses. Even by this "minimal" definition of treason, armed insurrection would be making war on the government of the United States, overtly, and would have hundreds or thousands of witnesses. Where is the "right" to do this stated in the document?

A third place where insurrection is condemned in the Constitution is at Article I, Section 8, Clause 15: "The Congress shall have power . . . to provide for calling forth the militia to execute the laws of the Union, *suppress insurrections* and repel invasions" (emphasis added). The militia exists, in the Constitution's express mandate, not to engage in insurrection but to suppress it. That, by the way, is just what it did in the cases we looked at in the last chapter. When local militia groups sided with Shays, and with the Whiskey rebels, it was the state militia, led by its authorized commander (Governor Bowdoin in the one case and Mifflin in the other), that acted with the federal government. We must remember that only the state militias are recognized by the Constitution, which reserves "*to the states* respectively the appointment of the officers and the authority of training the militia according to the discipline prescribed by Congress"— Article I, Section 8, Clause 16, the fourth place where insurrection is condemned, since the training prescribed by the federal government will not include a direction to defy the government. Madison, writing to Washington about what he hoped the convention would accomplish, had said: "The militia ought certainly to be placed in some form or other under the authority which is entrusted with the *general* protection and defense" (M 9.384, emphasis added). That was done in Article I, Section 8, Clauses 15 and 16. Yet a legal insurrectionary like Glenn Harlan Reynolds can say that the National Guard, as presently operated, cannot be the militia intended by the Second Amendment since it "was never designed to resist a tyrannical government. . . . And they are required to swear an oath of loyalty to the United States government, as well as to the states."[14] Professor Reynolds seems not to have read any part of the Constitution except the Second Amendment. If he had, he would know what Article I says about the subordination of the state militias to the general authority.

The fifth passage in the Constitution dealing with insurrection is the extradition clause (Article IV, Section 2, Clause 2): "A person charged in any state with treason, felony, or other crime, who shall flee from justice and be found in another state, shall on demand of the executive authority of the state from which he fled be delivered up, to be removed to the state having jurisdiction of the crime." The men framing and ratifying that clause had a recent case vividly in mind—the way Shays rebels, who had committed treason by levying war on constituted authority, fled to other states and could not be rendered back by the terms of the Articles of Confederation. In the Whiskey Rebellion, which occurred after the Constitution was ratified, those who fled could be extradited, making it clear that insurrection was not an option allowed in individual states. The whole union would unite in returning insurrectionists to the scene of their crime. This passage, when read in conjunction with the treason clause, forbids insurrection, as does each of the other three clauses, even when they are read in isolation. Taken together, they make it overwhelmingly clear that the Constitution was framed to forbid, prevent, and punish insurrection against its own laws—as, indeed, any constitution that claims legitimate authority must do. How can professors of the law, men of otherwise composed minds, deny such clear constitutional directives?

4. Though insurrection is denied as a right under the Constitution, according to its own plain and reiterated provisions, the professors fall back on an argument from authority and tell us that *some* people thought, early on, that the right was provided for. That "some" mainly boils down to two, Tench Coxe and Joseph Story. Coxe, not otherwise known as a constitutional scholar, was a Federalist who wanted to allay Antifederalist objections to the Bill of Rights—in his words, "to promote harmony among the late contending parties" (M 12.239). He did this in an article for Philadelphia's *Federal Gazette* (June 18, 1789), which he sent to Madison and which contained this passage:

As civil rulers, not having their duty to the people duly before them, may attempt to tyrannize, and as the military forces which must be occasionally raised to defend our country might pervert their power to the injury of their fellow citizens, the people are confirmed by the next article [the Second Amendment] in their right to keep and bear their private arms.

As I say, Coxe is not known as a constitutional scholar, and there would be no reason to take his words seriously in the face of the five constitutional passages forbidding insurrection, but the professors claim that Madison approved Coxe's treatment of the Second Amendment, making it a kind of official interpretation. The evidence for this is that Madison wrote a letter acknowledging receipt of Coxe's article, which he hoped would be "of a healing tendency" (M 12.257). Madison does not address himself to any specific matter in the article, though he clearly would not have agreed with Coxe's claim, just before dealing with the Second Amendment, that the First Amendment's establishment clause is meant to restrain only "impious" and "self-righteous" religions. There is no reason to presume that he would have agreed any more with the reading of the Second Amendment. Madison's letter is polite and general, not a discussion of any substantive point Coxe made.

The second authority appealed to is Supreme Court Justice Joseph Story, who *was* an important constitutional interpreter. Story said in his 1833 *Commentaries on the Constitution of the United States* and his 1840 *Familiar Exposition of the Constitution* that the Second Amendment "offers a strong *moral* check against the usurpations and arbitrary power of rulers" (emphasis added). It does this, first, because the militia makes it unnecessary to "keep up *large* military establishments and standing armies in time of peace" (emphasis added) and, second, makes it possible to resist such usurpation if it does occur.[15] Sanford Levinson and others take this to mean that Story is defending insurrection, though the emphasis in both commentaries is on a "moral check." But even if Story is defending insurrection, he does not consider how that can be reconciled with the passages in the Constitution that forbid it. Moreover, important as he is in constitutional thought, Story is hardly infallible, as we can see from *his* interpretation of the First Amendment, that it means "Christianity ought to receive encouragement from the states."[16] Madison would not have agreed with that. Neither would Levinson. The argument from authority cannot be made a substitute for the evidence of the document itself.

5. One of the principal devices of the insurrectionists is to confuse the right of insurrection under (within) the Constitution with the right of revolution (which would overthrow the Constitution). Levinson says that the Second Amendment authorizes "a Lockean 'appeal to heaven' "

against unjust laws. And David C. Williams argues that the amendment embodies not a liberal right of resistance but a republican right of revolution.[17]

It is certainly true that the Americans who had just completed their own revolution believed in the right of revolution—as did almost every political theorist in the British tradition, including even a Tory like Samuel Johnson. A people can overthrow a government it considers unjust. But it is absurd to think that it does so by virtue of that unjust government's own authority. The appeal to heaven is an appeal *away from* the earthly authority of the moment, not *to* that authority. It makes no sense to say that I must overthrow this abomination, but only because it has given me permission to do so. Madison hammered at the distinction between insurrection and revolution when he was warning the South away from armed secession. To those who claimed a constitutional warrant for taking arms against the government, he said that "resorts within the purview of the constitution are not the same as the *ultima ratio*" of revolution.[18] He had said the same thing in *The Federalist* when he assured opponents of the Constitution that, if ever it should spawn a tyrannical government, the same thing would happen as during the Revolution. Referring to the Revolutionary committees of correspondence, he wrote:

> A correspondence would be opened. Plans of resistance would be concerted. One spirit would animate and conduct the whole. The same combination in short would result from an apprehension of the federal as was produced by the dread of a foreign [British] yoke (F 46.320).

The academic insurrectionists like to appeal to this as Madison's reading of the Second Amendment, but it is clear that Madison is referring to the "original rights" that pre-exist constitutions and can be neither granted nor obliterated by them. (The Second Amendment, needless to say, did not exist when *The Federalist* was written.)

This clear and obvious distinction, between insurrection and revolution, has repeatedly been spelled out by American authorities. Andrew Jackson, in his 1832 state paper on secession, proclaimed:

Secession, like any other revolutionary act, may be morally justified by the extremity of oppression; but to call it a constitutional right is confounding the meaning of terms, and can only be done through gross error or to deceive those who are willing to assert a right, but would pause before they make a revolution or incur the penalties consequent on a failure.[19]

Lincoln observed the same distinction in his first inaugural address: "Whenever they [the people] shall grow weary of the existing government, they can exercise their *constitutional* right of amending it or their *revolutionary* right to dismember or overthrow it" (L 2.222, emphasis in original). The revolutionary right, he argued, *cannot* be a constitutional right: "It is safe to assert that no government proper ever had a provision in its organic law for its own termination . . . it being impossible to destroy it except by some action not provided for in the instrument itself" (L 2.217).

David C. Williams is the scholar who has tried most strenuously to get around the treason clause in defending a constitutional right of revolution—what he calls "conservative revolution."[20] If the government departs from the Constitution, then a revolution to restore the Constitution acts within the Constitution. But the *constitutional* way to decide what is *un*constitutional is through the document's own machinery of Supreme Court review (if elections and amendments fail). If that machinery is unworkable, then the Constitution is defunct and one cannot be working under its authority. If one goes outside the Constitution to "defend" the Constitution, one is still acting *outside* it—that is, unconstitutionally. Almost every revolution begins as the American one did, by saying that the social compact has broken down—in our case, that the rights of Englishmen were not being protected because of parliamentary usurpation. But when one replaces the defunct machinery, it is with a new regime, which must (and does) establish its own constitutional rules. This is what common sense calls a revolution—and it does not derive its sanction from a disputed interpretation of an amendment with an altogether different purpose. It is what Sanford Levinson calls it, an appeal to heaven, a higher tribunal than the text of one document.

Since everyone agrees that the right of revolution antecedes and outranks the Constitution, why don't the professors just settle for that, and stop writing acres of analysis to say that revolution somehow got smuggled into a document that set up a government (for an obviously different purpose than providing for its own dismantling)? Besides the motive already glanced at—that they feel an American government must be anti-government—there is the desire to have just a little bit of revolution (like being a little bit pregnant) when it suits them to invoke violence over an injustice. After all, the Shays and Whiskey and John Brown insurrections were based on genuine grievances. Admittedly. But the Constitution worked to suppress those rebellions, and was bound to. And the militias, which the professors want to use in support of insurrection, were the instruments that put them down.

6. Here we come to another argument in the insurrectionary arsenal—that the militia that suppressed rebellions was not the "real," the original, militia of universal citizen warriors (something that never existed) but some bastardized modern substitute for it, the National Guard or the select levies of Governors Bowdoin and Mifflin. (Those governors raised militia troops exactly as they were raised before and during the Revolution.) Well, if the Second Amendment is, in Williams's words, an anachronism, why keep arguing that it allows for insurrection? Because Williams and others want the amendment to serve as a warrant for "equivalent" action preserving the "spirit" of the amendment. For Williams, that would be such republican and anti-governmental action as broader distribution of property, campaign finance reform, proportional representation, or universal service in welfare projects.[21] Anyone who can offer those as proper applications of the Second Amendment is invalidating all his earlier claims about it. If it is not for insurrection at the moment, then let's at least get some use out of it for doing community improvement—or for anything that the professor wants to accomplish under color of applying the Constitution. The academic insurrectionists deserve some kind of medal for their dogged ability to keep taking themselves seriously.

Akhil Amar also admits that the "original conditions" for a militia no longer exist, but he would apply the "spirit" of the amendment to abolish the draft, put gays and women in a voluntary military force, and make it impossible for the military to reject anyone who, while sound of mind and limb, wants to serve in it, no matter whether the service makes military sense (in an army where troop numbers are just one element in a defense system).[22] He, too, claims that this is a proper way of carrying out the mandate of the Second Amendment. For him, the draft's "possible" un-constitutionality is not based on personal freedom from involuntary servi-tude but on the fact that it deprives the *states* of their Second Amendment responsibility for self-defense. The Second Amendment set up "a military federalism in large part to protect the states from the federal govern-ment."[23]

Sanford Levinson believes that, even though a universal militia no longer exists, its spirit can be guaranteed by the Second Amendment when authorizing guerrilla actions by privately armed citizens against govern-mental abuses. "It is simply silly to respond that small arms are irrelevant against nuclear-armed states. Witness contemporary Northern Ireland and the territories occupied by Israel, where the sophisticated weaponry of Great Britain and Israel have proved almost totally beside the point."[24] What is really beside the point, as Charles Dunlap has proved, is the use of such examples to explicate the Second Amendment. The ability to make trouble in Northern Ireland has not "prevented tyranny," has not unseated or altered the British regime. The resort to terrorism, as we have seen, is a confession that insurrection has failed. And Palestinian guerrillas are not part of the constitutional order—their actions no more claim Israeli con-stitutional sanction than slave rebellions in the American South did.

Levinson's position is part of the romanticizing of the guerrilla that he found in the NRA literature he quotes from. Wayne LaPierre, for instance, the NRA executive, writes:

> The twentieth century provides *no example* of a determined populace with access to small arms having been defeated by a modern army. The Russians lost in Afghanistan, the United States lost in Vietnam, and the French lost in Indo-China. In each case, it was the poorly armed populace that beat the "modern" army.[25]

Dunlap points out that in none of those cases were the indigenous forces fighting alone or with their own "poor" arms. They were heavily armed by other governments with tanks, missiles, and heavy artillery—and, despite that fact, they won no major military victories.[26] The democratic colonial forces withdrew when they lost the stomach for foreign domination at a disproportionate cost. The situation would be far different if an insurrection were challenging those governments at home—as a Second Amendment insurrection would challenge the American government within our borders. In such cases, there can be no simple withdrawal. Fighting for its life, the government would use whatever resources were needed to prevail. Trained specialists in military intelligence, logistics, maneuver, and sophisticated weaponry would make guerrillas as ineffectual as Thomas Dorr's nineteenth-century troops were in Rhode Island.

7. Akhil Amar turns the romanticized militia into another of those "climate of opinion" arguments for the Second Amendment's assumed values. He says that the nation meant to rely primarily on its militias since the age abominated regular troops. This is a theme he cannot sound often enough. He tells us that the very "word army connoted mercenary," a force "consisting of aliens, convicts and other misfits," a place for "lackeys and hirelings (mercenaries, vagrants, convicts, aliens and the like)," making the standing army a mere "collection of misfits."[27] As usual, the insurrectionists read only the Antifederalist literature, and assume that this was the entire climate of opinion. Certainly Washington's veterans did not consider themselves a bunch of misfits. They, the regular army—and not, as Amar still thinks, the militias—won the War of Independence. Nor, despite the republican literature of England, did the opposed royalist and Cromwellian armies of the English Civil War—who were that country's main experience of standing armies—think they were mere hirelings.

It is true that regular armies sometimes supplemented their numbers with mercenaries. But, as John Shy and others have shown, militiamen too had to be bribed, given bounties, or dragooned into filling up the ranks needed for even minimal performance of duties—and it was often the vagrant, the idle, the "dregs" who were most easily swept into the militia net. Amar is falling for the illusion of "yeoman virtue" as superior to trained professionalism that was manifested (at great cost) in the early days of the Revolution. We saw how that illusion was revived by Daniel Shays and David Bradford in their "yeoman revolts"—which crumbled at the first encounter with trained troops. Bad history serves bad logic in the arguments of the insurrectionists. But that is a regular occurrence when people want to preserve the emotional values of anti-governmentalism even in the structure of government itself.

VI.

Vigilantes

Vigilantes stand at a pole opposed to insurrectionists. The latter take arms against the government because it is too repressive. The former take arms to do the government's work because the authorities are not repressive *enough*. Those "vigilant" for the good rush to impose it where the government is too slow, indifferent, or lax.

When the government treats a criminal with slow due process, "coddling" him with procedural niceties, vigilantes speed justice along with a lynching. When disorderly or unwanted people come into an area—immigrants or "shiftless" folk—and the government does not exclude or discipline them, vigilantes feel they must rectify that omission. When the Reconstruction governments were considered too lenient in treating freed blacks after the Civil War, the Ku Klux Klan had to create a secret government for punishing them.

When government was not assiduous enough in ferreting out communists, citizen groups had to make sure that all domestic "Reds" were exposed and driven from their jobs. When the government abets "baby killing," vigilantes must protect the young by executing the doctors who commit such murder. There is ample work for the modern vigilante.

Vigilantism can be embraced by individuals as well as groups, at least in some of our favorite cultural myths. Before governmental procedures were regularized on the American frontier, order had to be kept by lone heroes making law with a gun—the cowboy against the rustler, the marshal against any drunk terrorizing a saloon, the homesteader against a trespassing drover.

And urban cowboys in our own day believe that government cannot protect an individual's freedom. That must be done by each person, keeping law and order in private ways, with private guns. Isn't that what the

Second Amendment was created for—to make each of us a vigilante, imposing law with our gun, like our glorious forebears on the frontier? For many Americans, vigilantism is a particularly appealing form of anti-governmental government.

18.

Groups:
From Regulators to Clinic Bombings

To give a sense of the range of vigilantism throughout our history, I have singled out six examples of group activity—the South Carolina Regulators of 1767–69, the San Francisco Vigilance Committee of 1856, the Ku Klux Klan of 1866–70, the Wyoming range war of 1886–92, McCarthyism in the 1940s and 1950s, and anti-abortion terrorism in the 1980s and 1990s. Each of these movements targeted people who were thought to upset the moral order of society—the "intruders" in South Carolina, Irish immigrants in San Francisco, freed blacks in the South, small ranchers in Wyoming, communists or their sympathizers in the 1950s, and abortion providers in recent years.

South Carolina Regulators (1767–69)

The association of vigilantism with frontier conditions arose from the fact that the earliest identifiable vigilante force of any great importance was the Regulator movement in the backcountry of South Carolina in 1767–69. ("Regulation" was the normal word for "vigilantism" in the late eighteenth and early nineteenth centuries—an appropriate term for the imposition of a *regula*, or rule). The backcountry of that state was disorderly, an aftermath of the vicious and unsettling local war with the Cherokee Indians in 1760–61. Fanatical religious cults effervesced in the apocalyptic atmosphere of that war.[1] Vagrants were shaken loose upon the land, to the distress of its first settlers, who were trying to protect their struggling cotton plantations. In the absence of anti-vagrancy laws, these "solid citizens" drew up the Regulation for taking law into their own hands. To protect their power to do this, they thwarted other channels of rule—the militia, or the courts and legislature in "lowland" Charleston. They meant to impose order more rapidly and efficiently.

> If the Regulation was to proceed free of misguided and legalistic interference from the outside, it was necessary to erect a barrier between the Back Country and the capital. Charleston judges, possessing only imperfect knowledge of Back Country conditions, might be unduly influenced by enemies of the Regulators. By nullifying the authority of the provincial criminal and civil courts, the Regulators established themselves as the supreme rulers of the Back Country. They sealed off their dominion from Low Country interference and created a regime in which they were free to impress on their communities the ideals of honesty, industry and the security of property.[2]

The eastern part of South Carolina looked with a lenient eye on the Regulators at the outset. They were a buffer against the Indian menace, and their harshness toward free blacks and other "shiftless" people discouraged slave escapes or lower-class restiveness in the coastal region. But after a year or so of Regulator dominance in the west, the state's acting governor, William Bull, tried to suppress the vigilantes, on the grounds that they had done all the real work against criminals that was useful; but the sympathy of too many people was involved by that time, and Bull had to soften his own proclamation.[3]

The extremism of the Regulation itself led to the formation in the western sector of a counterforce called the Moderation. When Regulators tried to bully the Moderators, the latter resorted to violence in their turn, under a ruffian named Joseph Coffell (who would later lead Loyalist forces in the Revolution).[4] Vigilantism was descending to the level of an organized feud, and the government had to step in. Its first target was not the original offenders, but the Moderators. Yet it could not put down that group without asserting authority over the first one as well. This pattern would recur—of the government looking the other way during the first stages of vigilantism (since the enemies of both were the same), only to see its own legitimacy undermined by the "law and order" lawbreakers.

San Francisco Vigilance Committee (1856)

This was an urban, not a frontier, phenomenon. Even in the 1850s, San Francisco was a cosmopolitan city, with its trade contacts to the Orient, a developed local culture (exemplified by the Jenny Lind Theatre), and even its own urban machine politics.[5] It was this last point that roused the conservatives' ire. In other cities of the time, reformers tried to overthrow the machines that deployed immigrant voters. The business interests of San Francisco, by contrast, fought fire with fire—they hired goons to outmuscle the Irish toughs who served the voting districts of the local boss, David C. Broderick.

Broderick was an Irish Catholic, the son of immigrants, who had grown up in the rough Five Points area of New York. Initiated early into the ward politics of the town, he hoped to build a national career on that shaky foundation, reaching toward the United States Senate. When his ambitions were thwarted at home, he took the longer route through California politics, where the newly formed state legislature (which elected senators at the time) might prove more manageable—as it did: Broderick reached the Senate in 1857, after only eight years in San Francisco.[6] His first task on arriving in California was to provide himself with an economic base. He did that by coining gold and trading real estate. Then he organized the immigrant wards as in New York, gathering votes from saloons, volunteer fire departments, and loading areas at the docks. His organization was called Tammany Hall, and it provided the network of individual and community services with which urban machines bought or placated lower-class voters. Broderick was not interested in holding city office himself—his eyes were on Sacramento and the votes for senator. This meant that he was less visible than other bosses. His aura of mystery frightened others. Resentment of machine corruption could be focused on him, since his power was so vague that it grew ominously in his foes' imagination. Roger Lotchin has demonstrated from election records that Broderick's centrality was much exaggerated at the time.[7]

The principal exaggerator was James King of William, a failed banker who poured bitterness over his failures into a newspaper, the *Daily Evening Bulletin*, that he began to edit in 1855. That was an explosive year, when resentment flared at a hung jury in the trial of a gambler named Charles Cora. This man had shot a United States marshal, William Richardson, while defending the "honor" of a prostitute. The "respectables" of the city claimed that this showed how the riffraff on a jury could thwart justice. King of William began a series of omnidirectional accusations that called for the cleansing of the city. Favorite targets were the machine enforcers known at the time as "shoulder pushers," who were largely Irish. The American party, whose nativist element led to its being called "Know-Nothings," was strong in the reform movement of San Francisco, and King of William emphasized the ethnic ties of his whipping boys. When he published the prison record of James P. Casey, an Irish operator (who had actually worked with the Know-Nothings), Casey shot King down in the street.[8]

The reformers feared that Casey would "get off" as Cora had in his first trial. They made sure that would not happen by taking Casey out of prison and lynching him. To settle the complete account, they lynched Cora, who was in jail awaiting a retrial, along with Casey. The hanging was an open and well-attended affair, held in front of the San Francisco Vigilance Committee's headquarters. The Vigilance Committee had been founded in 1851, but had lain dormant after that year. Now it came explosively back to life, hanging another two people and holding kangaroo trials for many of those identified as "shoulder pushers" by King of William. Those convicted were ordered out of town.[9]

The reformers had just been waiting for an opportunity to take over the political organization of the city from the parties and the machines. They launched the People's Party, which put up citizen candidates (i.e., nonpoliticians). The vigilantes policed the polls more successfully than shoulder pushers ever had. "The use of terror was real enough, but it was supported by the mass of people and wielded by the acknowledged community leaders, the merchants."[10] Businessmen, lawyers, and other professionals ran for office claiming to stand above party politics. It was crucial for many that the new party take control, since thousands had been implicated in the lynchings and expellings, and a resurgent Democratic party could have served indictments on them all. In a circular process, the Vigilance Committee had created the People's Party, which in turn indemnified the Vigilance Committee.

Broderick, after unsuccessful attempts to save some of his minions and to negotiate with the Vigilance Committee, traveled around California looking for votes at the next legislative session in Sacramento, which would safely remove him to Washington the following year. The People's Party became a regular party in time and upheld the laws its creators had violated. The vigilance movement was glorified in the subsequent history, and looked upon as a moral reformation of the city. Vigilantes often cloak their activities in the need to protect community morality. The Regulators of South Carolina even flogged abusive husbands. The Vigilance Committee of San Francisco said it was making the streets safe for good women to walk abroad without the humiliation of seeing prostitutes on the street. The Ku Klux Klan would say it was saving white women from black lust. The business interests of Wyoming would lynch a prostitute.

But under the San Francisco vigilantes' claims to be bringing morality to the frontier was a deeper social war. Richard Maxwell Brown reaches a measured conclusion:

> Allegedly concerned with a crime problem, the San Francisco vigilantes of 1856 were, in actuality, motivated by a desire to seize control of the municipal government from the Democratic political machine that found the nucleus of its support among the lower-class, Irish-Catholic workers of the city. Basic to the vigilance movement was the desire to establish a business-oriented local government which would reduce expenditures, deprive the Irish-Catholic Democrats of access to municipal revenues, and lower taxes. To a considerable extent, the San Francisco vigilante episode of 1856 represented a struggle for power between two religious, class, and ethnic blocs. Thus, the vigilante leadership of upper- and middle-class, old American, Protestant merchants

was aligned against a political faction supported by Irish-Catholic lower-class laborers. Such were the social and economic tensions that typically enlisted the violence of neovigilantism.[11]

Ku Klux Klan (1866–70)

The Ku Klux Klan is the most famous of the vigilante movements in our history, because it was even more successfully glorified than the others, as part of the great myth of the slaveholding South—that it had seceded in defense of freedom from central government oppression. Thomas Dixon's novel *The Clansman* and D. W. Griffith's movie made from it were praised by Woodrow Wilson—and no wonder. This president with a doctorate in history from the Johns Hopkins University had written, in his multi-volume history of the United States, that the South, after the Civil War, had to resort to illegality as a way to preserve its honor:

> The white men of the South were aroused by the mere instinct of self-preservation to rid themselves, by fair means or foul, of the intolerable burden of [state] governments sustained by the votes of ignorant negroes and conducted in the interest of adventurers. . . . There was no place of open action or of constitutional agitation, under the terms of reconstruction, for the men who were the real leaders of the southern communities. . . . They could act only by private combination, by private means, as a force outside the government, hostile to it, proscribed by it. . . . They took the law into their own hands, and began to attempt by intimidation what they were not allowed to attempt by the ballot or by any ordered course of public action.[12]

That attitude toward the Klan has not entirely disappeared. Even Shelby Foote, whose commentary on the Ken Burns TV special about the Civil War made him an icon of southern nostalgia for nonsoutherners, told an interviewer that the original Klan "was very akin to the Free French Resistance to Nazi occupation . . . [it] was anti-black but not opposed to all black people. It was trying to keep illiterate blacks from occupying positions like sheriff and judge."[13] It was also trying to keep all blacks illiterate—as when it forcibly closed black schools in Mississippi, twenty-six in one county, eleven in another, threatening and whipping teachers who tried to keep them open. One superintendent was flogged so viciously that his shirt was sent north and displayed by Massachusetts congressman Ben Butler on the floor of the House—giving rise to the expression "wave the bloody shirt."[14] Foote, I am sure, would not defend these school raids, but Wilson did:

> Many of the teachers who worked among the negroes did in fact do mischief as deep as any political adventurer. The lessons taught in their school seemed to be lessons of self-assertion against the whites; they seemed too often to train their pupils to be aggressive Republican politicians and mischief-makers between the races. The innocent and enlightened among them suffered in the general opinion from the errors of those who deliberately sowed discord.[15]

Wilson was right in saying that the Klan began more as prank than policy. Six Confederate veterans in Tennessee, in May or June of 1866, began a secret society in the spirit of a college fraternity. Even their name was taken from the Greek word *kuklos* (circle) used by fraternities like the Kuklos Adelphon (Brothers' Circle) of the University of North Carolina. Secret rites and grandiose titles led to pranks in public, with members using various disguises and masks at first and communicating by the use of whistles, so as not to betray their own voices. They began to favor white robes and hoods after noticing their ghostly effect.[16] Wilson enters into the fun: "It threw the negroes into a very ecstasy of panic to see these sheeted 'Ku Klux' move near them in the shrouded night; and their comic fear stimulated the lads who excited it to many an extravagant prank and mummery."[17]

Within a year at most of its founding the possibility of turning black "comic fear" into a systematically terrorized condition had occurred to the original Klan and its rapidly proliferating bands of imitators throughout the South. It was the original group in Tennessee that saw the importance of making the Klan a kind of shadow Confederate army. Celebrants of the Klan claimed that they tried to get Robert E. Lee to take command, and that he blessed the effort without joining it.[18] Be that as it may, they did get the second best of surviving Confederate generals, the man Shelby Foote calls one of "the two authentic geniuses of the Civil War" (Lincoln being the other)—Nathan Bedford Forrest, the cavalry hero famous for getting there first with the most.[19] There was no reason to doubt Forrest's ruthlessness toward blacks. He had been a slave trader before the war, a calling looked down on even by slave owners, and during the war he allowed, if he did not encourage, the massacre of black prisoners after the capture of Fort Pillow.[20] By the spring of 1867 he had become the Grand Wizard of the Klan.

Forrest's leadership of the Klan was an open secret. Though he would not admit to his membership (which was against the rules of the order), he defended the organization in public, telling a reporter in 1868: "It is a protective, political, military organization. I am willing to show any man the constitution of the society. The members are sworn to recognize the government of the United States. It does not say anything at all about the government of the state of Tennessee."[21] In the very year he spoke, the Klan intimidated voters in the six months before elections in Arkansas by committing two hundred murders. In the six months before a Louisiana election, 1,081 murders were committed, 135 shootings, 507 floggings or other acts of violence. In three months before Georgia's election, there were thirty-one murders, five stabbings, fifty-five beatings, and eight whippings of three hundred or more lashes.[22]

Wilson justified these acts under a plea of necessity: "They backed their commands, *when need arose,* with violence" (emphasis added). When violence became excessive, according to Wilson, it was because non-members of the Klan hid themselves in the hood without recognizing the code of honor *real* Klansmen observed: "Reckless men not of their order, malicious fellows of the baser sort who did not feel the compulsions of honor and who had private grudges to satisfy, imitated their disguises and borrowed their methods."[23] Actually, the Klan was so loosely organized, and supplemented by so many other groups of white terrorists, that it cannot be blamed for all the violence, though it inspired and heartened others to commit it. The Klan's glamour cloaked every kind of vileness.

Foote, too, thinks the original nobility was betrayed and General Forrest "dissolved the Klan when it turned ugly."[24] Forrest's biographer agrees that the general distanced himself from the Klan in 1869, but mainly as a way of placating Republicans he needed for his new railroad ventures.[25] But his distancing did not "dissolve" the Klan. It took another three years for the federal government to rein in the Klan (without entirely erasing it). Organized terrorism continued in many forms, including irregular militia companies in Mississippi that made the state's governor complain, in 1875, of the "autumnal" (election season) terrorism that practically eliminated the black vote.[26] As literary critic Edmund Wilson concluded in 1962, "The Klan was completely successful."[27] Jim Crow laws just codified the conditions it had imposed.

Edmund Wilson is a good example of the way anti-governmental feelings can justify even this, the most murderous reign of vigilantes in our history. He sympathized with "the unfortunate south, which had been beaten but would not submit."[28] While glorifying the Klan, he argued that Lincoln was "an uncompromising dictator."[29] The myth of the Klan is hard, perhaps impossible, to kill. The city museum of Vicksburg, Mississippi, which is housed in the city hall, still has an 1860s Klan hood, with this information posted by it: "The Klan's purpose was to rid the South of the carpetbag-scalawag-black governments, which were often corrupt. Atrocities were sometimes attributed to the Klan by unscrupulous individuals."[30] That is because the Klan was embedded in that nest of values I have been describing—including religion. When an alleged black rapist was lynched in 1868, the *Tennessee Observer* editorialized: "We know not who did it, whether the Ku Klux or the immediate neighbors, but we feel that they were the instruments of Divine vengeance in carrying out His holy and immutable decrees."[31] We get the whole mindset in that homey phrase "immediate neighbors." As President Reagan liked to say, people know best how to handle their own affairs. The only anti-government value the Klan could not observe was candor—but even its secrecy shut out only others. The neighbors knew.

Wyoming Range War (1886–92)

The Wyoming vigilantes of the 1880s and early 1890s were glorified in Owen Wister's famous novel *The Virginian* (1902), in several movies based on that book, and in Michael Cimino's film *Heaven's Gate* (1980). The hero of Wister's novel is admired as a man of honor because he has to lynch his best friend for joining a rustler gang. But the truth about the Wyoming affair was not so much a matter of honest cowmen against rustlers, but of business interests against labor. The beef business had grown explosively in the 1870s, thanks to foreign investment of large amounts of capital.[32] In 1879, the major owners formed the Wyoming Stock Growers' Association (WSGA) to keep prices up, cooperate on roundups, and discourage competition from small landowners. They also tried to control the labor force, their cowboys. Despite a certain prickly independence endemic to their work, the cowboys formed a union, which the WSGA meant to break. When labor went on strike in 1886, the strike leader, Jack Flagg, was blackballed by the WSGA. Unable to work on any of the large spreads, Flagg started his own small ranch. To punish those who tried to imitate him, the WSGA sponsored laws that made it impossible for non-members of their organization to join roundups, sell to buyers at auction, or bid for cattle there. (A prohibitively large bond was required for buying at auction.) Since mavericks (unbranded calves) strayed off or were lost before roundups, the WSGA tried to prevent their addition to independent herds by getting a compliant legislature to declare that all mavericks belonged to the WSGA itself, to be auctioned for the maintenance of inspection officers (often detectives in the employ of the WSGA).[33] Ironically, these controls were probably unconstitutional invasions of the rights of business and trade—but the businessmen themselves resorted to them.

The cattle barons ran into the same problem that frustrated the San Francisco business community. Juries were reluctant to convict some of the underdogs they were prosecuting. The WSGA responded by branding the jurors, and even their judges, as rustlers themselves, or as sympathizers with the rustlers. So they took the same course that the San Francisco vigilantes had—making themselves judge, jury, and executioner. A man who was active against the WSGA was lynched, along with the prostitute in his company, in 1889. Owen Wister met one of the suspects in this lynching on a train leaving Wyoming and said he looked like an honest fellow—the kind of "good vigilante" he would glorify in his novel. But witnesses who could have implicated the suspect disappeared as fast as he did, or they were silenced.[34]

This marks the great difference between the California and Wyoming vigilantes. The latter worked in secret, like the Klan. Though business interests directed the terror, they did not have a dense urban crowd to manipulate. Holders of the large ranches were often resented for absentee ownership, clannishness (most belonged, when in the state, to the exclusive Cheyenne Club), and arrogance. So they could not seize the organs of law themselves. They struck in the dark, or used hired guns. The most famous instance of the latter is the invasion of Johnson County, the stronghold of the independents, by a train in which twenty-two Texas assassins were hidden. They had a hit list of seventy men they were supposed to dispose of, but they got bogged down in the siege of one house where two men were holding out. By the time the house had been set on fire and the occupants shot, Jack Flagg, who came on the scene by chance and escaped a fusillade from the besiegers, was able to alert the countryside. Now it was the gunmen's turn to be besieged—warned that superior forces were converging upon them, they holed up at a ranch that was quickly surrounded.[35]

The Republican governor of Wyoming, an ally of the businessmen, wired President Benjamin Harrison that he needed federal troops from nearby Fort McKinney to put down an "insurrection" of Johnson County, making the gunmen's intended victims the violators of law. The troops arrived, effected a surrender by the vigilantes, and took them by train to Fort Russell. The hired guns, released on bail (with WSGA money for their bond), went back to Texas. Local citizens involved in the "war" were never brought to trial.

McCarthyism (1940s and 1950s)

The era of communism as a pervasive force in American life—of the "enemy within"—was a concomitant of the foreign threat from the Soviet Union. This fear led to excesses that are normally considered a *governmental* aberration. It was, after all, the Truman administration that fired security risks in the State Department and elsewhere, the Congress that investigated suspected communists and jailed some of them for contempt, the courts that convicted Alger Hiss and Julius and Ethel Rosenberg. Since vigilantes work outside the government, these acts cannot be chalked up to vigilantism.

But there was a penumbra of nongovernmental activity, accompanying these official policies, that can qualify as vigilantism, since it not only went beyond what the government was doing, but did so out of a distrust for the government. These vigilantes were responding to the public agitation of Senator Joseph McCarthy, who charged that the government was not purging itself of the communists who had infiltrated it. Various groups—veterans organizations, Catholic clubs, private monitors of the entertainment industry—compiled lists of dangerous people to be hounded out of their jobs. These and other private agencies account for more victims of McCarthyism than did official agencies.

Ten leftist moviemakers were questioned and jailed by federal authorities, but approximately 250 were fired or denied the chance to work on the studios' own initiative.[36] The government dismissed scientists from federal work on nuclear projects, but private schools and universities fired teachers, or refused to hire or promote them, in far greater numbers. The government put suspect organizations on the Attorney General's List of communist fronts, but ordinary citizens denied those groups halls to meet in or outlets for their advertising. The government demanded loyalty oaths for those working on sensitive assignments, but universities demanded such oaths from people teaching any subject at all, on the grounds that Karl Marx might be smuggled into mathematics lessons, or that a teacher might do the Kremlin's work just by teaching poorly. As one anti-communist zealot said, "Inadequate and improper teaching of any subject could be considered as subversive."[37]

Clinic Bombings (1980s and 1990s)

As the Ku Klux Klan lynched blacks who violated white society's orderly regime, anti-abortion terrorists in the last two decades have harassed, bombed, or shot people who conduct what the terrorists call a "holocaust" of murdered babies. Like all vigilantes, they feel they must provide the law enforcement the government has ceased to exercise since the 1973 Supreme Court decision, *Roe* v. *Wade*, which made women the arbiters of their own pregnancies. In the immediate aftermath of that decision, political protest took the form of agitation and propagandizing in the arena of public opinion, largely conducted by the Catholic Church's hierarchy and adherents. But beginning in the 1980s there was an increase in violent campaigns against abortion clinics and their staffs, with evangelical Protestants leading the way. Some social scientists connected this development with the election of Ronald Reagan as president, an election that evangelicals felt had been won by their crucial support at the margin of voter majorities.

> Following President Ronald Reagan's election in 1980, the number of violent incidents against clinics and clinic personnel, including vandalism, death threats, assault, arson, bombing, and invasion, increased by almost 450 percent. President Reagan's speeches to anti-abortion groups were interpreted by radicals as tacit approval for their vigilantism.[38]

An abductor of a doctor who performed abortions claimed that his allies felt "they have a green light from the president." Lawyers for clinic bombers adduced in court a Reagan letter that demanded "something be done" to stop abortions.[39] When Reagan's rhetoric against abortion was not followed by actions after he won office, some felt that they were expected to take the steps that he desired but could not implement because of an obstructive Congress. The scholars Dallas Blanchard and Terry Prewitt wrote in 1993:

> Our point is not to cast Reagan as leading a "call to violence" but to cite the effects of Reagan's failure to issue a call *against* violence in the

context of the ideological struggle that intensified after the 1984 election. Reagan's re-election was interpreted by Jerry Falwell and others of the religious Right as a renewed mandate for their position.[40]

We have here the situation that often arises where vigilantism is concerned—the authorities either turning a blind eye on the extra-legal "enforcement" or seeming to do so. That impression was confirmed when George Bush's Justice Department entered a 1991 protest against a district judge's injunction against Operation Rescue activists who had blocked three clinics in Wichita, Kansas, shutting down their operation. The Bush administration also supported Operation Rescue's 1992 plea before the Supreme Court that interfering with access to clinics did not suspend women's rights.[41]

Violence over abortion, though it was widespread, seemed (like Klan violence) to be especially common in the South. This can be seen in the pivotal role played by Pensacola, Florida, in the development of the anti-abortion war. In 1984 two young evangelicals blew up the main abortion clinic in that town, demolishing it beyond further use. When the clinic was reestablished elsewhere, the same men, with the help of one's wife and the other's fiancée, blew up that building and the offices where two doctors performed abortions. The triple explosion occurred on Christmas morning, as what the perpetrators called a "birthday present for baby Jesus."[42] It was commonly thought that revulsion at violence would discourage other opponents of abortion from endorsing such tactics. But that was not the case in Pensacola, where John Burt, from an Assembly of God congregation, and David Shofner, a Baptist minister, organized demonstrations in favor of the "Pensacola Four," supporting their right to interfere with the murder of babies. They clearly believed what the lawyer for the accused men was pleading in court—that these were all-American boys ("Tom Sawyer and Huck Finn") who were simply doing what God told them to do, and that the real judgment must weigh upon a society that tolerates abortion:

When Jesus was on trial, the government won in the case and Jerusalem fell. Socrates was tried and Athens fell. If Tom Sawyer and Huck Finn are convicted, America will be the loser. We cannot take those losses impending on us now.[43]

Tom and Huck were convicted and sentenced to five years in prison, but the sentence was suspended and they were required to pay for the damage done at $100 per month. They and their supporters took this as a sign that the community was with them in spirit, since it imposed only the lightest possible rebuke. Pensacola had become the capital of anti-abortion activism. Leaders of the movement flocked to the city, including the Catholic Joan Andrews, who engaged in nonviolent sabotage at clinics (sealing doors with Super Glue, planting stink bombs, wrecking equipment, and the like).[44] She slipped into a Pensacola clinic and was arrested while damaging a medical suction machine. She, too, was given a suspended sentence if she would promise not to return to the clinic she had damaged. She refused—in fact, she would cooperate in no way with the authorities whose system supports abortion. She did not comply when asked to come into court, move about in the prison, or answer questions addressed to her. She had to be carried everywhere, and was eventually left in the cell she would not budge from on her own. Her reputation for sanctity grew when Mother Teresa, the famous missionary in India, expressed an admiration for Andrews. The authorities even offered to release her in Mother Teresa's custody. Mother Teresa agreed to this plan, but Andrews would not accept it.[45] Now Pensacola attracted Joan celebrants to come and demonstrate in her honor.

It was at such a demonstration that the evangelical activist Randall Terry established the key organizational links for launching his Operation Rescue, in effect taking the anti-abortion leadership away from the Catholic Andrews and widening the movement among Protestants in the South (though Terry is from New York). Terry targeted the South for his attempts to block access to clinics and disrupt their operation, mounting what he called "the siege of Atlanta," filling jails there in the late 1980s. Atlanta continued to be a center for anti-abortion terrorism. In 1997 a clinic was bombed in the suburb of Sandy Springs, as was a lesbian nightclub, with letters from "the Army of God" taking credit for the blasts. Letters delivered to the *Atlanta Constitution* also claimed the Army's responsibility for the 1998 bombing of a clinic in Birmingham, Alabama, where one person was killed.[46] It is now alleged by the FBI that the fugitive Eric Rudolph, a fundamentalist "Christian Identity" believer, may have been involved in these bombings, as well as in the 1996 bombing of Atlanta's Olympic Park that killed one and injured over a hundred people. Rudolph became a folk hero in 1998 for his ability to elude capture in the wilds of his native North Carolina, where local residents laughed at federal attempts to run him down.

Pensacola had returned to the news in 1993, when Dr. David Gunn was murdered there by a pistol shot outside his clinic, and in 1994 when Dr. James Barrett and the man driving him to his clinic were killed with shotgun blasts.[47] Even when the violence moved north, with the 1998 murder of a doctor, Barnett Slepian, in Amherst, New York, the man sought as a material witness to this crime—and to three other shootings of doctors over the Canadian border—had been arrested in Atlanta as part of Terry's "siege of Atlanta" and in Pensacola demonstrations.[48] A computer web site based in Carrollton, Georgia, ominously ran a slash line across Dr. Slepian's name after his murder, the seventh such mark through the name of a doctor killed for performing abortions. The God-fearing owner of the web site, Neal Horsley, did not disguise his pleasure at the death.[49]

· · ·

There are other examples of vigilantism too numerous to be considered here—for instance, the use of the Pinkerton Detective Agency and other "private police" forces to break up union organizing and strikes in the late nineteenth and early twentieth centuries. Union organizers were branded as un-American, outsiders acting on the basis of foreign ideologies. Modern militias that arm themselves for opposition to a government aligned with the United Nations or with other foreign entities are also "vigilant," watching for signs of the "takeover."

At first glance, vigilantism may not seem to fit with the anti-governmental values we find in other activities listed in this book. Vigilantes favor *more* "law and order" than the government is providing. But they do this for the kind of "community values"—religion, social homogeneity, tradition—that can be aligned against the actual government at any time. The Klan and McCarthyites, clinic bombers and the Militia of Montana, are opposed to the government as too cosmopolitan, too secular, too disrespectful of traditional mores. Even union busters felt, in the past, that government was too soft on anarchical immigrants outside the American tradition, not making them conform to the American way, to the traditions of American capitalism. Here, as often, business has it both ways, offering freedom from "big government" while doing its own regimenting and empire building.

19.

Individuals:
Frontier

Vigilante *groups* are less common, now, than that peculiarly American phenomenon, the *individual* vigilant for his or her own safety, armed to provide for it, not delegating the task to faceless groups or agencies. The rest of the world is bemused or appalled at the guns that float everywhere in our society, as many guns as there are people. But we are assured that they are a necessity, that taking a gun from a man is depriving him not only of safety but of freedom, of manhood, of the right to be an individual. This belief, idiosyncratic in others' eyes, is central to the American value system. It expresses the desire for self-sufficiency that is at odds with government control. It is fed by a whole series of myths, of which the frontier myth is perhaps the most obvious.

According to that myth, the American man (more rarely, woman) was freest when he went west, armed to remain safe while he invented himself, freed from the pressures of conformity, of deadening civilizational habits. The frontier has always been with us—it was at the Atlantic Ocean's edge when the first settlers arrived on this continent. It was pushed westward through the seventeenth, eighteenth, and nineteenth centuries. But the imagination has fed on one time as the pre-eminent era of the frontier—oddly, the time when the frontier was filling up rapidly, when the lone individual was less isolated than before, when a countdown was taking place to the year 1893, when the historian Frederick Jackson Turner ominously announced that the frontier was closed. That period, from the Civil War to the close of the nineteenth century, was celebrated by its end in a spate of dime novels, lurid biographies, and traveling spectacles like Buffalo Bill's Wild West Show. A trio of friends—Theodore Roosevelt, Owen Wister, and Frederic Remington—kept the myth alive long enough for it to pass into the history of cinema, where it became what French critics have described as the quintessential American movie, the western.

All through this process, the gun is credited with a leading role in the "taming" of the West. It was the main tool by which men held their own against nature, Indians, and other frontiersmen. There is some basis for this hugely inflated tale. The Civil War had been a great accelerator of gun technology, use, and expertise. Americans, who had not (despite myths about the early militias) been universally familiar with guns, acquired some familiarity from service in the war. When the troops on both sides were mustered out, many of them illegally kept the guns they had been issued.[1] Besides, the spurt in technological invention and improvement of guns continued right through the century, as Samuel Colt and Oliver Remington came up with new models meant to flog sales at ever faster rates. The guns were now tooled with greater precision. The wholesale shift from muzzle-loading to breech-loading guns was accomplished. Ammunition was improved, both the powder and the casings. In 1871, two Union army veterans, William Conant Church and George W. Wingate, set up the National Rifle Association, to encourage soldiers to improve their marksmanship with the latest expertise about guns.[2] They held shooting contests between the army and the National Guard (established in 1879), awarding prizes and distributing educational material on weapons development. There was a close alliance between the NRA and the National Guard— George Wingate, the NRA founder, became the president of the National Guard Association. That union was reflected in the declaration of principles enumerated by the *National Guardsman* of 1877: "We believe in rifle practice as an important element of National Guard education."[3]

The title of the NRA is important—it was a *rifle* association. The rifle was the most effective, reliable, and used weapon of the time. One would never guess that from the myths of the West, especially as they have been embroidered in the twentieth century. These focus almost entirely on the handgun, the "six-shooter." The picture of "the gunfighter"—a term that did not come into general use until this century—is of the fast-draw artist, whose weapon is always with him, strapped to his side, almost a part of him, something he can practice with in idle moments, or show off to admirers, or compare with other men's personalized models, and—of course—whip out at the slightest affront or challenge.

This gun has become truly magical in the hands of literary figures or movie actors. It can be effective when "thrown" (with a motion flipping it from one's ear toward the target, near or far), or fired from the hip, or with its hammer "fanned" (the palm of the left hand slapping it while the right hand holds it steady, a process that is supposed to speed the rate of firing), or accurately fired from a galloping horse, or fired from both hands at once by "two-gun" marksmen. The point of all these maneuvers is to show that the shooter does not have to aim along the barrel with his eye. The fast-draw artist cannot take the time or trouble to do that, even though the gun was designed to be used that way—which is, after all, why the six-shooter had a sight at the end of its barrel. Samuel Colt said he designed his revolver barrels to remind the user of a finger, so it would be pointed like one. We do not normally point at something by putting our hand to our belt and sticking one finger out at that level. We point with extended arm, our finger at the end of it.

Despite improvements, the nineteenth-century revolver was still an imperfect weapon, and all its shortcomings would be added to by the antics of the movie cowboys. A "thrown" shot is a vague gesture, inclusive of most things but the target. It is impossible to get real accuracy when firing from the hip. And fanning the gun (which can be done *only* at hip level) would bounce it around and hose the area with shots. Nor is one arm steady enough to hit a target from a moving horse. As for shooting with two guns (often "throwing" both), even ambidextrous people will be really aiming only with one, wasting the other's shots and endangering standbys. Besides, the smoke caused by the black powder used then would blind the guns' wielder if he pumped out shots at the rate of the "two-gun" heroes of the movies. That same smoke made it impossible to perform the marvels that are a staple of westerns—such as keeping a can bouncing with a succession of shots, or keeping an object in the air by hitting it repeatedly. The thick smoke from the gun would make such continued accuracy impossible.[4]

The smoke helps explain the amazingly low casualty rate in encounters where several people were shooting revolvers at close range. A notorious gunfight of 1879, which took place in Dodge City's famous Long Branch saloon, went like this. Two men quarreling over a woman drew their guns. They were standing so close to each other that "their pistols almost touched each other." Neither man took the time to aim, so both managed to miss with their first shots. One man stepped back, took aim, and hit the other. But the wounded man kept firing, until one more hit (out of two more shots) put the wounded man down. In the smoky fray, eleven shots were fired at practically point-blank range, and nine of them missed. This was not unusual, or caused by the fact that these men were amateurs (one was a buffalo hunter famous for his accuracy with both pistol and rifle—and he was the one who lost).[5]

In a more famous gunfight, the shoot-out at Tombstone's O. K. Corral (actually, behind the corral)—the only gunfight Wyatt Earp ever took part in—"nine men and two horses are suddenly gathered in a lot perhaps eighteen feet wide."[6] They turned revolvers, a shotgun, and a Winchester rifle on each other in this small area, which was quickly filled with smoke, and only three of the men were killed. When Earp's brother Morgan—who survived the O. K. Corral—was later shot in the back while playing pool, Wyatt took revenge in the customary manner: he killed one man with a shotgun pressed against him and cut another almost in two with the same gun, not indulging in any nonsense about "quick draw" with a revolver.

The fight that made James Butler ("Wild Bill") Hickok's fame, at Rock Creek, Nebraska, in 1861, occurred when the landlord of an overland coach station, David McCanles, came to collect money from the station manager. The twenty-four-year-old Hickok, who worked in the station stables, exchanged angry words with the landlord in the yard before going into the station. When McCanles challenged Hickok to come back out, he was shot dead by a rifle at one of the windows. One man who was with McCanles tried to run into the house, but Hickok wounded him as he was coming through the door and a woman in the station bashed his head in. Another of McCanles's men, along with McCanles's twelve-year-old son, ran off into the woods. The man was chased and pinned down by a bloodhound kept at the station, and someone with Hickok killed him with a shotgun. No one in McCanles's party had fired a gun. The presence of the child shows they had not come looking for violence. When Hickok told the story of this slaughter of three men to a credulous journalist, he claimed that McCanles, who had nine other men with him, had charged into the station firing a gun, and Hickok killed him with his rifle. Then the gang burst in through two doors, and Hickok killed four of them with his revolver, before he killed the others with a knife. That is the story that made Rock Creek the best-known gunfight after the O. K. Corral. In later versions, Hickok's ten dead men grew to twice and even to thrice that number. Actually, he killed eight men at most (giving him credit for several of the kills at Rock Creek) in the whole course of his life.[7]

If much shooting just caused much smoke, why did cowboys carry two guns? We know they did so from contemporary photographs. Some carried three or four. It was not to use them simultaneously, but to pull the other if the first one misfired—as it often did, for a variety of reasons. Those who carried three or four did not even trust the second one to work properly. Those who expected to be using a revolver were wise if they fired it just beforehand, cleaned it, and checked the cylinder pin, the percussion cap, and the flash hole:

> A serious drawback to all percussion caps of the era was the fulminate of mercury, which soon corroded the nipples. When checking his weapon, the experienced pistol man also regularly inspected the nipples. To guard against misfire, at each loading he pushed a pin or spike through the flash hole to remove any dirt or unburned powder. . . . Hickok also made a practice of periodically firing and reloading his pistols to avoid overnight dampness, which affected the salt-laden black powder of the day.[8]

Proper loading was a problem. Until the 1870s, many had to rely on loose powder and caps. Improvements came, but they made the individualist rely on anonymous factory workers: "Metallic ammunition became commonplace in the 1870s, but it was of poor quality and subject to misfire."[9] If the first bullet misfired, the gun could jam from a cap falling into its mechanism, and after a few shots powder could foul the works.

When modern experts tried to verify reports of sharpshooting with nineteenth-century Colt revolvers, they went through a careful ritual before each shot, making sure the antique gun was in perfect condition, not relying on mass-manufactured ammunition, but measuring each ball taken from the gunmaker's own molds:

Before each test great care was taken to load the weapons correctly, and grease-soaked felt wads were placed under the balls, which were themselves smeared with grease when rammed into the chambers to reduce the leading in the rifling. Even then, fouling from the black powder affected the weapons' accuracy. Consequently, it may be assumed that only if owners of cap-and-ball were careful to keep them extremely clean, well oiled and properly loaded could they expect to achieve reasonable accuracy with them.[10]

Despite all these modern precautions and advantages, "It is regrettable that few reports of the prowess of old time pistol shots can be substantiated."[11] One nineteenth-century target shooter whose skill *was* verified (by matches he won in England in 1897) was able to use the new smokeless ammunition and a personally designed sight, and he had time to aim along the barrel with each shot. Even so, he said, the pistol is not an accurate weapon for actual use beyond a few yards.[12]

It is natural, then, that when a man intended beforehand to use a gun, he would take a rifle, carbine, or shotgun, whose longer barrel gave him greater accuracy and whose shoulder stock and two-handed hold gave him greater control. That is how Hickok hunted down the men suspected of killing his brother. But what of the quick-draw duels in the street that form the climax of so many movies? The answer is simple. That never, ever, happened. For a number of reasons. The holsters of that time were not designed for quick drawing. In fact, some of the most famous gunmen wore no holster at all. Hickok wore his guns tucked into a sash. The guns were worn at belt level (not in low-slung holsters along the thigh), their butts forward to keep the barrel out of the man's groin. One drew from the right with one's left hand (or vice versa). Whoever moved first would automatically win any hypothetical speed contest (the reaction time to another's move is a prohibitive disadvantage, modern tests have shown). The only "fair fight" would have been one, like modern contests, where a referee gives the signal to both men at the same time.[13] Quick draws are, in fact, a modern phenomenon. The first important record was set in 1934, and the game did not really catch on till 1954, by which time special holsters had been designed for it.[14] If the first to draw is going to be the winner anyway, the only sensible thing to do was to come into a dangerous situation with a weapon already drawn.

Given all these obstacles to pistol use, why was the handgun so popular in the West? Men clearly found it comforting to have a gun they could wear without carrying it or even thinking about it. Rifles have to be put down if you are going to do a chore, have a drink, or simply move about. But having the gun always there at one's waist was itself an obstacle, so far as community peace was concerned. It was there for instant use by drunks, hotheads, or panicky people. That is why handguns were banned in the cattle towns. The "Wild West" was the birthplace of strict gun-control laws. Far from the gun being the tamer of the West, the West had to tame the gun in order to be civilized. Kansas, after its bloody experience in the John Brown days, had made it a state law that no vagrants, drunks, or former Confederate soldiers could carry "a pistol, bowie-knife, dirk or other deadly weapon." The cattle towns made the restriction much tougher, collecting guns from cowboys and drovers when they came inside the city limits. (Wyatt Earp and his men went to the O. K. Corral because they heard the Clantons had not given up their guns in town.) Famous "gun cities" like Dodge had a year or two of violence when the herds were first driven to them in the early 1870s, but they quickly imposed the gun laws that cut homicide rates spectacularly. In 1877 and 1882, there were no killings in Dodge City during the cattle season. In the other years, the average was one and a half killings, some of those accidental or unconnected with cowboys or marshals.[15]

These results were not attained by a lone marshal awing bad guys with his quick draw (Earp mainly used his revolver as a club when arresting people).[16] The cattle towns hired police forces of five or so men who acted as a team (like those going with the marshal, Virgil Earp, and his deputy, Wyatt, to the O. K. Corral). When cowboys were not coming into town, the police were a sanitation and repair work force—Wyatt Earp repaired boardwalks in the off season.[17] The cattle towns were run by a business elite, since the towns formed a nexus between large-capital investments in herds and in the government-supported railroads. They needed a controlled climate in which gambling and prostitution were regulated (secretly taxed but protected, to keep the cowboys coming up from Texas) while safety was guaranteed (to keep buyers and agents in town for the large cash or banking transactions involved in shipping such huge amounts of property).

In general, the settlement of the West was not a matter of individuals going off into the wilds. The modern frontier was marked by the advance of a technologically more sophisticated culture into a backward one.[18] The technology of the western settlers—in mining and drilling equipment and expertise, railroad expansion, cavalry intelligence and maneuver, coordination of market information by telegraph, and a steady influx of manufactured goods—was at the core of settlement. One reason the railroads were eager to buy cattle was to fill the trains that had been running back empty to the East after bringing huge amounts of equipment, stores, weapons, and commercial products to the West.[19] The western endeavor depended on an eastern base, both capitalistic and governmental. The army was especially important and desired by the supposedly unregimented individuals of the West. The network of forts often set the pattern of civilian settlement (Dodge City began as a mere adjunct to Fort Dodge). And the army's weapons had more to do with conquering the West than any lone gunmen did. The trained teamwork of the cavalry was seen in the way it deployed to fire at Indians. Even rifles were not accurate from bouncing horses, so the cavalry rode into range of the foe, dismounted in designated groups of four, with one man deputed to hold the horses while the others fired (from natural props or cover if possible). Indians also dismounted to shoot. The wild charges of men shooting from the saddle are the creations of Hollywood.[20]

Although raw settlements did have unstable conditions at the outset, especially when in conflict with Indian, Mexican, or renegade groups, there was a massive social effort to quell those conditions as rapidly as possible. That is why Prohibition, gun control, and women's suffrage were pioneered in the West.[21] The most successful settlements were the most regimented (the Mormons were outstanding in this regard). Social institutions—churches, schools, newspapers, libraries, theaters, and "opera houses"—were introduced and supported by business interests and communal discipline. The federal government supported the whole enterprise with land grants, subsidies to the railroads, and maintenance of the army's logistical trains. Fiction is full of violent struggles when tracts of territory were thrown open to settlers making a run to stake their claims. When fifteen thousand people made the run into Oklahoma Territory, on the day when it was declared open in 1889, newspaper stories told of shootings, claim jumping, and bloodshed around Guthrie, the "instant town" where claims were recorded. But no one was killed or even wounded:

> Within thirty-six hours after everyone had arrived at the "Magic City" on the Prairie, this heterogeneous mob had elected a mayor and a council of five members, adopted a city charter, and authorized the col- lection of a head tax. Within a week, Baptists, and Methodists, and Presbyterians were holding church service in tents and planning the construction of permanent church buildings. . . . Six months passed before Oklahoma Territory recorded its first homicide.[22]

The historiography of the West has undergone a major shift on the subject of its violent and unregulated nature since 1968, when Robert Dykstra established the actual homicide rates in the cattle towns where gunmen were thought to have ruled. Dime novelists, it turns out, were not the only exaggerators of the West's individualism and self-protection. His- torians must bear their share of the sensationalism.[23] The textbook in which many students learned about the West—Ray Billington's perennial *Westward Expansion: A History of the American Frontier*—had to be revised in a 1974 edition to remove unsubstantiated claims like this: "Seldom did a group of drovers leave [town] without contributing to the population of boot hill."[24] (Billington's popular course at Northwestern University was nicknamed by its students "Cowboys and Indians.")

Much of the violent death rate in the West, as in the rest of the coun- try, was caused by that problem of all technologically advanced societies, the industrial accident, whether in mines or in railroad construction and operation. If one wanted to live a really dangerous life, the place to be was not on a cattle town street, facing a bad guy with a gun; it was in a mine, where slides, fires, and explosions gave you a fifty-fifty chance of being killed on the job if you stayed at it:

> One out of every thirty western miners was disabled every year in an accident. One out of every eight was killed. The hardrock miner could thus expect to be either temporarily or permanently disabled in one or

more accidents during his lifetime, and he had an even chance of being killed in one before he retired.[25]

This was one of the things that made people call any forlorn hope a "Chinaman's chance," since Chinese laborers were prominent among those who worked both the mines and the railroads. As for railroad safety at the time, 433 men died laboring at railroad couplings in 1893—143 more than died on both sides at Little Big Horn, the bloodiest by far of the cavalry's battles with Indians.[26]

The myth of frontier individualism—of the man whose gun made him his own master, free and untrammeled—dies hard. What is excitement for the movies is ideology for the National Rifle Association, which thinks gun control would destroy the frontier spirit that made America great. But the gun did not tame the West. The West had to tame the gun.

20.

Individuals:
NRA

Until recently the Second Amendment was a little-visited area of the Constitution. A two thousand–page commentary on the Constitution put out by the Library of Congress in 1973 has copious annotation for most clauses, but less than a page and a half for the Second Amendment.[1] There has been only one significant Second Amendment case decided by the Supreme Court—*United States* v. *Miller,* in 1939, where the National Firearms Act was upheld against a man who claimed that the amendment allowed him to keep and bear a sawed-off shotgun. The Court declared that a sawed-off shotgun is not a militia weapon.

We have seen that there has been a recent spurt of academic interest in the amendment as guaranteeing a right of militia revolution. But even before that, the National Rifle Association had launched an ardent campaign to argue that the amendment applies to private ownership of guns. This involved a historic reversal of the NRA's purpose. As we saw in the last chapter, the NRA was launched in conjunction with the National Guard, and was devoted to military marksmanship. Now the NRA denounces the National Guard, as not in any case a real militia, and says that the real purpose of the Second Amendment was to guarantee to citizens the right to own and use guns. Chronologically, the fearful assertion of a need for self-protection came out of the Cold War, while academic insurrectionism came out of the radical 1960s. The two have latterly joined forces, however, since the idea of a revolutionary purpose appealed to the anti-governmental instincts of those already defending the personal ownership of guns.

The case for Madison's sponsorship of an amendment devoted to private gun ownership is based on very slim historical materials, which have been spread and distorted in a wondrous way. We saw in Chapter 7 that there was a flood of argument about the militia as the object of a bill of rights—argument to be found in the ratification debates, in the recommendations for a bill of rights sent on to the Congress after ratification, and in the record of the amendment's passage. Since the amendment did not get rid of the standing army, people whom the NRA likes to quote, like Patrick Henry, lost interest in the amendment. (If Henry had all along been calling for *individual* possession, and if that is in fact what the amendment guarantees, then he should have been happy with it and supportive.)

Against all this material from the debates over militias, the new NRA can muster only one clear reference to private ownership from the ratification debates and one argument from the drafting of the amendment. Not much there, in either quantity or quality, since each of the two items is questionable.

1. Take the reference from the ratification debates. At the last minute, before the Pennsylvania convention voted to ratify the Constitution, a delegate named Robert Whitehill filed a list of fifteen changes to be made in the document, reducing it to even less authority than was granted in the Articles of Confederation (R 2.597–99).

> In the convention he resorted to every device to delay and defeat ratification. He insisted that there were inadequate safeguards against a tyranny and on the day of ratification attempted, without avail, to have fifteen articles incorporated as a bill of rights.[2]

The items on the list were never discussed in the convention, which went on to approve the Constitution. Five days after that vote, Samuel Bryan, who had not been a delegate in the convention, assembled some quickly obtained and miscellaneous objections to the Constitution—including Whitehill's list, along with some things that contradicted it—and published this under the misleading title *The Dissent of the Minority of the Convention* (R 2.617–49), under which title the NRA defenders cite it. Whitehill deals with guns in three of his fifteen headings. Article 8 begins: "The inhabitants of the several states shall have liberty to fowl and hunt in seasonable times. . . ." But the passage the NRA people like best is from article 7: "That the people have a *right to bear arms* for the defense of *themselves* and their own state, or the United States, *or for the purposes of killing game . . .*" (emphasis added). From this we are to conclude that this one man, who could not even get a discussion of his points started in the convention, is explaining to us the meaning of the Second Amendment, drafted by Madison, who was in total disagreement with every other thing in Whitehill's list (which returned total sovereignty to the states and reduced the federal judiciary's jurisdiction to extra-state relations). This violates the Jeffersonian maxim that we should expound a document's meaning from those who approved it, not those who disapproved.

But this is the least of the objections to the use of Whitehill. There is another item in his list which *is* relevant to the Second Amendment, in ways that articles 7 and 8 are not. Whitehill's article 11 reads, in its entirety:

> That the power of organizing, arming, and disciplining the militia (the manner of disciplining the militia to be prescribed by Congress) remain with the individual states, and the Congress shall not have authority to call or march any of the militia out of their own state, without the consent of such states and for such length of time only as such state shall agree (R 2.598).

If Madison had drafted the Second Amendment to agree with Whitehill's militia article, Patrick Henry would have been pleased, since that would have invalidated the constitutional provision for federalizing the militia (Article I, Section 8, Clauses 15 and 16). In fact, Whitehill's phrasing exactly reverses and cancels that of Clause 16, which gives Congress (not the states) the power "to provide for organizing, arming and disciplining the militia." This is what, it can be seen from their own representations, the real spokesmen for the minority wanted to accomplish by a right to keep and bear arms. Whitehill, here as elsewhere, not only gives Congress less power than it would have under the Constitution but less than it already possessed under the Articles of Confederation—since Articles VII and VIII of that document gave Congress the authority to lead militias out of state "for the common defense" (R 1.89). No one else in the minority that Samuel Bryan made Whitehill speak for was asking for *less* power than the Articles granted.

Rather than deal with Whitehill's article 11, the item clearly related to the Second Amendment, the proponents of private ownership go to other items distant in meaning from this, and claim that *they* of all things explain what Madison meant in the Second Amendment. It is a breathtakingly naïve (or cynical) maneuver—but what else are the private ownership folk to do? This *un*debated thing is the only passage they have to work with from the ratification debates.

Yet we should not let the matter rest here. The private ownership defenders have not asked why Whitehill treats militia matters in one article and hunting in two others. There are many signs that Whitehill threw together his objections in a hurry, simply to stave off the vote that was impending. Where did he get his objections? He flipped through the Pennsylvania constitution and took things from it. That constitution also treated the militia in one place (Declaration of Rights, Article XIII), offering it as a defense against standing armies (as "dangerous to liberty"), while it treated hunting in a later place (Frame of Government, Section 43). That later section explains why Whitehill's article 8 is so interested in the times and places of hunting. Here is Pennsylvania's Section 43:

The inhabitants of this state shall have liberty to fowl and hunt in *seasonable times* on the lands *they hold*, and on all other lands therein *not enclosed*; and in a like manner to fish in all boatable waters, and others *not private property* (emphasis added).

This is not a gun-freedom act, but a *restriction* meant to protect *property* rights. One can hunt on one's own land (but only in season), but not on others' property or on enclosed lands. Whitehill, patching together his objections, just dumps this in, along with the "killing game" permission of article 7, adding only that the federal government shall not infringe on the property rights spelled out in Section 43. Here is his article 8:

The inhabitants of the several states shall have liberty to fowl and hunt in seasonable times, on the land they hold, and on all the other lands in the United States not enclosed, and in like manner to fish in all navigable waters, and others not private property, without being restrained therein by any laws to be passed by the legislature of the United States.

Not even the NRA people have claimed that there was a groundswell of minority support for putting hunting territory restrictions into the Constitution, yet they continue to dignify Whitehill's odd document as the controlling authority on what the Second Amendment means.

2. They have even less to call on in the debates on the framing of the Second Amendment. Here they must rely on an argument from omission. While the Senate discussed the phrasing of the proposed amendment, "It was moved to insert the words, 'for the common defense' [after 'bear arms'], but the motion was not successful."[3] The record does not say why the motion was rejected, but Stephen Halbrook (often cited by the NRA people) is certain that he knows. For him, "common defense" means "for military purposes," showing that the amendment was meant to include *nonmilitary* matters (i.e., private use).[4] That is a very circuitous argument from what was *not* said, and it falls before the simple fact that "for the common defense" had a fixed legal meaning for the drafters. It was used in the Articles of Confederation to mean "for the joint action of the states," not (as Halbrook would maintain) "for any military use at all."[5] Including the phrase would have given the state militias power to bear arms *only* in conjunction with other states—which was clearly not the aim. Again, the little evidence at hand had to be drastically misread to give the NRA folk any pretense that private ownership came up in the drafting process.

There, in all its nakedness, is the historical argument for taking the Second Amendment to refer to private gun possession and use. To supplement its obvious inadequacy, NRA proponents turn to philology, examining the language of the Second Amendment. But if they are inadequate as historians, they are ludicrous as philologists, as one can see from the way they treat the term "bear arms." Don Kates writes in the *Michigan Law Review* that the amendment clearly refers to personal weapons, since "bear" means "carry," and a person cannot carry certain military weapons, like artillery.[6] This gets things exactly backward. "Bear arms" refers to military service, which is why the plural is used (based on Greek *hopla pherein* and Latin *arma ferre*)—one does not bear arm, or bear an arm. The word means, etymologically, "equipment" (from the root *ar-** in verbs like *ararisko*, to fit out). It refers to all the "equipage" of war. Thus "bear arms" can be used of naval as well as artillery warfare, since the "profession of arms" refers to all military callings. In fact, the only regular use of "arm" in the singular refers to branches of the military—the mounted arm, the naval arm, etc. William Shakespeare called war itself "arms," and Hamlet's "take arms against a sea of troubles" was a military metaphor.[7] (He did not mean to stab the sea with a bare bodkin.) A whole series of uses shows that "arms" means military service in general—to be under arms (*sub armis*), to call to arms (*ad arma vocare*), to take up arms (*arma capere*), to lay down one's arms (*arma ponere*).

Stephen Halbrook, as ingenious a lexicographer as Kates, replies that Noah Webster clearly referred to a *private* gun in a *pocket* when his dictionary (s.v. bear) listed "to bear arms in a coat."[8] Halbrook has missed the heraldic context. Webster is referring to a coat of arms (originally based on *military* shields) as family emblems. Halbrook also thinks that a law referring to the "bearing of a gun" in the hunt shows that "bear arms" can be used of hunting. He neglects the military and inclusive plural. A Roman hunter could "bear a bow" (*arcum ferre*) without changing the military meaning of *arma ferre*. One does not bear arms against a rabbit.

Desperate for examples of "bear arms" in a nonmilitary sense, the NRA's representatives resort to metaphorical or extended meanings. They bring up Whitehill's "right to bear arms for the defense of themselves," downplaying the fact that the sentence continues "and their own state or the United States." The verb "bear" goes with all these objects, by the rhetorical figure called zeugma, even though it may not be proper to each one individually. The same is true of the Pennsylvania constitution's Declaration, Article XIII: "The people have the right to bear arms for the defense of themselves *and the state*." Or they mention Tench Coxe's "bear their private arms," though we saw in Chapter 17 that he meant "private arms" only as used in militia service.

The tactic of the private ownership interpreters is to ransack any document, no matter how distant from the ratification debates, in the hope that someone, somewhere, ever used "bear arms" in a nonmilitary way, as if that would change the overwhelming body of military usage. That body of usage is enough to show that Madison must have meant the term in its normal sense *unless* he gave an explicit statement otherwise, or put the term in a clearly unmilitary context. Did he do that? Far from it. The context of the amendment as he drafted it is clearly military:

> The right of the people to keep and bear arms shall not be infringed; a well armed and well regulated militia being the best security of a free country; but no person religiously scrupulous of bearing arms shall be compelled to render military service in person.[9]

That last clause equates "bear arms" and "military service." Quakers and other conscientious objectors are exempted from bearing arms, which does not prohibit them from hunting rabbits with their privately owned muskets. The Congress actually strengthened the military context, by moving Madison's explanatory second clause into the first place, as a preamble stating the scope of the law (the regular function of a "whereas" introduction):

> A well-regulated militia being necessary to the security of a free State, the right of the people to keep and bear arms shall not be infringed.

Having failed in their first philological exercise, to change the normal meaning of "bear arms," the NRA troops make one last stab at linguistic analysis, focusing on the word "keep" in "*keep* and bear arms." Instead of reading keep-and-bear as conjunctive, they see the words as sharply disjunct. Robert Dowlut says: "The bearing of arms in a public place is different from the keeping of arms in the home on account of the home's special zone of privacy."[10] Don Kates agrees: "The term 'to keep' refers to owning arms that are kept in one's household . . . the words 'to keep' take on meaning *only* if what is being protected is the individual's own arms . . ." (emphasis added). Apparently Kates thinks that Article VI of the Articles of Confederation made no sense:

every state shall always keep up a well regulated and disciplined militia, sufficiently armed and accoutered, and shall provide and constantly have ready for use, *in public stores*, a due number of field pieces and tents, and a proper quantity of *arms*, ammunition and camp equipage (R 1.89, emphasis added).

It was a point of militia doctrine that it must keep its arms in readiness, while a king's army must "depone" its arms after a specific campaign, so as not to be "standing" in readiness: "The King must not be allowed to keep up a standing army."[11] John Trenchard, the British celebrant of militias, said that their arms must be "kept in every parish" (not every home).[12] Arsenals and armories were the normal repositories of arms, since—as we have seen—that term meant all the equipage of war. The private ownership school continues to think that plural "arms" means nothing but a singular "gun" for each individual, that every militiaman had his own gun, and that "keep arms" would be restricted to storing that gun at home. If the Congress had meant anything so outlandish, it could with great verbal economy have said "keep *at home* and bear. . . ." But it would have collapsed with laughter at its own absurdity. The militias had common stores of arms—not only guns but bayonets, artillery, ammunition, flags, drums, and all the *arma* (equipage) of war.

History, philology, and logic furnish no solid basis for thinking the Second Amendment has anything to do with the private ownership of guns. Those who believe there is a natural right to own guns can argue their case on many grounds—natural right, for a start—and the arguments might be sound or strong. It is just not a constitutional right (many of our rights are not constitutional ones). Why, then, does the NRA search so feverishly for a constitutional argument that eludes them? After all, many of the people who are devoted to the Second Amendment (as they construe it) are not such great lovers of other parts of the Constitution (like the Article I guarantees of the right to raise and renew armies or to federalize the militias). Some even say, with Charlton Heston, that this one short text is worth all the rest of the document. These are people who generally distrust government. Then why do they need a *governmental* basis for their activities?

Sanford Levinson gives away the reason when he says that flooding our society with guns is getting more difficult to defend on other grounds—of prudence, say, or safety, or social amity. But just as the First Amendment forces us to put up with speech that might otherwise be considered destructive or obnoxious, we have to put up with our gun culture because the Constitution tells us to.[13] But it doesn't.

VII.

Withdrawers

One does not need to resist government actively in order to express distrust of it, distaste for it, or resentment. One can simply withdraw, so far as that is possible, from all contact with it—not voting, not supporting its activities, not associating oneself with its values. This is different from the mere apathy of many nonvoters. It is a *principled* abstention, based on belief that contact with government sullies one's own purity. Some withdrawers from the government think of themselves as forming an alternative society, a one-person or one-sect government in exile—the internal exile of those too good for the gamey doings of power. This kind of purist usually puts great emphasis on individualism. The extreme position would lead to anarchism, but most advocates of purism settle for some form of libertarianism.

There is a more communal (and less snobbish) withdrawal from the government, best exemplified by various religious groups. Some cloistered Catholic orders have, in the past, ignored the secular world altogether. German pietists, whether Mennonite or Amish, were similarly detached. The withdrawal can be partial rather than complete—for example, the Quakers' refusal to take oaths or serve in wars. It can be conditioned on assumptions that the world is about to end, or that worldly affairs are below the notice of saints.

This section will deal with four examples of individuals withdrawing from governmental activity and two cases of communal withdrawal.

21.

Individuals:
From Thoreau to Mencken

The four men I shall be considering were different in talent and temperament—two of them were geniuses—and they all had periods of their life in which they dabbled, with varying degrees of seriousness, in political affairs. But each of them reached a carefully stated conviction that they were better off abstaining from the sordid maneuverings of democratic government. Two of them (the geniuses) are from the nineteenth century—Henry David Thoreau and Henry Adams. Two are from the twentieth century—Albert Jay Nock and Henry L. Mencken.

Thoreau

Patrician thinkers of the nineteenth century deplored the loss of what they felt was the properly deferential basis of society in the eighteenth century. At the outset of the Republic, it was claimed, politics was a gentleman's calling—and even gentlemen were not supposed to make it their full-time occupation, not (certainly) to make a living from it. That was one reason for rotation in office. When the game became more egalitarian, gentlemen found it hard to put up with what they perceived as an invasion of politics by vulgarity. John Quincy Adams, having been defeated for a second term as president, kept at his political duties from a sense of obligation, but he did not like what men like Andrew Jackson were doing to politics. Jackson was a slaveholding plantation owner like Washington, and he had been a military officer; but he was not what any Adams would call a gentleman.

When the president of Harvard asked ex-president Adams to be present when the university gave President Jackson an honorary degree, Adams replied that "as an affectionate child of our Alma Mater, I would not be present to witness her disgrace in conferring her highest literary honors upon a barbarian who could not write a sentence of grammar and hardly could spell his own name."[1]

Some (not all) of New England's transcendentalists felt this revulsion from anything so crass and undignified as the competition of louts for political prizes. At least some of the time this was the attitude of Ralph Waldo Emerson, who wrote in 1844 that the state would wither away when the level of "soul force" made every man his own government: "The wise man is the State. He needs no army, fort, or navy—he loves men too well; no bribe, or feast, or palace, to draw friends to him."[2] His ideal person would be one who "denied the authority of the laws on the simple ground of his own moral nature." Although that condition had not yet arrived, it was coming, Emerson felt: "The tendencies of the time favor the idea of self-government." In fact, "I have just been conversing with one man to whom no weight of adverse experience will make it for a moment appear impossible that thousands of human beings might exercise towards each other the grandest and simplest sentiments."

Some think Emerson was referring, here, to his friend Henry Thoreau, who would express similar views of soul force as a substitute for politics in his famous essay on civil disobedience. But that essay was five years in the future as Emerson wrote. Even the night in jail on which Thoreau based his essay was still two years off. But another friend of Emerson had gone to jail for the very same offense that Thoreau would—nonpayment of a poll tax—just the year before Emerson's essay on politics was published. This was the inspired teacher and holy fool Bronson Alcott, who, at the very time when Emerson wrote, was setting up an experimental commune (Fruitlands) where personal purity would be a substitute for politics.

Influenced by Emerson's essay on politics and by Alcott's personal example, Thoreau used his later experience in jail to institute a secession of one from the contamination of politics.[3] Later, as he reworked his experience, he would make it a protest against specific evils—namely, slavery and the Mexican War. But he admits that, at the time of his arrest, he had no specific abuses in mind: "It is for no particular item in the tax-bill that I refuse to pay it. I simply wish to refuse allegiance to the State, to withdraw and stand aloof from it effectually."[4] The snobbery in this attitude comes out when he describes those responsible for jailing him as behaving "like persons who are underbred." When one takes the highest view of morality, the state is not "worth looking at or thinking of at all . . . and I shall bestow the fewest possible thoughts on it." His goal is "to live aloof from it, not meddling with it, nor embraced by it."

Thoreau admits that lesser souls can be profitably engaged in politics, since they have no higher light to live by. But one should recognize the limits of such a life. Daniel Webster, for instance, made a fine defense of the entire Constitution drawn up in 1787 (which continued the existence of slaves), thus proving that "He is not a leader, but a follower. His leaders are the men of '87" (the framers of the Constitution). Webster stands by what already exists, instead of forging a new moral conscience for mankind. Such people are incapable of understanding the symbolism of Thoreau's own withdrawal from mundane concerns. He condemned even friends if they proved themselves obtuse to his higher purposes. They showed "that they were a distinct race from me by their prejudices and superstitions, as the Chinamen and Malays are; that, in their sacrifices to humanity, they ran no risks, not even to their property." Thoreau manages the clever feat of being a racist toward his own race.

Thoreau is contemptuous of the person(s) who paid his tax to get him out of jail—and kept paying it to keep him out. While his passivity allows him to accept this favor, he has to sneer at it:

> If others pay the tax which is demanded of me, from a sympathy with the State, they do but what they have already done in their own case, or rather they abet injustice to a greater extent than the State requires. If they pay the tax from a mistaken interest in the individual taxed, to save his property or prevent his going to jail, it is because they have not considered wisely how far they let their private feelings interfere with the public good.

Thoreau's aim is to detach himself from the sway of a majority of his fellow citizens and constitute himself a government in and for himself: "any man more right than his neighbors constitutes a majority of one already."

I have mentioned that Thoreau later added specific political wrongs his night in jail was supposed to protest—thus reentering the politics from which he had detached himself. This part of his revised essay has led to important results with people like Mahatma Gandhi and Dr. King. It will be considered when the subject, later, is civil disobedience. But those sections of Thoreau's essay are inconsistent with its deeper and more settled conviction, that one cannot reform government except by delegitimating it entirely. The pure rejection of government frees him from the need to advert to this or that specific thing done by the government. Thoreau protests the very existence of government. It is a duty to encourage contempt for it: "It is not desirable to cultivate a respect for the law so much as for the right."

> It is not a man's duty, as a matter of course, to devote himself to the eradication of any, even the most enormous wrong; he may still properly have other concerns to engage him; but it is his duty, at least, to wash his hands of it, and, if he gives it no thought longer, not to give it practically his support.

Thoreau even has his sophisticated way of saying "don't vote, it just encourages them."

> All voting is a sort of gaming, like chequers or backgammon, with a slight moral tinge to it, a playing with right and wrong, with moral questions; and betting naturally accompanies it.

If nonvoting leads to nongoverning, then Thoreau will have accomplished his purpose, since "that government is best which governs not at all."

For Thoreau, the best way to pay your debt to others is to cultivate yourself. The private, by a kind of Newspeak, becomes the public. The individual is most social when most detached from society: "It is not so important that many should be as good as you, as that there be some absolute goodness somewhere; for that will leaven the whole lump." It was to establish himself as that point of "absolute goodness" that Thoreau went to his well-advertised isolation at Walden Pond. He went there to listen to his genius, in a place where men could not "pursue and paw him with their dirty institutions."[5] Occasionally, going into the nearby village on some errand, he would observe his inferiors, "each as curious to me as if they had been prairie dogs, each sitting at the mouth of his burrow, or running over to a neighbor's to gossip." The people tried to trammel him in their silliness, but he slipped away from it:

> I escaped wonderfully from these dangers, either by proceeding at once boldly and without deliberation to the goal, as is recommended to those who run the gantlet, or by keeping my thoughts on high things, like Orpheus, who, "loudly singing the praises of the gods to his lyre, drowned the voice of the Sirens and kept out of danger."

Thoreau's high thinking cut him off from others so decidedly that even when there was someone he wanted to commune with, like Walt Whitman, he found his auditor drawing away from him: "[I told Whitman] that I did not think much of America or politics."[6] One can sometimes purify oneself right out of the company of men. Whitman's later comment about Thoreau, that he had a "disdain for men," is borne out by his difficulty in bearing their very smell. Thoreau told Emerson that "by night every dwelling house gives out bad air."[7] He caught the scent of a cigar being smoked even miles off in the outdoors. He was angry at a woman who gave him a manuscript to carry when it left a trace of her perfume in his pocket.[8] Even his moral condemnations took an olfactory turn, as when he said of the churches, "How they stink!"[9]

Thoreau's embarrassed avoidance of most references to sex made him, according to a fellow naturalist, Joseph Wood Krutch, a deficient observer of the very animals he celebrated.[10] When he chanced across a phallus-shaped flower, he recoiled in disgust: "Pray, what was nature thinking of when she made this? She almost puts herself on the level with those who draw in privies."[11] He praised solitude for winnowing one's acquaintance to a few friends, and even they were seen rarely. He told his mother that the mere sight of humanity in cities could blight a childhood: "It must have a very bad influence on children to see so many human beings at once—mere herds of men."[12] After a while he stopped taking his walking stick with him on his strolls, since it afforded "too much company."[13] By the end he drove most friends away.[14] Government, to such a man, must have been The Other in its most hideous form, a net of compromises with mediocrity that he spent his life trying to escape.

Adams

It may seem odd to compare Thoreau with Henry Adams. Though both men were from Massachusetts, and both were graduated from Harvard (Thoreau in 1837, Adams in 1858), their lives' external similarities end there. Thoreau, the son of an unsuccessful businessman, led a sheltered bachelor's life, rarely straying far from his native Concord, where he was intensely involved with spiritual strivers like Emerson and Bronson Alcott. Adams, grandson and great-grandson of presidents, was a world traveler who had been engaged in the nation's great affairs, first as his father's secretary on a diplomatic mission to England during the Civil War, then as a reforming journalist and political activist during the Grant administration. But after he became professor of history at Harvard he turned his attention more and more toward explaining the past and disdaining the present. His brother and his friends stayed active in politics, but Adams gently mocked them and lamented their thralldom to such low engagements.

Adams told the story of his own disillusionment with politics in his novel *Democracy*, the story of a rich widow who goes to Washington to understand the mysteries of government. She has "the feeling of a passenger on an ocean steamer whose mind will not give him rest until he has been in the engine room and talked with the engineer." After becoming involved with a corrupt senator who tries to use her position and money, she flees the seat of government as a fatal lure and corrupter of the soul. Her shrewd observations as she partly succumbs to the moral atmosphere around her echo Adams's own satirical comments on political life: "I have got so far as to lose the distinction between right and wrong. Isn't that the first step in politics?"[15]

In *The Education of Henry Adams*, originally planned as a private account of his life for friends, Adams speaks not through a fictional character but through the many masks of his own situation. He presents himself as a comic figure always being baffled in his hopes and efforts, discovering that he is as out of place everywhere as the rich widow was in Washington. He described the book this way to a friend:

> If you can imagine a centipede moving along in twenty little sections (each with a mathematical formula carefully concealed in its stomach) to the bottom of a hill, and then laboriously climbing in fifteen sections more (each with a new mathematical problem carefully concealed in its stomach) till it can get up on a hill an inch or two high, so as to see ahead a half inch or so, you will understand in advance all that the "Education" has to say.[16]

Having learned to shun "the malaria of power," he watches as others are turned into monstrous self-caricatures:

> The effect of power and publicity on all men is the aggravation of self, a sort of tumor that ends by killing the victim's sympathies; a diseased appetite, like a passion for drink or perverted tastes; one can scarcely use expressions too strong to describe the violence of egotism it stimulates.

When a friendly fellow historian, Theodore Roosevelt, becomes president, Adams reflects:

> Power is poison. Its effect on Presidents had been always tragic, chiefly as an almost insane excitement at first, and a worse reaction afterwards; but also because no mind is so well balanced as to bear the strain of seizing unlimited force without habit or knowledge of it; and finding it disputed with him by hungry packs of wolves and hounds whose lives depend on snatching the carrion.

When his closest male friend, John Hay, becomes secretary of state, Adams resigns himself: "His friends in power were lost, and he knew life too well to risk total wreck by trying to save them."

Adams inoculated himself against the sickness of power by treating politics as a spectacle, one he could observe with detachment, as if it were a play:

> The Senate took the place of Shakespeare, and offered real Brutuses and Bolingbrokes, Jack Cades, Falstaffs, and Malvolios—endless varieties of human nature nowhere else to be studied, and none the less amusing because they killed, or because they were like schoolboys in their simplicity.

Because he did not expect the multitude to share this exquisitely detached view, he told his friends that he would settle for a small elite audience:

> As my experience leads me to think that no one any longer cares or even knows what is said or printed, and that one's audience in history and literature has shrunk to a mere band of survivors not exceeding a thousand people in the entire world, I am in hopes a kind of esoteric literary art may survive, the freer and happier for the sense of privacy and abandon.

In this way did Adams withdraw into his art as a kind of hermitage, like Thoreau's Walden. Both men had pity or contempt for those not able to detach themselves from the strivings of a lesser purpose. Each tried to strip away all illusion and live with an ascetic minimum of goods or knowledge, protecting individual serenity by letting the masses plunge by, irredeemable.

Nock

For my purposes I have taken from the *Education* only those elements that apply to my theme of anti-governmentalism. There is much more there (and much more in *Walden*), but that only demonstrates that men of supe-

rior talent can be scornful of government. The same attitudes are culti-
vated by people of lesser gifts, and seem more appropriate there, as in the
writings of Albert Jay Nock. Nock is little known now, though he remains
a cult figure with some on the right. He wrote what William F. Buckley has
called his favorite book, and he is the spiritual progenitor of the magazine
most important to the surge of modern conservatism, *National Review*.[17]
After twenty years as an Episcopal priest, Nock deserted his church, his
wife, and his children to become a political activist for Henry George's
single-tax movement. In 1920, he founded *The Freeman*, a Georgist journal, for which Van Wyck Brooks was the literary editor.

Though the magazine soon folded (in 1924) over disputes with its financial backer, its writers and editors kept alive for decades the ideal of
what was reverently called "the old *Freeman*." Suzanne La Follette, an assistant to Nock, revived *The Freeman* in 1930. When that attempt at resusci-
tation failed, Frank Chodorov, the director of the Henry George School of
Economics, renamed that institute's newspaper *The Freeman*, in 1936. By
1950, after the title was vacated again, La Follette was joined by Henry
Hazlitt and John Chamberlain in still another attempt to revive Nock's
journal. In 1955, Bill Buckley tried to buy this last *Freeman*. When it proved
not for sale, Buckley began his own magazine, identical in format with *The
Freeman*, and with many of its editors and writers now working for him—La
Follette, John Chamberlain, Willi Schlamm, Frank Chodorov, Ralph de
Toledano, and Forrest Davis.

The odd thing is that Nock himself, while all these people were trying
to revive his culturally ambitious form of political journalism, had become
in the 1930s a theatrically detached dilettante. Since democracy was irredeemable, he said, one must talk to a small elite—like Henry Adams's audience—who would be "the saving Remnant" of civilization after the great
democratic experiment met its inevitable end. The book that best sums up
this attitude is Nock's *Memoirs of a Superfluous Man*, the only book that
Buckley says was formative of his own writing style. Buckley read the book
at the end of his prep school years, prompted to this by his father, who had
become a patron and admirer of Nock. In visits to the Buckley home, Nock
instilled in father and son his own attitude toward "mass-men," who cannot be treated as basically human. Reflection on this fact gives Nock an
equanimity he prides himself on:

One can hate human beings, at least I could—I hated a lot of them when that is what I thought they were—but one cannot hate sub-human creatures or be contemptuous of them, wish them ill, regard them unkindly. If an animal is treacherous, you avoid him but can't hate him, for that is the way he is.[18]

All forms of government that rely on the populace are doomed: "Indeed, if it be true that the mass-man is not a human being, never has been, and never will be, no such society can possibly be developed, and all our schemes for it are visionary."[19]

Since politics has become the arena of the mass-man, Nock fastidiously disdains the least connection with it, at least in the account of his own superfluity: "a decent person could find no place in politics, not even the place of an ordinary voter, for the forces of ignorance, brutality, and indecency would outnumber him ten to one."[20] His attitude toward voting (and toward Jefferson Davis) is given in this passage:

I once voted at a presidential election. There being no real issue at stake, and neither candidate commanding any respect whatever, I cast my vote for Jefferson Davis of Mississippi. I knew Jeff was dead, but I voted on Artemus Ward's principle that if we can't have a live man who amounts to anything, by all means let's have a first-rate corpse.[21]

Nock said he could not oppose women's suffrage. Since the vote is a futility, mass-woman has as much right to amuse herself with it as mass-man does.[22] Public education, on the other hand, wasted money as well as being futile: "As for raising the general level of intelligence, the sluicing-out of any amount of education on our citizenry would simply be pouring water on a duck's back."[23] Even in his later days, when he posed as indifferent to the world's folly, he betrayed his strong feelings where Jews were concerned.

Thinking over Hitler's antisemitism, one is forced to admit, I believe, that the Nazis could not have carried their program through and made it work, without clearing the Jews out of Germany. I do not think their program was ever worth carrying through, but they did; and admitting that, probably the only course open to them was the one they took. From 1918 to 1932, Germany's circumstances were such that her domestic organization had to be carried on pretty much on the honor system. Most of the Germans played the game fairly and loyally, as far as I have been able to find out; the Jews, on the other hand, cut every corner they could—and there you are.[24]

It is the mark of these individual purists that they feel their separate status should make them scholars. Adams became America's greatest historian. Thoreau planned a major work on the American Indians. Nock fancied himself a scholar on Rabelais, seeking out manuscripts and rare editions. He and Buckley's father decided that young Bill should be a scholar. The father wanted him to go to Oxford. For many years Buckley himself harbored the ambition to write a major book on José Ortega y Gasset (one of Nock's enthusiasms). But Buckley's gift is for witty polemic, not learned inquiry, and he listened to *his* genius. He also managed to shed the most deleterious effects of Nock's influence (especially the antisemitism). But occasionally some of the Nock hauteur would come through, as when Buckley called politics "the preoccupation of the quarter-educated" or proposed a qualifying test for voters with questions like "What is the United Nations?" (A poll at the time found that 28 percent of the people questioned could not identify the United Nations.)[25]

Mencken

Nock admired some of the people we have already encountered in the anti-government ranks—John Taylor of Caroline, Jefferson Davis, Thoreau. But he referred to no contemporary with more praise than he lavished on Henry L. Mencken, who published some of his articles. Mencken was a verbal vaudevillian whose satirical approach to politics was suggested when he said that there is only one way the journalist should look at the politician—down. Many people, who took such remarks as the hyperbole of a comedian, were surprised to find antisemitism and other forms of bitterness in Mencken's posthumously published diaries.[26] The three volumes of Mencken's journalistic memoirs had given the impression of a genial and tolerant man. But Mencken, a Germanophile in all ways, admired the German talent for scholarship and wanted to imitate it. One form this took was his multi-volume study of the American language. But another manifestation of the urge to be systematic, one often overlooked, was his set of treatises attempting to give a broad statement of his own philosophy. This was spelled out in five main books—*The Philosophy of Friedrich Nietzsche* (1908), *In Defense of Women* (1918), *Notes on Democracy* (1926), *Treatise on the Gods* (1930), and *Treatise on Right and Wrong* (1934). These are profoundly anti-democratic documents, and they prove that Mencken's attacks on the politics of his time were not the genial joshings of a satirist but expressions of a contempt for mass-man (whom he called "the booboisie") as complete as Nock's own.

Mencken's book on Nietzsche praises him for being a social Darwinian who placed his hope in elite Supermen, not in "the drudge class" of mankind:

> That this natural incompetence of the masses is an actual fact was observed by a hundred philosophers before Nietzsche, and fresh proofs of it are spread copiously before the world every day. Whenever universal suffrage, or some close approach to it, is the primary axiom of government, the thing known in the United States as "freak legislation" is a constant evil.[27]

Nietzsche's belief that superior men need a drudge class to work for them is confirmed in America, according to Mencken:

> The history of the hopelessly futile and fatuous effort to improve the Negroes of the southern United States by education affords one such proof. It is apparent, on brief reflection, that the Negro, no matter how much he is educated, must remain, as a race, in a condition of subservience; that he must remain the inferior of the stronger and more intelligent white man so long as he retains racial differentiation. Therefore, the effort to educate him has awakened in his mind ambitions and aspirations which, in the very nature of things, must go unrealized, and so, while gaining nothing whatever materially, he has lost

all his old contentment, peace of mind and happiness. Indeed, it is a commonplace of observation in the United States that the educated and refined Negro is invariably a hopeless, melancholy, embittered and despairing man.[28]

In Nietzsche's scheme of things there are not only inferior races and classes but an inferior gender. Women, to compensate for their physical weakness, turn all their cunning into the effort "to deceive, influence, sway and please men." Since they feel they begin at a disadvantage, they find it necessary to take every moral shortcut, so that "a woman seldom manifests any true sense of justice or of honor."[29] This is different from the Superman's freedom from lesser men's morality. Women use law and government to bind man down, while the Superman transcends such empty forms: "Government, in its very essence, is opposed to all increase of knowledge."[30]

Mencken's "defense" of women simply expands what he said in the *Nietzsche*. Here he says that woman is inferior to man not only in strength but in beauty. Their "deplorable deficiency in design" gives them a dumbbell shape: "Below the neck by the bow and below the waist astern there are two masses that simply refused to fit into a balanced composition."[31] (A fastidious man despite all his beer and cigars, Mencken seems to have had the same view of sex's messiness that Thoreau did. Despite a lapse into marriage during his sixth decade, when he had lost the companionship of his brother, he claimed that most men of genius are bachelors.) Mencken "defends" women by praising their cunning, which allows them to overcome so many handicaps—though the intelligent man sees through their ploys, and the unintelligent are infuriated into "so called wife beating."[32]

Notes on Democracy blames Marx for inspiring the inferior four-fifths of mankind to seize power from the superior one-fifth. Mencken is no better at distinguishing welfare assistance from Marxism than is any *Homo Boobens* on a congressional committee, and he anticipates the argument that giving the poor governmental aid will just make them overbreed.

The *Treatise on the Gods* makes the connection between religion and democracy that led Mencken to his fury at William Jennings Bryan, a champion of both—and a man who, according to Mencken's boast, died of the ridicule he (Mencken) heaped on him.[33] According to the *Treatise*, the eighteenth century was an age of reason triumphant, but the nineteenth century made the mistake of giving the vote to the masses. Along with the mob, "popular religion surged up from its sewers and polluted every rank of society save the highest."[34] In America, this catastrophe was worsened by "an invading horde of moron Catholics, swarming in from Ireland and French Canada."[35]

The *Treatise on Right and Wrong* is Mencken's most ambitious philosophical work—it has, for instance, a long history of the controversy over free will. For him, there are three grounds for establishing moral obligation—revealed (Yahweh), rational (Aristotle), and evolutionary (Darwin). He considers a test case, that of slavery. Religion did nothing to abolish slavery. Reason helped, but only as it estimated the profit of getting rid of slavery. Evolution decreed the survival of the fittest, some of them slaves, some not—and only it achieved any real measure of success.

Though Mencken said he had never changed the views expressed in his Nietzsche book, he muted them over the years as a result of the nation's anti-German sentiment during and after the two world wars. Many found it hard to take seriously what seem such outrageous prejudices, and they preferred the buffoon to the thinker. But even as clown he helped feed the fashionable anti-governmentalism, as I know to my regret. At a time in the late 1960s, when I admired his journalism, and partly because of its influence, I stopped voting. It seemed a feckless enterprise.

•　　•　　•

These four men are a motley human collection—America's most influential nature writer, our greatest historian, a mediocre journalist, a brilliant journalist. It is extraordinary, then, how similar in attitude they can be on one side of their lives—the scornful opposition to democratic government. Despite this similarity, they fit less than others into normal polarities of feeling about the government—news they would, in their exceptionalism, welcome. They were cosmopolitan, not provincial; and only one of them was religious—Thoreau mixed his transcendentalism with Indian pantheism. But they certainly considered themselves authentic in both their realism and their idealism—as contrasted with people who lived by

authoritarian prescriptions of what they should believe. They were spontaneous, organic, and personal in their thought, as opposed to the mechanical and impersonal operations of government. They carried localism so far
as to find no government acceptable outside the counsels of their own
heart. Each was a majority of one, and the whole vast rest of the world
shrank to a single minority.

22.

Groups:
From Brook Farm to Hippie Communes

Elite *groups* can withdraw from political life for motives resembling those of the elite *individuals* just studied. They are anti-governmental in the sense that merely abiding by the law does not offer an enlightened form of social life. Sometimes this puts the group in opposition to laws, as when Mormons defied marriage laws. More often the groups just want to withdraw from political life and have nothing (or as little as possible) to do with its processes.

For the purposes of this book, two outbreaks of this communal purism have most relevance, those of the 1840s and the 1960s. The period of the 1840s is particularly instructive, since the groups' withdrawal from government was connected with the individualist transcendentalism of Emerson and Thoreau. By 1840, a number of tendencies met, blended for a while, then parted. At the centers of American religious learning, old Calvinist doctrines were being deserted in the name of liberal values. Congregationalism and Presbyterianism yielded, in many places, to Unitarianism, which led to transcendentalism. This last school responded to the nature mysticism of the romantic movement, the aesthetic revulsion from the industrial revolution, and an anti-materialist attack on the values of capitalism. (Henry Adams's novel *Esther* recalls all these forces and how they worked upon each other.) The spiritual socialism of the French reformer Charles Fourier led American groups to set up utopian communities.

In New England, some of those who admired Emerson could not accept his radical individualism. They felt they could live a higher life of the mind and reach spiritual peace by simplifying their lives in *common* activities. The most famous of these bodies, Brook Farm, had the support (though not the membership) of Emerson, of Thoreau, and of the female transcendentalist Margaret Fuller, while Nathaniel Hawthorne actually joined and lived with the group—he later wrote a disillusioned novel about the experience, *The Blithedale Romance*. Another disciple of Emerson, Bronson Alcott (who had set the example of going to jail for Thoreau), decided in 1843 to set up a perfectionist community of his own, Fruitlands, which continued his radical ideas for educating children.

Most of these experimental communities tried to combine manual labor and spiritual discipline—as that Scottish hero of the transcendentalists, Thomas Carlyle, put it, they wanted to "reform the world by growing onions."[1] Hawthorne, out of bitter experience, put it even more harshly:

> While our enterprise lay all in theory, we had pleased ourselves with delectable visions of the spiritualization of labor. It was to be our form of prayer, and ceremonial of worship. Each stroke of the hoe was to uncover some aromatic root of wisdom . . . [but] clods of earth, which we so constantly belabored and turned over and over, were never etherealized into thought.[2]

Intimate living arrangements were often based on, or led to, novel attitudes toward property and marriage. Monogamy in its contemporary form was considered possessive, exclusive, and property-obsessed. Alternatives were explored—sometimes celibacy, sometimes open marriages, sometimes polygamy or polyandry—and it was difficult for members of the group to reach agreement on the proper alternative (or mixture of alternatives). High thinking did not quench eros, since (as Hawthorne recorded) "the footing on which we all associated at Blithedale was widely different from that of conventional society . . . [and] seemed to authorize any individual of either sex to fall in love with any other, regardless of what would elsewhere be judged suitable and prudent."[3]

At Alcott's Fruitlands, the community was torn apart when its second most influential leader, Charles Lane, challenged the founder (and his wife) with a call for mandatory celibacy, or at least for the dissolution of the normal marriage bond.[4] The most enduring of these communities born in the 1840s was the polygamist Mormons. Another group that had a substantial if temporary success was founded by John Humphrey Noyes, and took its name from its final settlement (in 1848) in New York State at Oneida. The Oneida community adopted Noyes's doctrines of male continence or "complex marriage." Love was to be diffused equally through all the community, not restricted to "special loves." Women were not to be taxed with too frequent childbirth. The community would decide when, and with whom, the woman should conceive, and children would be held by all as the whole community's offspring.[5] The group aspired to realize St. Augustine's vision of Eden as a place where passion was entirely at the disposal of reason.

Oneida's comparative success (it lasted, in some form, into the 1880s) came in part—like that of the Shakers, the Amish, and Mormons—from the sale of profitable products. Shorter-lived groups like Brook Farm treated work as a form of spiritual exercise rather than a business. Such groups were often at the mercy of the idealists who financed them (as Charles Lane did Fruitlands) and who could therefore meddle in their affairs.

An even greater problem was that of charismatic leadership. Most groups had come into existence by the energetic efforts of a leader, often (like John Humphrey Noyes) an ordained minister discontented with the legalism and spiritual deadness of the established churches. These men yearned for a more spontaneous and anti-authoritarian life, but they either carried over from their former position an assumption of personal authority, or they had that attitude forced on them by the difficulty of holding together a community with little constitutional structure. This is an old problem for perfectionists who try to live outside the normal types of human government. Catholic religious orders, for instance, were founded by charismatic figures—Benedict, Dominic, Francis, Ignatius, and so on—whose followers found it necessary to adopt regulated procedures, betraying (in many people's eyes) the freedom and spontaneity of the original days. On the other hand, an attempt to retain charismatic leadership led to complaints that egalitarianism was being betrayed by what a later age would call the "cult of personality."

This problem, which was at the heart of these communal efforts to be free of structure yet sturdy enough to endure, shows how thoroughly what I have been calling anti-governmental attitudes were embraced by the utopians. They wanted to be totally candid (some engaged in mutual criticism sessions), totally voluntary (which made work assignments difficult), rotating ownership and privileges (including that of begetting children with different women), acting with organic spontaneity. Government represented the very things these people were fleeing—it was mechanical, regulatory, based on division of labor rather than sharing, on remote and often secret processes of arranging other people's lives instead of letting them arrange everything themselves.

•　•　•

It is fascinating to observe almost all the elements of the 1840s movement playing themselves out again in the 1960s. That, too, was a time of discontent with conformism, of a search for more authentic ways to live. The enemy was no longer the 1840s industrial revolution but a 1960s "warfare state," one that inculcated social disciplines in order to wage the Cold War. People in the 1840s felt that their churches had gone lifeless. Students in the 1960s felt that their universities—spiritual heirs to the nineteenth century's intellectual authority—were soulless diploma mills, where the student was less cared for than his punch-card computer record ("Do not fold, bend, or mutilate"). The end of ideology had been declared. "Consensus history" praised the nation that was "the leader of the free world."[6] Questions were not to be explored but facts imparted, by those competent to do the imparting. Amid prosperity, there was suspicion—the ever-present fear of subversion or nuclear one-upmanship. Amid religiosity, there was spiritual aridity—the businessman's gospel of Norman Vincent Peale.

The signs of spiritual unrest had been evident in the 1950s. As Thoreau had turned to Indian pantheism, the "dharma bums" of the beat ("beatific") movement turned to oriental mysticism, to Allen Ginsberg's form of contemplation, to the Zen philosophy of Alan Watts (a former Episcopalian priest), to Hermann Hesse's *Siddhartha*.[7] As Americans of the 1840s had experimented with Fourierism, so did coffeehouse poets try on French fashions in existentialism. By the 1960s the "God is dead" fad really meant that old-fashioned theology was dead, to be replaced with "authentic" Christianity preached by civil rights evangelicals, by the Catholic Workers of Dorothy Day, by pacifists trained in divinity schools (like A. J. Muste and David Dellinger). As John Humphrey Noyes and others had experimented with new sexual moralities, Norman Brown and Paul Goodman brought a new view of eros to the young, making modern students

—according to Richard King—"the New Transcendentalists."[8] Women at places like Brook Farm, where the old sexual roles were placed in question, became more creative.[9] The same thing happened with women who rebelled against doing the "housework" in communes.[10] Some of the original transcendentalists aspired to a new "mentalism" typified by mesmerism. The students of the 1960s sought visions in LSD, or with gurus like the Maharishi, or the shamanism of Native Americans.

Most Americans remember the student movement of the 1960s as highly political, inclined toward hedonism, violence, and obscenity. But much of it was, in the early days, just a way of "dropping out" of what was called "the system." Students were "turned off" by what J. D. Salinger's hero Holden Caulfield called the phonies. The search for authentic experience took many forms, and a thousand "flower children" did seem to bloom. By 1970, the *New York Times* reported that there were two thousand communes in America. The National Institutes of Health (which had to monitor problems of disease and nutrition in the communes) said that three thousand was a more accurate figure. The anti-materialism of the old transcendentalists found its echo in gestures like Abbie Hoffman's scattering of dollar bills from the gallery of the New York Stock Exchange.[11] New attitudes toward property were signaled in the title Hoffman gave his own book, *Steal This Book*.

Critics of the student movement had trouble finding what it was *about*. The issues it confronted—well before the draft threatened to take them off to Vietnam—did not look like the old bread-and-butter issues of the left. Were they truly rebelling just for the right to use dirty words at Berkeley? Old-fashioned liberals said the students could not really be objecting to the quality of their education, since the unrest began at the best schools, where no one could question the credentials of the professors. But the whole credentialing system was what the young had challenged. The quality of the life they were being channeled into was felt to be numbing. Alternative forms of being together, or conceiving themselves, underlay the gestures of revolt (long hair, pot, rock music). As a placard at Berkeley put it, THE ISSUE IS NOT THE ISSUE.[12] Not doing but being was at stake. Paradoxically nonprotesting nondemonstrations were called, simply, "be-ins" or "happenings." The irony is that the culture these youths were attacking had itself declared "the end of ideology." It could not cope with the reality of certain people actually *living* that condition.

Under the confusion of new terms and attitudes among the young, old value clusters were at work, the anti-governmental standards professed by other movements considered in this book. It is not surprising that these values would reassert themselves at a time when government had become more powerful and intrusive than at any time in our history. Now there was not simply a "standing army," but a worldwide network of nuclear delivery systems. To protect that network abroad, CIA agents had to monitor the countries near key installations or transfer points around the globe, altering or overthrowing governments if they posed any threat to these bastions of "the free world." To protect the network at home, information had to be classified, citizens had to be "cleared" for initiation into the ultimate secrets of the nuclear age. Campuses had to be kept under surveillance to protect government research. Soviet sympathizers had to be identified and isolated. Vast amounts of government money were poured into the educational system, after the success of the Soviet space vehicle *Sputnik*, to make sure America was not losing the brains race as one aspect of the arms race. Large corporations and expanding "multiversities" were part of this immense apparatus of free-world guidance.

Historian Michael Sherry has described very well this totally saturating militarization of our culture.[13] It was an apotheosis of governmental values—expert, authoritative, confidential, articulated, duties-oriented, regulatory, delegative, based on highly articulated divisions of labor (whence the need for specialization and exotic skills in the university of the future). Why be surprised, then, when attitudes historically opposed to governmentalism found a vehicle for their expression? The nation's conservatives, who had ordinarily been harsh critics of big government (especially in the South), found their hands tied by the justification for the new concentrations of governmental power. They were there to fight communism, the conservative's favorite devil. In fact, when a challenge to this fighting machine arose, the conservatives switched their whole set of values for the duration. In order to suppress "the kids," they now favored secrecy and dispatch, "law and order," expertise not to be questioned, efficiency not to be blunted. Vice President Spiro Agnew led the attack, telling the New Transcendentalists, "You may give us your symptoms; we will make the diagnosis and we, the Establishment, will implement the cure."[14] Expert authority will act, and the governed will passively accept whatever is prescribed.

The response of "the kids" to this smug assurance was traditional and religious in a radical way—going back to older traditions of the Eastern mystics or the West's Native Americans. As Emerson had said of the transcendentalists, who looked disturbingly new and faddist to their contemporaries: "The first thing we have to say, respecting what are called new views here in New England at the present time, is that they are not new but the very oldest of thought cased into the mould of these new times."[15] The natural and organic was put up against the artificial and mechanical. Homogeneity was pushed to the limits of tribalism. The youth culture was above all "participatory." Everyone was supposed to put his or her two cents' worth into every discussion, decision, or public statement. Rotation of labor among amateurs made everyone take turns at the chores on a commune—guaranteeing bad food on the days when bad cooks were at the stove.

This lifestyle led, predictably, to the same kind of problems faced by the original transcendentalists. A nonauthoritarian structure led either to chaos or to a need for charismatic leadership. In those circumstances, as sociologist Andrew Greeley said, "only an extraordinary leader can avoid being caught in the father-figure booby trap."[16] The effort to extricate himself (few communes had female leaders of topmost influence) from that trap led to elaborate structures of pretense—a claim that the leader was not really the leader. This reintroduced a note of the "phony" into lives meant to be totally "authentic." The communes I observed at the time all suffered from this problem (which is the problem of anti-governmentalism in a nutshell): they were saying they were not governed when, in fact, they had to be governed in order to survive. I wrote about a commune of draft evaders in Canada, where one "grown-up" figure held more spontaneous members to the minimal scheduling needed to function at all.[17] In an academic commune at Harvard, I could get few helpful answers to my questions when the leading figure, sociologist Christopher Jencks, was absent. In the religious commune around Philip Berrigan in Baltimore, not even Berrigan's outspoken wife, Elizabeth McAlister, had a voice equal to his.

The sixties communes resembled those of the 1840s in another way.

Spontaneity and anti-authoritarianism made it difficult for the commune to support itself with any productive kind of labor. Most of those forming such groups came from an affluent background and expected unearned amenities. The life they led was expensive, especially when drug costs were added in. Drugs had more to do with the failure of the counterculture than did any repressive action against it. Peter Coyote, a veteran of the Haight-Ashbury section of San Francisco, spoke what was in effect the epitaph of the village's "flower children":

> It was a daunting task we set out to do. It killed us. In the first place, we have introjected the culture that we're trying to change. We're a product of it. So every time you would come up against a form or a limit, you didn't know whether it was legitimate or something you'd been taught. So you'd have to break through to see what would happen. And the way that you would fuel your imagination to go through, unfortunately, was drugs.[18]

No wonder the communes of the 1960s were as short-lived as those of the 1840s. The nineteenth-century ones had more literary than social effect. Those of our century had a deeper social effect. On their political side, which I address in my next chapter, the "kids" of the sixties were a failure. Antiwar activities may well have prolonged the Vietnam War. But 1960s attitudes toward sex, marriage, authority, and religion have perdured. Campuses are entirely different now, with students participating in decisions, grading their teachers, demanding explanation of actions that were considered guild secrets when I began teaching in 1961. Some believe that this massive challenge to authority loosened the whole fabric of our society—though these are the same people who, on other matters, like to attack "big government" themselves. The values of anti-governmentalism, always with us, can take surprising turns.

No better proof of this is the way some conservatives switched back, in 1993, to praising the anti-government values of a commune. The commune at issue was the home of David Koresh's "Branch Davidians" in Waco, Texas, seventy-four of whom died in an attack by federal agents.[19] This splinter group from the Seventh-Day Adventists had mystical notions, odd sexual relations, a charismatic leader—just like the communes of the 1960s. Admittedly, Davidians were armed, expecting an attack from diabolic forces at the millennium; but that, far from disqualifying them for sympathy, increased right-wing support from the NRA, militias, and "Second Amendment fundamentalists." Federal agents had, just a year earlier, killed a religious extremist's wife in a raid on his home. This man, Randy Weaver, was a member of the antisemitic "Christian Identity" movement, and he had defied a court summons. But that hardly seemed a reason for the military assault on his home. Weaver and Koresh appealed to the spirit of armed self-sufficiency that is deep in our view of ourselves. Few compared the Waco settlement to hippie communes. Yet it resembled them in trying to create an ideal society outside the monitorings of government, and such communal purism is an authentic expression of anti-governmentalism.

VIII.

Disobeyers

In most of the cases so far considered, opposition to the government has not been successful in any long-range sense. Nullification, secession, and insurrection failed outright. Some forms of vigilantism (like the Ku Klux Klan) prevailed for a while, but were ultimately folded back into the government, or became governmental (like the Mormons). Withdrawal from contact with the government affected the purists who withdrew, but did not purify the government they were criticizing. In fact, the purists themselves—whether at Brook Farm or on hippie communes—could not sustain their experiments for very long, not (usually) because of government interference but from internal contradictions in their ideal, which was to live as an orderly community without the discipline of any government.

But there is one form of selective resistance to government that has been part of successful agitation for change—the disobedience to specific laws in order to reform government. This was engaged in by abolitionists (in the underground railway, for instance) in such a way that the ground was prepared for opposition to slavery in the Civil War and the dissolution of slavery by the Thirteenth Amendment. It was engaged in by labor unions, whose illegal strikes led to legislation recognizing union rights. It was engaged in by woman suffragists, who disrupted political meetings and chained themselves to the White House gates, making opponents realize that this intense movement was not going to fade away. It was engaged in, during the 1960s, by the civil rights movement and the anti–Vietnam War movement, with differing results that this section will assess.

Given this record of at least occasional success, civil disobedience, though it opposes government on at least one point, breaking a specific law, can be seen as an American tradition, with some claim to legitimacy as tested by results. If we ask why this anti-governmental activity can succeed where others fail, part of the answer comes from the fact that the movements involved did not oppose government as such or in toto. The laws targeted were presented as dissonant with the spirit of the government itself. The whole governing structure did not need to be shaken down. In fact, the purpose of the disobeyers was to provoke action *by* the government to right a wrong it was equipped to deal with. Thoreau announced that government of itself is ignoble, and only then got around to finding certain laws he objected to even more than most. Martin Luther King Jr., though he thought of himself as a disciple of Thoreau, had an entirely different approach. He called government back to its own noble professions—to the Declaration of Independence and the Gettysburg Address.

If this kind of disobedience does not oppose government itself, but only particular abuses, can it rightly be placed among the anti-government activities that fill the rest of this book? It can, though only with reservations. It is a borderline case when conducted with Dr. King's kind of restraint. Even in that case, authority is defied and its legitimacy challenged. More important, this kind of disobedience slides easily into the whole cluster of anti-governmental sentiments that afflict the other movements. It is a dangerous thing, as Dr. King found out—some of his own followers chafed at the limits he placed on their acts, succumbed to hatred of the government itself, and committed acts of violence. That dynamic was even more disastrously illustrated by the degeneracy of the antiwar movement that opposed our engagement in Vietnam. Borderline anti-governmentalism became full-blown hatred of "the system."

23.

From Dr. King to SDS

An appreciation of the distinctive character of Dr. King's campaign for civil rights is best achieved by contrasting it with the approach of Henry David Thoreau, with which it has been too often confused. Thoreau disobeyed every one of Dr. King's rules of disobedience. In his "Letter From Birmingham City Jail" of 1963, King laid out seven directives for constructively breaking the law:

1. *Collect facts to establish there has been a serious injustice not corrected by the law.* At the time of his arrest in 1846, Thoreau had not published, nor (so far as records indicate) reflected on, what exactly he would be protesting if he refused to pay a state poll tax. Earlier he had protested a church tax and been exempted from paying it.[1]

2. *Negotiate with officials over the injustice.* Thoreau had not notified state officials that he had any reason for refusing to pay the state poll tax.

3. *Investigate one's motives, purging any purely selfish or destructive aim.* Thoreau thought all his acts were pure, and that very fact made it impossible for him to take an adversary scrutiny of his refusal's meaning.

4. *Take "direct" action, as opposed to indirect actions like voting or pamphleteering, in order to target a specific wrong.* Thoreau did not initiate any action at all. He was surprised by his arrest, since he did not think he was breaking one law, just ignoring all law. Thoreau did not target a specific

wrong his refusal to pay was meant to remedy. The real wrong was, for him, the existence of government in the first place.

5. *Act openly*. For six years, without notice to anyone, Thoreau had simply (as Carlos Baker puts it) "ignored his poll-tax obligation."[2]

6. *Act lovingly*. Thoreau saw nothing more in his incarceration than the "pawing" of "persons who are underbred."[3]

7. *Show willingness to accept the penalty for one's act.* On the contrary, Thoreau showed anger at the jailer for not releasing him on the night of his arrest (as Bronson Alcott had been released) even though the penalty was paid by then.[4]

Dr. King said that actions so disciplined are "expressing the very highest respect for law,"[5] whereas Thoreau meant all his acts to express a disrespect for government itself, arguing that people should be "no-government men." Thoreau did no more to test government by disobedience after his night in jail, a sentence Baker calls "among the shortest in Middlesex County's penological history."[6] Alcott, by contrast, tried again to be arrested for nonpayment of taxes, and was thwarted—a fact that made it look safe for Thoreau to ignore the tax with that precedent before him.[7] Theodore Baird noted how absurd it is that Thoreau's few hours in the village pokey should be remembered in the annals of human suffering, put up there with the death of Socrates or the condemnation of Galileo.[8] I say this less to rebuke Thoreau than to emphasize the genius of Dr. King in explicating the rules that have made constructive disobedience so successful in our history. Others followed his outline only partially or by intuition. He made it a matter of declared principle, spelled out for the knowledge of the authorities as well as for those trying to effect reform of the law by disobedience to the law. (He generally informed all the relevant governmental bodies about what he intended to do before he did it.)

It did not hurt, in Dr. King's case, that the disobedience he supported was based on religious reflection and duty. That is not essential to conscientious disobedience, but it has often been a help to civil disobeyers, simultaneously strengthening conviction and imposing moral restraint.

Most abolitionists and some woman suffragists acted from religious motives. Thoreau was religious in his mystical devotion to nature—his pantheism drew on Eastern religions. But he nowhere adduces that in his essay on civil disobedience. There he says only that the state is unworthy of touching his personal integrity. There were, by contrast, some religious traditions at work in the early antiwar movement.

In this respect, as well as others, early proponents of the New Left of the 1960s were close to Dr. King's model of reform—not surprisingly, since some of the student leaders had worked in the civil rights movement, before the Student Nonviolent Coordinating Committee expelled whites from leadership positions there. (Abbie Hoffman was especially upset at this move.)[9] Dr. King's evangelical background was not the only religious influence on white political activists, as Doug Rossinow has emphasized. He points especially to the most important center of student activism between the two ocean coasts—the YMCA and the Faith-and-Life Community at the University of Texas in Austin, under the leadership of (respectively) Frank Wright and Joseph Mathews. The star of the many activists to come through that program was Casey Cason, a young woman prominent in the National Student Association who became more famous when she married Tom Hayden, the author of the Students for a Democratic Society's founding document, "The Port Huron Statement." Hayden and Cason were married at a Faith-and-Life service in Austin.[10] Other religious influences included the Catholic Worker movement and priests like the Berrigan brothers and Father Bernie Gilgun (whom the "Yippie" Abbie Hoffman called his "rabbi").[11]

The responsible approach to civil disobedience was obvious in "The Port Huron Statement," issued in 1962 by the SDS, the most influential student body on the left. The New Left was a serious political movement that should not be confused with the hippie communes (see Chapter 22), which were more concerned with their own lifestyle than with the nation's policies. Tom Hayden's statement called for research (Dr. King's gathering of facts) as the basis for reform activities. On the basis of that research, reforms should be openly identified and worked for: "Any new left in America must be, in large measure, a left with real intellectual skills, committed to deliberativeness, honesty, reflection as working tools."[12] Only on that reflective basis should protests be mounted, targeted to the real agencies of change: "Demonstrations should be held at every congressional or convention seating of Dixiecrats. A massive publicity and research campaign should be initiated, showing to every housewife, doctor, professor and worker the damage done to their interests every day a racist occupies a place in the Democratic Party."[13] Thoughtful arguments were mounted for long-scale disarmament negotiations, and for domestic reforms like congressional changes meant to break legislative "deadlock." Much has been made of the influence of the radical sociologist C. Wright Mills on the statement. But mainstream works also left their stamp—John Kenneth Galbraith's book on the affluent society, for instance, or James MacGregor Burns's book on Congress.

Many antiwar protests took place in the Vietnam era that were entirely in the spirit of Dr. King's rules for civil disobedience—the burning of draft cards by Benjamin Spock and others, for instance. That was an open and symbolic act, for which the perpetrators stood trial and accepted the outcome, asking only to explain their protest. Daniel and Philip Berrigan broke one of Dr. King's rules—not openly saying beforehand what they intended to do—when they poured their own blood on draft records in Catonsville, Maryland. They could not have won access to the records if they had announced their plan ahead of time; but they waited for arrest afterwards and did not try to evade the authorities.[14]

One act of civil disobedience typical of many was undertaken by Redress, a group that twice demonstrated at the Capitol. Carefully drawing up a petition for redress of grievance, giving arguments why the war in Vietnam was unconstitutional (it was not declared by Congress), a hundred or so people blocked the entrance to the House and, on a later date, the Senate, to ask that the war not be funded or supported by Congress. Such petitioning is a right guaranteed in the First Amendment. The protesters blocking entrance to each chamber did not leave when told to, and they went to jail for that symbolic emphasis on their conviction about the constitutional point. They had proclaimed their intent beforehand, and appealed to individual members of Congress, some of whom supported them.[15]

Why did the civil rights movement succeed in its first aim, of changing the climate of opinion on segregation, while the antiwar movement failed?

Martyrdom is one answer. The vicious response of some southern officials to Dr. King's efforts, leading to bombings and beatings, to the loosing of dogs and spraying of high-pressure hoses, even to murder, sickened parts of the country that witnessed the oppression on television. Though sections of the black community turned to violence in response, Dr. King held the movement to nonviolence long enough for its case to be made. Where the war was concerned, however, the establishment was not so manifestly evil. Though some tried to diabolize Lyndon Johnson, he was (in the eyes of most Americans) mistaken at the worst, not vicious. When four students were killed by the National Guard at Kent State in Ohio, the guardsmen seemed more frightened than evil. In the same way, policemen who lost their heads at the 1968 Democratic convention were trying to defend order, not racism. People were confused about the rights and wrongs of the war in ways that they could no longer be about blatant racism. The antiwar protesters were not making their case. On the contrary, they began to initiate violence themselves.

Some on the left continue to think they helped end the war in Vietnam. The best evidence is that they helped to prolong it. Before they resorted to violence, even some on the right were having doubts about Nixon's war, especially after he restored diplomatic relations with "Red China." *National Review,* for instance, was on the verge of opposing his reelection in 1972.[16] But the right's resentment of an increasingly clamorous and undisciplined drumbeat of protests against Nixon swung these conservatives' sympathies back to him. The nation's mood hardened as ex-SDS people like the Weathermen engaged in bombings or bomb threats. Civil disobedience had degenerated into terrorism. Any loon could now disrupt ordinary persons' lives with a credible threat. After bombs went off in three corporate headquarters in New York, on March 12, 1970, four hundred bomb threats were issued in the next twenty-four hours. At federal buildings alone there were 592 bomb threats in 1970, forcing 226 evacuations of the threatened buildings, at a taxpayer cost of $4 million.[17] Campuses were another favorite target. ROTC buildings were torched. I was then teaching at Johns Hopkins, and several times my class had to leave the building because of such threats. One of my classes was of adult students in the night school—people who had to get baby-sitters to attend, or make other sacrifices—and their bitterness at the intrusion into their lives outran their doubts about the wisdom of our Vietnamese venture.

On the other side, protesters less disciplined than the Berrigans were frustrated by the endless killings in Vietnam. They lost all sense of control or of communication with those who supported the war. They found in violence a drug even headier than heroin. They gave up the effort to persuade others in the name of expressing their own rage. Faculty members who had supported the students found it harder and harder to make a case for them, while those opposed became enraged themselves. In this cycle of mutual irritation the neoconservative movement was born, of ex-Democrats telling themselves horror stories about the young barbarians who had taken over whole universities.

Vietnam undid the New Left. It gave a focus for anger and attracted new members to the radical movement, but it blurred the original aims of that movement. "The Port Huron Statement" of 1962 ignored Vietnam, which was still a minor engagement of United States military "advisers." The statement was more concerned with quality-of-life issues. It addressed the growth of a rigid and hierarchical government during the crisis years stretching from the Depression through the Cold War. It might have been possible to reach ordinary Americans on such matters, especially since a break had been made with the Old Left and its communist connections: "the dreams of the older left were perverted by Stalinism, and never recreated."[18] The SDS saw its task as a form of teaching: "A new left must transform modern complexity into issues that can be understood and felt close-up by every human being."[19]

At the meeting where "The Port Huron Statement" was adopted by SDS, the socialist Michael Harrington was dismayed by the neglect of bread-and-butter issues like trade unionism. He tried to cut off support from the League for Industrial Democracy, out of which the SDS had emerged as a student branch.[20] This hastened the break with the Old Left. Before Vietnam became the issue, charges of collaboration with communism would have been hard to sustain against this body of students. Their movement did not start with class analysis, but with the psychology of affluent alienation. It was middle class, not working class, in its emphasis, centered around campuses, not around union halls. But when opposition to the war devoured the whole left agenda, two charges were launched with great effect—that the students were, after all, helping the communists in North Vietnam, or that (for all their talk of idealism) they were just running from the draft.

The differing outcome of disobedience by Dr. King's Southern Christian Leadership Conference and by the SDS illustrates an important truth about civil disobedience: it may express anti-government values like authenticity and participation, but it has little chance of succeeding if it attacks government itself rather than focusing on reforms *within* government. It should respect the general values of government while attacking abuses that undermine even those values. Dr. King told businessmen that segregation was *inefficient* as well as unjust, that it held back *progress* in the South, that it offended *cosmopolitan* views around the nation and the world, that it was *unpatriotic* to smirch the name of America with this offense.

The SDS began with similar protestations. It was trying to make the campus and the nation work more efficiently for all concerned. Rather than adopting a Thoreauvian contempt for all politics, it asked "that politics be seen positively, as the art of collectively creating an acceptable pattern of social relations."[21] It strove to break stalemate in Congress, to relax the brain-lock over Cold War issues, to build on civil rights successes. But there was no structure of discipline to hold the movement to these initial goals. Charismatic leadership was expressed in dramatic gestures against the war. Opposition was personalized in a hatred of Presidents Johnson and Nixon. Dr. King had voiced his own patriotism in his "I have a dream" speech, mingling the words of the old spirituals with the hymns of the nation: "My country, 'tis of thee." The New Left degenerated into expressions of support for Ho Chi Minh's despotism and the burning of the American flag. Anti-governmentalism of this sort does not destroy government. It destroys itself.

IX.

A Necessary Good

If anti-governmentalism has been, in most cases, so unsuccessful, should we just congratulate ourselves on being lucky enough to have any kind of government at all and stop grumbling? Obviously not. Like any human institution—like the family, or the university, or the labor union—governments fail and become dysfunctional or destructive at times. Even the best of governments will show on occasion most of the faults that governments are accused of—becoming wasteful, inefficient, impersonal, rigid, secretive, oppressive. But when marriages fail, we do not think it is because marriage is an evil in itself. Government is a necessary good, not a necessary evil; and what is evil in it cannot be identified and eliminated from the good if the very existence of the good is being denied at every level.

The view that government is a necessary evil, a concession to human frailty and viciousness, is often buttressed by quoting James Madison: "If men were angels, no government would be necessary" (F 51.349). But if men were angels, they would need no sexual partners, no education, no cooperation to feed and raise families. An angel (that fiction) has no body, no ignorant youth to be enlightened, no need for others. We do not conclude from this that sex and the family and education are evil in themselves. Being human is not an evil condition, but one needing completion from others, in love and companionship, in teaching and learning, in mutual support and correction—in all of which government has a part to play.

Why is it so difficult for Americans to admit this fact? One reason is that the semi-official philosophy of government we absorb, with various degrees of conscious articulation, is a vulgarized theory of John Locke's social contract, which teaches that government is founded on a necessary *loss* of freedom, not on the *enhancement* of liberty. Another reason is that a prudent watchfulness over governmental pretensions *is* imperative, and people fear that we will "let down our guard" if we grant that government is good in itself. To admit an essential goodness in government is not to say that everything governments do is good. But such a simplistic conclusion is encouraged as the only safeguard against a surrender to despotism. This section will consider these two matters separately—first the good of government in itself, then the need for vigilance against abuses of that good.

24.

The Uses of Government

The view that government is a necessary evil is assumed by many Americans because our dominant rationale for government in general has been a faded version of John Locke's theory of the social contract.[1] Our revolution leaned heavily on Locke's justification for what became the English Revolution of 1688 (bringing in a new monarch to replace the Stuart king, James II). Our popular conceptions subtly vulgarize Locke's theory since he said that human beings exchange a state of natural liberty for a state of social *liberty*; but his own language suggested—against his more nuanced views—that one was exchanging liberty for bondage:

> The only way whereby anyone *divests himself of his natural liberty and puts on the bonds of civil society* is by agreeing with other men to join and unite into a community, for their comfortable, safe and peaceable living, one amongst another, in a secure enjoyment of their properties and a greater security against any that are not of it (*Two Treatises* 2.8.95, emphasis added).

My students have taught me over the years that the way Locke is popularly misunderstood substitutes for his qualitative terms (one *kind* of liberty for another) merely quantitative ones: one gives up a part of one's potentially disruptive liberty in order to enjoy more security in one's possessions. If that is the case, then forming a government is a trade-off based on a continual calculation: how do I give away the least amount of my liberty, in return for the least burdensome amount of governmental security to life, limb, and property? This is a grudging grant—no matter how little liberty is given up, that still amounts to a deprivation of freedom. Government, no matter how necessary, has to be seen as a necessary *exaction*. We play a zero-sum game: whatever power accrues to the state is subtracted from the citizen's powers. One must be constantly vigilant, therefore, to see that the state takes away as little of one's freedom as possible. Government labors under the constant suspicion that it will exact more from the citizen's freedom than its services are worth. A person must resist it, make it justify any increase of its energy, be fearful of its every move. This is the theoretical justification for what I have been calling anti-governmentalism, and a great many Americans—perhaps most—think that this is the only theory of government entertainable in a modern democracy. Old religious and monarchical views were different. But the social contract has replaced those, just as Locke's majoritarianism replaced the authoritarianism of his principal theoretical opponent, Sir Robert Filmer, the author of the 1680 *Patriarcha: The Natural Power of Kings*.

Social contract theory begins, in Locke's view, with an assumption that the individual in a hypothetical pre-social condition would be complete and self-sufficient, like an enclosed circle centered on private interest. It is only the rub and challenge of others, equally intent on self-interest, that makes the individual cut away a bit of his or her circular completeness, as a concession that not everyone can get his or her way in a free clash of selfish interests. The state's power is an accumulation of these sacrificed bits of self-sufficiency. Thus *the other* is an enemy even before the state is formed. The inner self is violated by other selves, forcing it to the negotiated compromises of the social contract. Others, everyone outside my individuality, intrude upon my personal domain and make me sacrifice part of it to the state, in order to accommodate some minimal part of their demands, which are different from mine even when not directly opposed to me. Let me repeat that this position is not true to Locke's theories, or even to Thomas Hobbes's. But it is the attitude taken by our popular Lockeanism, and it approximates the views of some Lockean thinkers.[2] It is so prevalent that my students are surprised to hear that another theory of government can be taken seriously as more than an ancient superstition (e.g., the divine right of kings). They are especially surprised to hear that most thinkers in our Western tradition thought of government as a necessary good, not a necessary evil.

Modern social contract theory is, in fact, a bit of a latecomer (arising in the seventeenth and eighteenth centuries), conditioned by some historically circumscribed assumptions about psychology and anthropology. An older and still vibrant approach involves what might be called a division-of-labor theory of government. According to this view, the individual in a pre-social state is not free, but is imprisoned by unsatisfiable needs—exposed to the ravages of storm and beast (the sole *human* individual does not exist, even in hypothesis, apart from the rest of nature), unable to aspire above the animal level because of the cruelly attritive struggle to find, make, expand, or preserve things necessary to mere survival.

We should not, of course, think of the pre-social individual on the model of Robinson Crusoe. Daniel Defoe's character was post-social, in the sense that he brought with him into his accidental isolation not only many artifacts of the culture that formed him—guns, an axe, saws, nails, etc. from the shipwreck—but also the skills and concepts formed in that culture, his calculation of times and seasons, of means to accomplish tasks without a long process of trial and error over what works and what does not. He had an accumulation of practical knowledge (which things are edible, which animals are useful, how to make and control fire, and so on). The society he left not only made his axe, which is so useful to him as weapon or tool. It made *him*. He knows what to do with the axe, how to build with it, keep it from rust, turn it to things it can accomplish most efficiently. He learned all those things through prior social intercourse, before he was isolated. In order to imagine a truly *pre*-social individual, we would have to think of a Crusoe with total amnesia about the world he had left and without any artifacts from that world. Would such a person in fact be freer than he was back in England, no matter how undemocratic the government he had been living under?

One of the first theorists of a division of labor as the basis of society was Plato. In a thought experiment on how a state could properly be formed, he had Socrates, in Book II of *The Republic*, ask a series of questions suggestive of this line of reasoning: Would a farmer be better off raising all his crops himself, making his own plow, watching his own herds, making his own clothes and shoes, spinning his own fibers, skinning animals to make his own leather, felling the timber and forging the tools to make his own house, and so on—or would he be better off relying on others to do most of those things while he does the farming that they will rely on in exchange for the goods they supply him with? The answer is obvious, but Socrates indicates some of the reasons for this. Exigencies of time and season would make the farmer neglect his fields at crucial moments to do other urgent tasks. Unevenness of skill would make him waste time on things he does poorly and slowly, time wrenched away from tasks at which he is swifter and more productive. And no matter how productive he might be as a farmer, he could never create a surplus, since he must hurry off, once he had a sufficiency for his own immediate needs, to catch up with all the other tasks clamoring for his attention.

For Socrates in the dialogue, the pre-social individual is not a complete and enclosed system servicing one's own self. "The polity arises because each of us is not sufficient to our own needs, but deficient in many ways" (*Republic* 2.11). For him *the other* is not the enemy, something invading one's completeness. The other is needed to complete the individual's freedom. The self cannot be the self *without* the other. Richard Hooker was saying the same thing in the sixteenth century:

> But forasmuch as we are not by ourselves sufficient to furnish ourselves with competent store of things needful for such a life as our nature doth desire, a life fit for the dignity of man, therefore, to supply those defects and imperfections which are in us, living single and solely by ourselves, we are naturally induced to seek communion and fellowship with others.[3]

And this was David Hume's teaching in the eighteenth century. He writes in A *Treatise of Human Nature:*

> When every individual person labors apart and only for himself, his force is too small to execute any considerable work. His labor being employed in supplying all his different necessities, he never attains a perfection in any particular art. And as his force and success are not at all times equal, the least failure in either of these particulars must be attended with inevitable ruin and misery. Society provides a remedy for these three inconveniences. By the conjunction of force, our power is augmented. By the partition of employments, our ability increases.

And by mutual succor we are less exposed to fortune and accidents. It is by this additional *force, ability,* and *security* that society becomes advantageous (3.2.2, emphasis in original).

What has been described so far is just the exchange of goods. Why does that involve a government, the state? Hume said that the state's first function is judicial, to adjudicate equity in the division of labor and fairness in the exchange of goods. Our popular mythology makes the state the enemy of the free market. But without the state the free market could not exist. Market exchange is a form of contract, and the contracts would not be binding without some authority to enforce them. A businessman cheated by another businessman cannot form a private police force, to haul the accused into a court which consists of the aggrieved person judging his own case, and then to compel submission to the verdict. A third party must do that, in whom a sanctioning power has been recognized. And the standards by which its judgments are handed down must be codified as rules acceptable to all sides—whence the legislature. And the penalties must be exacted, the rules implemented—by an executive. The state, far from being an enemy of the market system, is both the market's product and its perpetuator.

So far we have discussed mainly physical exchanges, the division of labor in matters of the economy. But Aristotle had another, higher conception of the division of functions. For him, the incompleteness of man is not so much a matter of physical need as of intellectual and spiritual separation. What sets man apart is language, and that necessarily calls for exchanges at a deeper level than the marketplace of exchangeable *things*. Without a partner to some dialogue, the individual is, simultaneously, a signal sent out without any receiver, and a receiver that no signal is reaching. A human being's highest capacity is frustrated, not given its function, if he or she is kept in isolation. Such people are like isolated chess pieces, without either a board to move on or other pieces to make their moves meaningful. That is why Aristotle defines the human being as an "of-the-polis creature." Without intellectual interchange one cannot explore the nature of one's own capacities and virtues, teach and be taught, and then exercise those virtues. All the higher forms of communication—music, dance, the plastic arts—depend on mutual instruction, training, and performance based on language skills. Those who have traveled where there is no common language at all know how less-than-human one feels in such a situation. It is not that one cannot make one's physical needs known and satisfied—the currency of the place is itself a sign system that is easily recognized by all parties. Rather, the intimacy of communication of any but a fairly robotic nature seals off all that is best in human expressiveness and mutual enlightenment.

So far, on a kind of ladder of interchanges, we have moved up from physical marketing to intellectual dialogue as the basis for government. Is there a higher level to be reached? Without a stable society, where approachableness is assured by the disarming of apprehension, the benevolent instincts could not be satisfied. In that way the state makes love itself possible. As Hume says,

> In all creatures that prey not upon others and are not agitated with violent passions there appears a remarkable desire of company, which associates them together, without any advantage they can propose to reap from their union. This is still more conspicuous in man, as being the creature of the universe who has the most ardent desire of society, and is fitted for it by the most advantages. We can form no wish which has not a reference to society. A perfect solitude is perhaps the greatest punishment we can suffer (2.2.5).

For Hume, even deeper than the advantages society bestows in the form of physical satisfaction, there is a human sympathy that demands company and that works to make that companionship orderly. The need for love and affection shows that humans are incomplete without a respondent to that affection—as in Plato's myth that humans were primordially cut in two by Zeus and must seek out their other half through love.[4] The social order created by government is a necessary condition of that quest:

> By means of these two advantages in the *execution* and *decision* of justice, men acquire a security against each other's weakness and passion, as well as against their own, and, under the shelter of their governors, begin to taste at ease the sweets of society and mutual assistance (3.2.7, emphasis in original).

Saint Augustine, too, based the state on love. Since he felt that people were too divided (e.g., between Christianity and paganism) in ultimate orientation, he thought they could not base society, as Cicero maintained, on philosophical agreement. But even pagans and Christians can agree on their love for shared goods, and work together to protect them (*City of God* 19.24). The goods he is referring to are not only social peace and the treasured parts of one's cultural legacy, but the language of one's fellow citizens, along with the social amenities and comforts Hume listed. This shared love of what we possess in common is what we normally call patriotism, and even those who have anti-governmental instincts are often self-proclaimed patriots (an odd conjunction of attitudes).

On three levels, then, the physical, the intellectual, and the affectionate, the state can be seen as a positive good, not an invasion of the individual's domain but a broadening of his or her horizons—what Hume called the "expedient by which men cure their natural weakness" (3.2.7). All this may seem a little high-minded and vaporous to people who are complaining about their taxes, the bureaucracy, or business regulations. The arbitrary and petty acts of government are enough to make anyone grumble. But all human relationships grate or gall at times—which does not make us call the parent-child relationship, or the husband-wife bond, or friendship, mere necessary evils. They are necessary goods that do not uniformly please. Love itself is a bondage. But the inability to love would stifle and imprison far more cruelly.

Often people seem more resentful of government the slighter its intrusions are. I know men who feel they have lost their liberty if they are obliged to wear a seat belt or a motorcycle helmet. It is odd that they cavil at this while they submit to far more stringent restrictions. What could be more arbitrary, less founded on any point of justice or principle, than the order to drive only on the right side of the road (or the left, according to the country)? And that is just one of a series of disciplines imposed on drivers of cars or riders of motorcycles. You must be licensed by the state to engage in either activity, and you can be banned from the road entirely if you are not old enough, not able to read and write, too clumsy to pass a road test, too blind to see signs, or so defiant of such rules as to incur multiple violations. One must stop on the command of an inanimate red light or stop sign, yield to other drivers in a number of circumstances, drive at prescribed speeds (a maximum speed imposed everywhere, though at different levels place by place, and a minimum speed set on some highways). We are told where we *cannot* drive (the wrong way on one-way streets, the sidewalk, certain bus lanes, certain downtown areas at certain times). Truckers are even more thoroughly regulated, and must stay off many kinds of thoroughfare. We are told exactly how much (how little) alcohol we can drink if we are to be allowed to drive. The very vehicle must be licensed, and the license periodically renewed. A car must have a mandated quantity and kind of lights, mirrors, windshield wipers, and unobstructed windows. Its width and turning capacity are determined by the state. It must have functioning brakes, mufflers, horn, and other parts. It must pass pollution tests. The car itself and its action upon others must be insured to prescribed levels. The accumulation of minor impositions is really quite staggering when one stops to add them up. Adding a seat belt seems trivial next to all this prior regimentation. How can we really be free when we are continually triggered to obey on so many fronts?

Actually, these rules are immensely liberating. On the first level of social intercourse, they reflect a high degree of divided labor. We do not have to build our own cars, create their safety features, test their efficiency. Standardization of requirements means that we do not normally even think about how many mirrors or lights we must have. They are provided us by the economy of scale achieved in the manufacture of cars and motorcycles to expected specifications. Second, we do not have to create our own roads, or trespass on the patchy efforts of other individuals at making their own roads, or bump across a roadless landscape. We have roads provided us, of engineered contour, with freedom of passage through or around private property—roads cleared, maintained, and lit at night. If we all woke every morning, took out cars of uncertain performance, and tried to drive every which way, not heeding (nonexistent) signs or a right-side requirement, any speed laws or rules of precedence at crossings, we would either be crashing constantly, or would be immobilized by a fear of crashing or being crashed into. Because specialized activity has provided the roads and the rules as well as the vehicles, we speed on efficiently.

So much for the physical advantage of regulated social teamwork. Can a higher claim be made for the road rules? Well, we have a special language, a sign system, made up of the car's stoplights and turn signals, the hanging stoplights and roadside signs, the rules governing the side of the road to drive on, the times and places for stopping, the permissions to proceed. We are not simply obstructed or ordered about by inanimate things. We use those things to talk to each other, signaling our intent by the side of the road we drive on, the way we make turns, the way we slow down. If we lapse in consciousness, we stop "talking" and others are alerted that something is wrong (if, for instance, I am driving on the wrong side of the road or speeding through a stoplight). All this is a quiet triumph of human communication. And it enables us to get to places we could not otherwise reach—to school, or work, the library, the concert. We are all intellectually enriched by the rules of the road. That applies, *mutatis mutandis,* to other forms of transportation—to the safety drills, and equipment, and right-of-way procedures for boats, or to the metal detectors and other procedures for airplanes. Air travel broadens our intellectual horizons.

Would it be going too far to say that the rules of the road foster the social affections that Hume and St. Augustine spoke of? If cars get us to the library, they also get us to Grandmother's house. Planes rush us to loved ones who are sick or need help. But, more fundamentally, observing the road rules is a way of expressing one's concern for others' well-being. I know a man who accidentally killed a person with his car. Without reason he felt a burden of guilt ever after. Absent rules of the road, we would all inflict suffering not only on those hit or hurt or killed, but on those who would have to live with the thought of having been the agent of another's death. It is an act of compassion and mercy to spare both the victim and the driver that kind of misery. That is itself a form of social affection.

I have deliberately taken something rather trivial to illustrate the blessings of government. We do not often reflect on the multiple ways that government insensibly affects (and improves) our lives. We tend to advert to rules only when irritated by some peripheral annoyance connected with them. Is it too much to freight minor rules, like those of the road, with such meaning? Not, I suppose, if you are a person whose loved ones were killed by people defying the rules. But my point was to bring down the grander philosophical insights of Plato or Aristotle to a humbler level. If the philosophers are satisfying enough in themselves, you can be content with them. But I have employed these mundane examples just to work out, in a prosaic way, what G. K. Chesterton put in a brief parable, to show that social restraints can be liberating:

> We might fancy some children playing on the flat grassy top of some tall island in the sea. So long as there was a wall round the cliff's edge they could fling themselves into every frantic game and make the place the noisiest of nurseries. But the walls were knocked down, leaving the naked peril of the precipice. They did not fall over, but when their friends returned to them they were all huddled in terror in the center of the island; and their song had ceased.[5]

25.

The Uses of Fear

Despite all the good things government can do, it often ends up doing harmful and destructive things. So regular is this occurrence that some critics *personify* it as an evildoer. "Government always aggrandizes itself. Government preys on the weak." They talk as if government were some hypostatized entity apart from the people who direct it. Government can do nothing of itself. It needs human agents—kings, elected officials, appointed committees—to act with and for it. One and the same act of government will be seen as edifying or destructive by people who are included or neglected in the benefits of the act. Most such acts are not completely good or completely evil, but uneven in their effect. Because so many people are affected by anything governors do, the reports on their activity are always contradictory.

There are many things that limit what services governments can perform. For one thing, we often impose conflicting demands on them. We want our government to be efficient yet we want it to be accountable. The one, if it does not preclude the other, continually impedes it. It slows anyone down if he has to keep explaining what he is doing while he is doing it. Our criminal justice system is complicated and laborious, because its procedures must be tested every inch of the way. Trials drag on, it seems, forever. It would be far more efficient just to lynch people charged with a crime. Our pharmaceutical companies could produce medicine at greatly reduced cost if they did not have to meet government regulations. Of course, in the one case you might lynch the wrong man, and in the other you might take medicines defective enough to be poisonous. That is the cost of efficiency divorced from accountability. The cost of accountability divorced from efficiency has been demonstrated in a number of the investigations undertaken by the Office of the Independent Counsel.

Sometimes, of course, we get the worst of both worlds—no accountability *and* no efficiency. Senator Daniel Patrick Moynihan has provided many examples of this in his book *Secrecy*—cases of weapons developed or bought in secrecy so as to be more effective, but where the very secrecy hid from Congress and the public a *lack* of the weapons' effectiveness.[1] Secrecy has been the great enemy of accountability in our government since World War II, and the source of the greatest danger to democracy itself. It got an unmerited boost from the Manhattan Project, which developed the atom bomb during World War II. In most respects that project was a miracle of efficiency, precisely because accountability was suspended. The government did not have to explain or justify its commandeering of resources. It could order the nation's top physicists to give up their own research projects, report for work at Los Alamos, submit to military supervision (their phones were tapped, their mail opened), and perform as directed while cut off from their normal communities.

Though there was military accountability of the scientists and other workers to the officers over them, there was no political accountability to Congress or the voters—money was secretly devoted to the project, a project whose wisdom could not be discussed, reviewed, or made the subject of electoral approval. Of course, secrecy in wartime is normal, is so expected that it would have been extraordinary if the atomic project had not been kept secret. Nonetheless, just because it was taken for granted, the problem of secrecy has not ordinarily been addressed with regard to the Manhattan Project. It is worth asking just what was supposed to be accomplished by the secrecy.

The Constitution, which demands from Congress an open accounting of the money it dispenses and the debates it conducts, allows for "*secrecy and dispatch*" in the executive branch (F 64.434–46). The President must deal with foreign governments, both friendly and hostile, where confidentiality is needed in diplomacy (the prevention of war) and strategy (the waging of war). An actual enemy should be prevented, so far as that is possible in a free government, from knowing our military resources, intentions, and schedules. In the case of the atom bomb, German knowledge of the state of our research and the intensity of our effort might have led to a new level of concentration on their own atomic research. (On the other hand, at a stage too late for others to catch up, knowledge of our capacity might have weakened the will to fight on.)

There was a further reason for keeping this new weapon secret from others, beyond our enemies of the moment. The bomb was destructive on such a scale that it could not be trusted to others, who might not use it as responsibly as we felt ourselves to be doing. Even a nation that could use the scientific capacity and economic resources to replicate our development might not bring itself to devote so much of its vital national treasure to this one effort, unless it were given a shortcut around all the initial obstacles by access to our secrets. This meant that the bomb would remain shrouded in secrecy even after the war, with most nations excluded from information about its creation.

There was a third reason for the secrecy, not part of its official rationale, that became more important as time went on, both during and after the war. If American politicians and voters knew what was going on at Los Alamos, they would probably, given the wartime atmosphere, have acquiesced in the project's purpose; but they would have wanted to know more about its chances of success, among other things to make sure men and materiel were not being diverted from other efforts of more certain outcome. Some might even have objected to the use of such a weapon on moral grounds (as they would have objected to the use of poison gas or bacteriological war). Having to explain or justify its action, the government would have disseminated information useful to the enemy. But even aside from that, the effort at justifying the task would get in the way of concentration on the task, accountability warring once again with efficiency.

Looking back at the secrecy of Los Alamos, we can see that it was only moderately successful in its first aim. The Germans knew about our atomic effort, but for the period when they might have done something about it, they did not suppose our success would come soon enough to win the war, and they knew that diverting their own attention to a matching effort would reduce the chance of prevailing with conventional arms, before we had time to produce a usable bomb. They were confirmed, in a sense—we did not have the bomb by the time war in Europe was over, though that was the arena it was being designed for. Only the extra months of war with Japan gave us an opportunity to get the hoped-for return on our investment.

As for secrecy's second purpose, keeping knowledge of the bomb's manufacturing secrets from other countries (and especially from Russia, our distrusted but necessary ally), that was a stupendous failure. Klaus Fuchs and David Greenglass, working at Los Alamos, found ways to smuggle information to Russia by way of Julius Rosenberg and others. Another spy at Los Alamos probably did even more damage—Theodore Alvin Hall, whose role only recently became public knowledge, though the FBI had discovered it in 1950, by which time Hall was teaching physics in England.[2] Thanks to Fuchs and Hall, the Russians—who could have built the bomb on their own by 1948—were able to test a successful atomic explosion in 1947. In this area, despite the most thorough security procedures at Los Alamos, secrecy was a terrible flop.

But the third area was a total success—the American people were served without having to waste time explaining what was being done on their behalf. Since it was not known yet that some secrets were already stolen by Russia, the Manhattan Project offered a very tempting model for future government action. It seemed the way to accomplish great things in a hurry, behind a veil of "national security" that precluded scrutiny by outsiders, American citizens as well as foreign nationals. The American people had to be both excluded from knowledge of the bomb's secrets and convinced that continuing secret research (even though that posed dangers of radiation from domestic tests) was vital to their safety and power. The government embarked on a mission to "sell" the bomb. Our future as a superpower rested on our monopoly of this weapon, and it would have maximum effect only if we could make a credible threat to use it again. If it was moral to use it twice, a need for it could arise again.

Revulsion against the bomb, it was decided, should not be allowed to accomplish what was done after World War I with mustard gas—the banning of such a weapon from *all* future use. (We proposed, in the Baruch Plan, that *others* not be allowed to develop a nuclear capacity.) The elements of opposition to use of the bomb were emerging, to the horror of James B. Conant, the president of Harvard who had been a supervisor of the Manhattan Project. He quarreled with his admired mentor, the "realistic" theologian Reinhold Niebuhr, when the latter signed a statement by church leaders that use of the bomb on Hiroshima and Nagasaki was "morally indefensible."[3] Conant became more panicky when John Hersey described the horrors of Hiroshima in *The New Yorker* and Norman Cousins called for its total abandonment in *The Saturday Review*. Conant arranged for answers to be published—by MIT president Karl Compton (in *The Atlantic*) and by former secretary of war Henry L. Stimson (in *Harper's*).

The Stimson article was important because quasi-official. President Truman's endorsement of it was sought and gained. Conant would not leave the composition of it to the seventy-seven-year-old Stimson, who expressed great reluctance at writing it. Conant got a draft from Stimson by way of McGeorge Bundy, who was ghostwriting Stimson's memoirs. Then Conant thoroughly rewrote the draft, leaving out things like Stimson's suggestion that the Japanese could have been offered the chance to surrender while retaining their emperor ("the problem of the Emperor diverts one's mind from the general line of argumentation," Conant wrote).[4] The letter used a shamelessly inflated projection of American casualties if the bomb had not been used (a million men, *ten times* the military's own estimate for killed, wounded, or missing).[5] Conant, a university president, was afraid that professors would mislead students, so he engaged in some pre-emptive misleading, his way of guarding against people who are "sentimental and verbally minded and in contact with our youth." McGeorge Bundy gloated that the Stimson letter would silence such professors, "one or two of my friends who fall into Mr. Conant's unkindly classification of the 'verbal minded,' " and he concluded: "I think we deserve some sort of medal for reducing these particular chatterers to silence."[6]

Secrecy had been used to develop the bomb. Deception would be used to sell it. The American people would be told only what was good for them. In the testing of weapons over the next two decades, lies and evasions and cover-ups were used to minimize the effects of fallout. Stewart Udall has called this "the most long-lived program of public deception in U.S. history."[7] The purpose of such secrecy was not to deceive the Russians, who soon had their own fallout to measure, but to keep from the American people an awareness of the threat to their safety and health. This became the pattern of future secrecy. Fidel Castro knew that the CIA was plotting and performing sabotage in Cuba before Soviet missiles were placed there. Nikita Khrushchev knew it, too. Only the Americans did not. And Kennedy had to lie about that, saying there was no American aggression to provoke Castro into such an act. Our enemies knew what we did not. Secrecy almost always entails not only the withholding of truth but also positive acts of deception, like Kennedy's.

The "secret bombing" of Cambodia in 1970 was no secret to the Cambodians. You tend to know about bombs when they are being dropped on you. But the American people had to be fooled, since they might have protested an action being taken in their name. In the same way, we could not be told when foreign leaders were ousted or assassinated with our government's complicity or control.

Who could be told? Only a band of initiates cleared to read classified information, the high priests of a mystical "national security." For years Americans were assured that they would see the wisdom of the Vietnam War if only they were qualified to know the secrets our leaders were privy to. When the Pentagon Papers were leaked, the Nixon administration tried to prevent their publication, not because of any secrets they could reveal to an enemy, but because they showed that our leaders did *not* have any clear and convincing rationale or justification for their bumbling into war. Once the priesthood is installed, preventing embarrassment to the initiates is a continuing reason for secrecy, long after the immediate occasion for it has disappeared. Being privy to secrets becomes not only a mark of distinction in itself but also a great reason for keeping out the uninitiated, who might see that the high priest has no clothes. When Admiral William Crowe, the former chairman of the Joint Chiefs of Staff, expressed doubt about President Bush's launching of the Gulf war to a Senate committee, Secretary of State James Baker told the committee that the admiral no longer had access to classified cables. That was supposed to be enough to disqualify Crowe's views. And if he, with his experience of government and the military, had no right to an opinion, then you and I, mere citizens, have less than no right. We have surrendered the entire decision-making faculty to the rituals of secrecy.

Often secrecy itself prevents the use of information gathered and stored away from the public. The government had evidence of the guilt of Alger Hiss and the Rosenbergs, but it was gleaned from Russian messages published, long after, as the Venona intercepts—and the government would not disclose the information for fear of revealing that we had cracked the code. The recurrent irony works even here—the Russians already knew we had cracked the code because a cipher clerk, William W. Weisband, working at Arlington Hall, the Venona decryption station, had informed them.[8] As at Los Alamos, the government had locked the public out and locked a spy inside. Once again, only our citizenry was fooled.

When John Kennedy, campaigning against the Eisenhower administration, accused it of letting a "missile gap" widen, Eisenhower could not answer that U-2 flights had discovered there was no Russian missile superiority—there was, in fact, a great inferiority—because he did not want to reveal the existence of the U-2. The Russians knew about that plane. It flew above their rockets, but not above their radar. They were working to bring it down—and eventually did. We were kept in the dark so there could be no discussion of air rights. Not the enemy but the friend is to be deceived in such a case.

Senator Moynihan argues persuasively that misguided policies were formed and clung to in secret because the chance to air opinions about them, to hear criticism of them, to justify them in debate, was precluded. And once mistakes or crimes are committed, the urgency to conceal them becomes even more intense. Secrecy has an inner dynamic of inevitable growth. The more you have of it, the more you need. That is why the end of the Cold War did not, as one might logically have expected, lead to a decrease of secrecy but to "a stunning 62 percent *increase* in new secret documents."[9] When Augusto Pinochet was held in England for a possible trial for atrocities he committed in Chile, we could not fully cooperate with the world tribunal, since that would entail the revelation of our part in bringing down Salvador Allende to make way for Pinochet. Efforts to find out about the murder of Jesuits and nuns in El Salvador could lead to embarrassing discoveries about our actions there. We have an immense backlog of things to hide.

One of the things accountability is meant to do is reassure the public that its interests are being properly served. Withholding information creates a general air of suspicion that has corroded public trust in government, giving an especially bitter new edge to our tradition of anti-governmentalism. One of the reasons there are so many conspiracy theories about everything from the death of President Kennedy to the downing of various air-liners is that we have found, too late, that many things we thought we understood were actually the result of secret actions we were never supposed to know about. If it has happened so often before, why not again, why not now?

So, there is ample reason to fear and distrust government, to probe it, make it come clean, demand access. This is as true of the little lies of the bureaucracy, and the campaign managers, and the crooked congressmen, as of the big lies that we were fed during the Cold War. The necessary good is betrayed by those who work against its very nature as a representative system, who deny accountability. We can stand some inefficiency when it is the necessary concomitant of accountability. To get neither is the curse of a government machinery that protects itself more than the people it is meant to serve. But only paranoia can turn these truths into a belief that government is in itself a necessary evil, inevitable in its denial of freedom, to be attacked on all counts and at all times. The values that the opponents of government espouse—populist and rights-oriented authenticity—can be defended without assailing the other values that government can legitimately embody (expertise, division of labor, authority). The sterile opposition noticed in the examples I have given from history arises only when the government is perceived as always and in all things the enemy.

Most of the forms of fear and resistance traced in this book were futile. Some of them tried to meet force with force, and were outnumbered. Others tried to deny the power of government to do harm by denying it the power to do much of anything. A few tried to use secrecy themselves in order to fight secrecy. Others met poor performance on the government's part with indifference and abstention on their part, matching contempt for the government with a contempt for the people. The cures were worse than the ills they addressed.

The snobbish withdrawal from politics, the Menckenian cynicism, may at times be more corrosive than dramatic opposition of John Brown's sort. He at least began with a hope that citizens might respond to a moral appeal. Where he erred was in his manner of appealing to them, not in any belief that they should be the arbiters. Charles Dunlap, in his criticism of NRA appeals to a right of armed insurrection, makes an excellent point. He says it is not the armed citizen but the unarmed one who has been a real threat to modern governments. Government power grows in an atmosphere of threat and violence, as recent tyrannies have shown. But unarmed protest throws those in government off balance:

> The civil rights struggles of the 1960s were won not by force of arms, but by peaceful protest and civil disobedience. Where the government tried to use force against unarmed resisters, the results were often counterproductive. The spectacle of fire hoses and police attack dogs employed against civil rights protesters galvanized public opinion against discriminatory practices. Similarly, when National Guardsmen fired upon unarmed students during anti-war protests at Kent State University in 1970, the tragedy became an important influence in reversing policy on Vietnam.[10]

No one had better excuse for distrusting or hating government than Dr. King, not only for its long history of racial injustice but because of its specific acts against him. He was spied on and bullied by the FBI, actively plotted against by local and state officials, sometimes abandoned by the federal government. But he appealed to the government itself, to its promises, to the Declaration of Independence, the Gettysburg Address. He never gave up his hopes for the government, though God knows he had reason (or at least the temptation) to do so. He never concluded that the proper response to hate is anything but love. The corrective to the flaws of government, that necessary good, is more good.

Conclusion

How are we to explain the deep-seatedness of the anti-government tradition in our history? I have suggested some of the confluent influences in the course of this book—the lack of a symbolic center (religious or political) at our origins, the air of compromise in our Constitution's formation (which made it vulnerable to the reversal of Federalist and Antifederalist values), the Jeffersonian suspicion of the Constitution (which Madison abetted at one stage), a jostling of competitive states' claims (reaching a climax in the secession of the South), a frontier tradition, the "Lockean" individualism of our political theory, a fervent cult of the gun. All these were added, in overlapping layers, to the general anti-authoritarian instincts of mankind. Our history gave a particular twist to each strand in the skein of our past.

But the instinctive urge that kept all these forces quick to the touch was that cluster of anti-government values identified at the outset of this book. These grew out of the elements just listed, but they took on a life of their own, especially as they cross-pollinated in mutually confirming ways. Their strength came from the fact that no one can really challenge them as valuable parts of the human outlook. Who, after all, can deny that authenticity, amateurism, spontaneity, candor, tradition, rights, and religion are important to human society? But by persistently bringing these qualities to bear directly on debate over *government,* we indulged in a confusion of categories.

Take one of the more astounding assumptions of our political life, the belief that government should be inefficient. It is true that the citizenry in general, we political amateurs, should choose representatives to govern us, and that those who represent us should be "like us" in basic values. But it is a wild leap (though a common one) to think that our representatives should be no more professional than we are in political matters. We should choose our own doctors, but we do so in the expectation that they are *unlike* us in their training and skills. We do not want inefficient doctors to treat us, inefficient lawyers to represent us, inefficient teachers to educate us, inefficient pilots to fly us. Why should we want inefficient politicians to govern us?

The answer too readily offered is that a government unable to do much of anything will be unable to oppress us. Inefficiency is to be our safeguard against despotism. History offers no warrant for this hope. Inefficient governments are often the most despotic. Just look at the Soviet Union, or at its tsarist predecessor. In your own observation of life around you, has inefficacy been a protection against the arbitrariness of an employer, the random vindictiveness of a teacher, the insecure bluster of a physician?

We turn money over to our government for certain tasks. Do we want that money to be wasted? Do we want inefficient soldiers and law enforcers? The government compiles information on the basis of which we make vital decisions. Do we want inefficient reports on air accidents, the healthiness of meat, the rate of unemployment, the growth of inflation? Whatever the virtues of the amateur in other areas of life, we want a certain expertise in these matters.

The same is true of the other anti-governmental values constantly brought to bear on political discussion, where they have less worth than elsewhere. Localism is a virtue in the social life of a community. But in any more extended government, being locked within the locale of one's residence creates a clash of local views without the release Madison found in a *removal* from local pressures. Religion is a vital aspiration of the soul; but government works best when it does not reach into the recesses of the soul, but keeps a secular practicality about it. This is proved by the fact that America, the first country to adopt the separation of church and state, is the most religious country in the industrialized West.

This should give us an important clue for dealing with the polarized values that kept asserting themselves in this history of our attitudes toward government. The "anti-governmental" value of religion is best protected by a "governmental" secularism in the state. The same will be found to be true with other values in our list. The anti-governmental values are protected within their proper sphere when governmental attitudes are stressed more vigorously in the realm of the state. Spontaneity is safer in private life when there is predictability in the public order. "Authentic" emotion will find less vent for lynchings, in that case; and trials will be more impersonally authoritative; but freedom will be the greater for this "faceless" proceduralism.

Populism should give everyone a voice in government; but once that voice has elected certain officials, they become an "elite" (the word is just "elected" in French), and it makes no sense for the people to resent what they have themselves brought about. What they have a right to resent is an official who does *not* act like a professional chosen for his qualification to do a job. Who can attack a doctor for being too skilled?

What has crippled our political discourse is a long-indurated habit of demanding from government qualities that should be sought, primarily, in other aspects of our social life. Government plays a limited role in human activity, and it should have the aspects suited to its limits. It cannot be the family, the church, the local club, the private intellectual circle—all of which show the anti-governmental qualities some seek to impose on the state. When government does not show all the human virtues, it is rejected as contributing to none of them. That asks too much of government, as a preliminary to expecting nothing of it. This is admittedly an American tradition. But it is a tradition that belittles America, that asks us to love our country by hating our government, that turns our founding fathers into unfounders, that glamorizes frontier settlers in order to demean what they settled, that obliges us to despise the very people we vote for. Our country, our founders, our representatives deserve better. So do we, who sustain them all.

Notes

Introduction

1. Henry David Thoreau, "Civil Disobedience," in *Walden, and Civil Disobedience*, edited by Owen Thomas (New York: Norton, 1966), p. 224.
2. *Meyers v. United States*.
3. *United States v. Brown*.
4. Walter Bagehot, *The English Constitution* (Oxford: Oxford University Press, 1974), p. 2.
5. Arthur O. Lovejoy, *Reflections on Human Nature* (Baltimore: Johns Hopkins University Press, 1961), pp. 46–47.
6. Carol M. Rose, "The Ancient Constitution vs. the Federalist Empire: Anti-Federalism from the Attack on 'Monarchism' to Modern Localism," *Northwestern University Law Review* 84 (1990), pp. 74–105.
7. Henry Cabot Lodge, *The Works of Alexander Hamilton*, vol. 1 (New York: Putnam's Sons, 1903), p. ix. Claude Bowers, *Jefferson and Hamilton* (Boston: Houghton Mifflin, 1925). For Roosevelt's endorsement of the Bowers thesis (in the only book review he ever published), see Merrill D. Peterson, *The Jefferson Image in the American Mind* (New York: Oxford University Press, 1960), pp. 351–52.

Part I. Revolutionary Myths

1. Minutemen

1. William Pierce, the secretive author of *The Turner Diaries*, was a former assistant to George Lincoln Rockwell in the American Nazi party. See the 1995 Anti-Defamation League Research Report, *William L. Pierce, Novelist of Hate*.

2. The militias' use of the Vietnam analogy is described by James William Gibson in *Warrior Dreams: Paramilitary Culture in Post-Vietnam America* (New York: Hill and Wang, 1994), pp. 142–47. The analogy occurred in William Pierce's *The Turner Diaries* (Gibson, p. 222).

3. Wayne LaPierre, *Guns, Crime, and Freedom* (Washington, D.C.: Regnery, 1994), pp. 19–20.

4. W. Scott Thompson and Donaldson Frizzell, *The Lessons of Vietnam* (Bristol, Pa.: Crane, Russack, 1977), p. 279. As early as September 1972, Hammond Rolph was writing in *Asian Survey* (p. 785) that "We are no longer studying a true guerrilla insurgency. A regular professional army is operating outside its borders in conventional style. . . ." A year later, Chalmers Johnson wrote: "In terms of the first sense of guerrilla warfare—the one in which the concepts of peasant mobilization, an anti-imperialist national front, clandestine munitions and possible sanctuary support from allies, and protracted war are central—none of the people's wars of the sixties did very well, including the one in Vietnam" (*Autopsy on People's War* [Berkeley: University of California Press, 1973], p. 46). See also Harry G. Summers Jr., *On Strategy* (Novato, Calif.: Presidio, 1982), pp. 71–92.

5. J. Bowyer Bell, *The Myth of the Guerrilla: Revolutionary Theory and Malpractice* (New York: Knopf, 1971), pp. 255–57.

6. For President Kennedy's fascination with "counterinsurgency" see Douglas S. Blaufarb, *The Counterinsurgency Era: U.S. Doctrine and Performance, 1950 to the Present* (New York: Free Press, 1977), pp. 52–88.

7. Cecil B. Currey, *Edward Lansdale, The Unquiet American* (Boston: Houghton Mifflin, 1988), pp. 153–55.

8. Don Higginbotham, *War and Society in Revolutionary America* (Columbia: University of South Carolina Press, 1988), pp. 155, 170.

9. William Casey, *Where and How the War Was Fought: An Armchair Tour of the American Revolution* (New York: Morrow, 1976), p. 9.

10. Gen. John R. Galvin, U.S. Army, *The Minute Men*, 2d ed. (Dulles, Va.: Pergamon-Brassey's International Defense, 1989).

11. Gary Hart, *The Minuteman: Restoring an Army of the People* (New York: Free Press, 1998), p. 77.

12. Akhil Reed Amar and Alan Hirsch, *For the People: What the Constitution Really Says About Your Rights* (New York: Free Press, 1998).

13. Charlton Heston, Speech to National Press Club, Sept. 14, 1997 (on NRA web site): The right to bear arms "is the right we turn to when all else fails. That's why the Second Amendment is America's first freedom."

14. John Shy, *A People Numerous and Armed*, rev. ed. (Ann Arbor: University of Michigan Press, 1993), p. 39.

15. W. W. Abbot et al., *The Papers of George Washington, Colonial Series*, vol. 3 (Charlottesville: University Press of Virginia, 1984), pp. 106–11; and Fred

Anderson, *A People's Army: Massachusetts Soldiers and Society in the Seven Years' War* (Chapel Hill: University of North Carolina Press, 1984), pp. 75–76.

16. David Hackett Fischer, *Paul Revere's Ride* (New York: Oxford University Press, 1994), pp. 156, 161.
17. Michael A. Bellesiles, "The Origins of the Gun Culture in the United States, 1760–1865," *Journal of American History*, September 1996, p. 429.
18. Margaret Burnham Macmillan, *The War Governors in the American Revolution* (New York: Columbia University Press, 1943), p. 36.
19. Bellesiles, pp. 426–28.
20. M. L. Brown, *Firearms in Colonial America: The Impact on History and Technology, 1492–1792* (Washington, D.C.: Smithsonian Institution, 1980), p. 307. Even in the early nineteenth century, American gunsmiths still tediously created the entire gun, without division of labor—see Merritt Roe Smith, *Harpers Ferry Armory and the New Technology: The Challenge of Change* (Ithaca, N.Y.: Cornell University Press, 1977), pp. 52–68.
21. Brown, p. 337.
22. George F. Scheer and Hugh F. Rankin, *Rebels and Redcoats* (Cleveland: World, 1957), p. 86.
23. Ibid., pp. 66–67.
24. Brown, p. 306.
25. Bellesiles, pp. 428, 432.
26. Fischer, pp. 170, 168–69, 143–44.
27. Shy, p. 35.
28. The "slave patrol" mission given to the militias in southern states is typified in Georgia's 1755 militia act, empowering the militia "to disperse, suppress, kill, destroy, apprehend, take, or subdue . . . any company of slaves who shall be met together or who shall be lurking in any suspected places where they may do mischief, or who shall have absented themselves from the service of their owners." See A. Leon Higginbotham, *In the Matter of Color: Race and the American Legal Process: The Colonial Period* (New York: Oxford University Press, 1978), p. 259; and John Hope Franklin, *From Slavery to Freedom: A History of Negro Americans*, 5th ed. (New York: Knopf, 1980), pp. 135–36.
29. Shy, p. 37.
30. Ibid., p. 40.
31. James Kirby Martin and Mark Edward Lender, *A Respectable Army: The Military Origins of the Republic, 1763–1789* (Wheeling, Ill.: Harlan Davidson, 1982), p. 19.
32. Douglas Southall Freeman, *George Washington*, vol. 1 (New York: Scribner's, 1948), pp. 330–31.
33. Robert A. Gross, *The Minutemen and Their World* (New York: Hill and Wang, 1976), pp. 59–61, 69–71.

34. Ibid., p. 60. Fischer, p. 153.
35. Charles Royster, A *Revolutionary People at War: The Continental Army and American Character, 1775–1783* (Chapel Hill: University of North Carolina Press, 1979), p. 11.
36. Ibid., p. 71.
37. Ibid., pp. 37, 41.
38. Dumas Malone, *Jefferson the Virginian* (Boston: Little, Brown, 1948), p. 344.
39. Elisha P. Douglass, "Thomas Burke, Disillusioned Democrat," *North Carolina Historical Review,* 1949, pp. 185, 174.
40. Higginbotham, p. 116.
41. Martin and Lender, pp. 132–33.
42. Royster, p. 326.
43. Ibid., p. 67. The corruption ran up from the lowliest to the highest, from the recruiter who gave bounties to nonexistent enlistees (p. 71) to the secret and "extra-legal" land grants Governor Patrick Henry made to George Rogers Clark to induce him to take his rangers into the western theater (Malone, pp. 308–309).
44. Higginbotham, p. 114.
45. Shy, pp. 239–43: "Popular military service was as old as the colonies, but never before had its performance or avoidance defined political categories. . . . The broad popular basis of military organization forced thousands of more or less unwilling people to associate themselves openly and actively with the cause."
46. Ibid., p. 240.
47. Pauline Maier, *From Resistance to Revolution* (New York: Knopf, 1972), pp. 28–84, on "disciplined collective coercion" as opposed to mob action.
48. Steven Rosswurm, "The Philadelphia Militia, 1775–1783: Active Duty and Active Radicalism," in *Arms and Independence,* edited by Ronald Hoffman and Peter J. Albert (Charlottesville: University Press of Virginia, 1984), pp. 75–118.
49. Martin and Lender, pp. 17–19.
50. Higginbotham, p. 108. For the bad relations of militias and Regulars in the French and Indian War, see Anderson, pp. 111–41.
51. Royster, pp. 346–47.
52. Martin and Lender, p. 197.
53. John C. Fitzpatrick, ed., *The Writings of George Washington*, vol. 8 (Washington, D.C.: U.S. Government Printing Office, 1931–44), pp. 203–204. The importance of preachers on the local level is seen in Chapter 4 of Gross.

2. Term Limits

1. David Hackett Fischer, *The Revolution of American Conservatism* (New York: Harper & Row, 1965), pp. 31–32.
2. Alexis de Tocqueville, *Democracy in America,* vol. 1, edited by Phillips Bradley (New York: Knopf, 1976), p. 62.
3. Fischer, p. 4.
4. David Hackett Fischer, *Albion's Seed: Four British Folkways in America* (New York: Oxford University Press, 1989), p. 198.
5. *The Works of John Adams,* vol. 2 (Boston: Charles C. Little and James Brown, 1850), p. 144.
6. Charles Francis Adams, *Three Episodes of Massachusetts History,* vol. 2 (Boston: Houghton Mifflin, 1893), pp. 966–67.
7. John Fairfield Sly, *Town Governments in Massachusetts* (Cambridge: Harvard University Press, 1930), pp. 54–57.
8. An example of the caucusing Adams did with his allies at the Continental Congress was the "club" that held weekly meetings to change the supply system for the Continental Army. See H. James Henderson, *Party Politics in the Continental Congress* (New York: McGraw-Hill, 1974), p. 113. Even after the Constitution was adopted, secret caucuses provided contingency plans for defeating certain measures, maneuvers John Quincy Adams called "evidently the result of consultation out-of-doors" (when out-of-doors influence was condemned). See Robert M. Johnstone Jr., *Jefferson and the Presidency* (Ithaca, N.Y.: Cornell University Press, 1978), pp. 123–24.
9. Margaret Burnham Macmillan tells the story of Clinton's efforts in *The War Governors in the American Revolution* (New York: Columbia University Press, 1943), pp. 129–30.
10. Henderson, pp. 339–40.
11. Ibid., p. 405.
12. Ibid., pp. 157–58, 283.
13. Dumas Malone, *Jefferson the Virginian* (Boston: Little, Brown, 1948), pp. 342–43.
14. John McAuley Palmer, *General Von Steuben* (New Haven: Yale University Press, 1937), p. 253.
15. Malone, p. 347.
16. Macmillan, pp. 216–17.
17. Malone, p. 361.
18. Macmillan, p. 76.
19. Ibid., pp. 78–79.
20. Ibid., p. 91.
21. Jackson Turner Main, *The Sovereign States* (New York: Watts, 1973), p. 194.

22. Ibid., p. 194.
23. Benjamin Perley Poore, *Federal and State Constitutions*, vol. 1 (Washington, D.C.: U.S. Government Printing Office, 1877), p. 958.
24. George F. Will, *Restoration: Congress, Term Limits and the Recovery of Deliberative Democracy* (New York: Free Press, 1992), p. 110.

Part II. Constitutional Myths

3. Sovereign States

1. Ronald Reagan, *An American Life* (New York: Simon & Schuster, 1990), p. 196.
2. *The Works of James Wilson*, vol. 2, edited by Robert Green McCloskey (Cambridge: Harvard University Press, 1967), p. 829. Elbridge Gerry, FC 1.467. Nathan Dane, *A General Abridgement and Digest of American Law*, Appendix, vol. 9 (Boston, 1829), pp. 10–54. John Quincy Adams, *An Oration to the Citizens of the Town of Quincy, on, 1831 the Fourth of July*. Joseph Story, *Commentaries on the Constitution of the United States* (Boston: Little, Brown, 1891), pp. 157–58. *The Papers of Daniel Webster*, vol. 1, edited by Charles M. Wiltse and Alan R. Berolzheimer (Hanover, N.H.: Dartmouth University Press, 1986), p. 251. Andrew Jackson in James D. Richardson, *A Compilation of the Messages and Papers of the Presidents, 1789–1902*, vol. 2 (Washington, D.C.: U.S. Government Printing Office, 1905), pp. 1203–19.
3. Pauline Maier, *American Scripture: Making the Declaration of Independence* (New York: Knopf, 1997), p. 123. Though Maier admits the states showed "deference" to the Congress (p. 75), she refers repeatedly to the state instructions as declarations of independence in their own right.
4. Ibid., pp. 63, 75.
5. Richard B. Morris, "The Forging of the Union Reconsidered," *Columbia Law Review* 74 (1974), p. 1089. Morris notes that the Continental Congress performed such sovereign acts as demanding an oath of allegiance (p. 1085), trying for treason to itself (p. 1084), adjudicating war prizes (p. 1081), and—above all the rest—declaring a state law unconstitutional (p. 1081).
6. Benjamin Rush, writing as "Nestor," *American Herald*, June 19, 1786.
7. Merrill Jensen, *The Articles of Confederation* (Madison: University of Wisconsin Press, 1940), pp. 161–76.
8. Jensen's simplistic division of the delegates at the Continental Congress into reactionaries and radicals is destroyed by a sophisticated voting analysis of

the Congress's actions in H. James Henderson, *Party Politics in the Continental Congress* (New York: McGraw-Hill, 1974), pp. 130–56.

9. Merrill Jensen, *The Documentary History of the Ratification of the Constitution*, vol. 1 (Madison: State Historical Society of Wisconsin, 1976), pp. 124–25.

10. Elisha P. Douglass, "Thomas Burke, Disillusioned Democrat," *North Carolina Historical Review* 26 (1949), pp. 162, 150.

11. John Locke, *Two Treatises of Government*, 8th ed., II, 95–98.

12. Rush.

13. Lois G. Schwoerer, *No Standing Armies: The Antiarmy Ideology in Seventeenth-Century England* (Baltimore: The Johns Hopkins University Press, 1974), p. 5. See also p. 33 on the locus of sovereignty shifting with control of the military.

4. Checking Efficiency

1. George Washington, *Writings* (New York: Library of America, 1997), p. 643. See also pp. 622, 635, 646.

2. Aristotle, *Politics* 1252b33.

3. Charles F. Hobson, "The Negative on State Laws: James Madison, the Constitution, and the Crisis of Republican Government," *William and Mary Quarterly*, 1979, pp. 215–35.

4. The first audience for *The Federalist* was the voters for delegates to the New York ratifying convention. Madison speaks for New York at F 41.275.

5. F 17.108, 18.110, 19.119, 120, 122.

6. John Taylor of Caroline, *New Views of the Constitution of the United States* (Washington, D.C.: Way and Gideon, 1823), p. 168.

7. Madison to Jefferson, June 27, 1823.

5. Co-equal Branches

1. F 18.110, 112, 20.124, 126 (twice), 22.138 (thrice), 139 (thrice).

2. *The Federalist Concordance*, which lists only two uses of co-equal, misses this one.

3. Balance of interests or motives: F 10.60, 54.372, 74.502. Society or government in general: F 2.10, 85.594 (quoting Hume). Trade: F 11.72, 35.216.

4. Organization of departments: F 37.237, 38.245, 42.282, 45.313. Distribution of powers: F 37.237, 41.268, 47.323 (twice), 51.349.

5. The President's reports were not exacted at a set date but "from time to time." That did not mean "occasionally" in the legal use of the framers. Like other reports—of money, of proceedings—the presidential reports might not be readily made on a predetermined schedule (e.g., in the midst of an interna-

tional crisis or delicate treaty negotiations). But "from time A to time B, from time B to time C" was understood—that is, leaving no period unreported. That is clear from the accounts exacted of moneys spent or of records kept, even though both of these, also, were to be rendered "from time to time." Whenever a report was made, it had to begin from the point where the last one ended. Compare Article I, Section 5, Clause 3 and Article I, Section 9, Clause 7 with Article II, Section 3. Madison spoke of a man elected "from time to time," which did not mean at disjunct or sporadic points in time, but "term after term" (M 17.316).

6. George Washington, *Writings* (New York: Library of America, 1997), pp. 749–50.

6. The Uses of Faction

1. George F. Will, *Restoration: Congress, Term Limits and the Recovery of Deliberative Democracy* (New York: Free Press, 1992), p. 4.
2. George F. Will, *Statecraft as Soulcraft: What Government Does* (New York: Simon & Schuster, 1983), p. 39.
3. Ibid., p. 39.
4. Ibid., p. 133.

7. Bill of Rights

1. Paul Finkelman, "James Madison and the Bill of Rights: A Reluctant Paternity," *Supreme Court Review*, 1990, pp. 328–33.
2. Bernard Schwartz, *The Bill of Rights: A Documentary History*, vol. 2 (New York: McGraw-Hill, 1971), p. 1027.
3. Ibid., p. 1032.
4. Ibid., p. 1113.
5. Jonathan Elliot, *Debates in the State Conventions*, vol. 1 (Philadelphia: Lippincott, 1941), p. 326.
6. Lester Cappon, *The Adams-Jefferson Letters*, vol. 1 (Chapel Hill: University of North Carolina Press, 1959), p. 279.
7. Schwartz, p. 1033.
8. Akhil Reed Amar, *The Bill of Rights* (New Haven: Yale University Press, 1998), pp. 145–62.

8. No Standing Army

1. J. R. Western, *The English Militia in the Eighteenth Century* (Toronto: University of Toronto Press, 1965), pp. 54–71.
2. Lois G. Schwoerer, *No Standing Armies: The Antiarmy Ideology in Seventeenth-Century England* (Baltimore: The Johns Hopkins University Press, 1974), pp. 33–38.
3. Ibid., p. 5.
4. Carl T. Bogus, "The Hidden History of the Second Amendment," *U. C. Davis Law Review* 31 (Winter 1998), pp. 309–408.
5. Wilson Armistead, *Anthony Benezet* (Philadelphia: Lippincott, 1859), p. 78.
6. Bernard Schwartz, *The Bill of Rights: A Documentary History*, vol. 2 (New York: McGraw-Hill, 1971), p. 1025.
7. Richard R. Beeman, *Patrick Henry* (New York: McGraw-Hill, 1974), pp. 170–73.
8. Robert E. Shalhope, *John Taylor of Caroline: Pastoral Republican* (Columbia: University of South Carolina Press, 1980), pp. 99, 119.

Part III. Nullifiers

9. John Taylor of Caroline: Father of Nullification

1. John Taylor, *An Inquiry into the Principles and Policy of the Government of the United States* (Indianapolis: Bobbs-Merrill reprint, 1969), chaps. 4 (Funding) and 5 (Banking). See C. William Hill Jr., *The Political Theory of John Taylor of Caroline* (Rutherford, N.J.: Fairleigh Dickinson University Press, 1977), pp. 112, 114: "Taylor was never willing to recognize any mitigating circumstances for banking. Its effects were thoroughly harmful. . . . Of all the Jeffersonians, few except for Taylor and John Randolph opposed all forms of banking, including state banking systems." Taylor so disapproved of credit and stock holders that he would have disqualified them for service in Congress—see Robert E. Shalhope, *John Taylor of Caroline: Pastoral Republican* (Columbia: University of South Carolina Press, 1980), p. 81.
2. Shalhope, p. 129.
3. John Taylor of Caroline, *Arator: Being a Series of Agricultural Essays, Practical and Political, in Sixty-Four Numbers*, 6th ed. (Petersburg, Va.: John M. Carter, 1818), pp. 94–95.

4. Shalhope, p. 23.
5. Rufus Ernst, *Rufus King: American Federalist* (Chapel Hill: University of North Carolina Press, 1968), pp. 200–202.
6. John Taylor of Caroline, *An Enquiry into the Principles and Tendency of Certain Public Measures* (Philadelphia: Dobson, 1794), pp. 53–56.
7. John Taylor of Caroline, *New Views of the Constitution of the United States* (Washington, D.C.: Way and Gideon, 1823), p. 68.

10. *Jefferson: Prophet of Nullification*

1. Jefferson's opponents, suspicious that he was plotting secretly against Adams, tried to find evidence of his "sedition" (RL 2.1000, 1009, 1071, 1108–1109, 1116).
2. Leonard Labaree et al., *The Papers of Benjamin Franklin*, vol. 4 (New Haven: Yale University Press, 1961), pp. 484–85.
3. Leonard Levy, *Jefferson and Civil Liberties: The Darker Side* (Cambridge: Harvard University Press, 1963), pp. 28–41.
4. The harshest sentence (eighteen months) went to a man who put up a Revolutionary liberty pole—though the man's partner in the "crime" apologized and was given six hours in jail.
5. The whole nation laughed when a man was put on trial for saying that a cannon shot fired as President Adams went by should have gone straight up his arse.
6. See Robert Murray, *Red Scare: A Study in National Hysteria, 1919–1920* (Minneapolis: University of Minnesota Press, 1955). For other laws worse than the Alien and Sedition Acts—including the Espionage Act of 1917 and the Alien Act of 1918—see John R. Schmidhauser, "Civil Liberties," in *Encyclopedia of the American Presidency*, vol. 1, edited by Leonard Levy and Louis Fisher (New York: Simon & Schuster, 1994), pp. 199–203.
7. Dumas Malone, *Jefferson and the Ordeal of Liberty* (Boston: Little, Brown, 1962), p. 405.

11. *Madison: Abettor of Nullification*

1. Irving Brant, *James Madison*, vol. 3 (Indianapolis: Bobbs-Merrill, 1941–61), p. 331.

12. *Nullification North: Hartford Convention*

1. J.C.A. Stagg, *Mr. Madison's War* (Princeton: Princeton University Press, 1983), pp. 3–47.

2. Forrest McDonald, *The Presidency of Thomas Jefferson* (Lawrence: University Press of Kansas, 1976), pp. 115–17, 137, 141.

3. Leonard Levy, *Jefferson and Civil Liberties: The Darker Side* (Cambridge: Harvard University Press, 1963), p. 119.

4. Henry Adams, *History of the United States of America During the Administrations of Thomas Jefferson* (New York: Library of America, 1986), p. 1106.

5. Levy, pp. 119, 137.

6. Merrill Peterson, *Thomas Jefferson and the New Nation* (New York: Oxford University Press, 1970), pp. 889, 913.

7. Ibid., pp. 913, 917.

8. Henry Adams, *The Life of Albert Gallatin* (Philadelphia: Lippincott, 1879), pp. 369–70.

9. Levy, pp. 211–14.

10. Louis Martin Sears, *Jefferson and the Embargo* (New York: Octagon, 1966), p. 187.

11. Adams, *Administrations of Jefferson*, p. 1211.

12. Sears, p. 185.

13. Herman V. Ames, *State Documents on Federal Relations* (Philadelphia, 1911), p. 370.

14. Adams, *Administrations of Jefferson*, p. 215.

15. Samuel Eliot Morison, *Harrison Gray Otis*, vol. 2 (Boston: Houghton Mifflin, 1913), pp. 63–64, 97–98, 151.

16. Ames, p. 58.

17. Stagg, p. 477.

18. Henry Adams, *History of the United States of America During the Administrations of James Madison* (New York: Library of America, 1986), p. 1092.

19. Ibid., p. 1061.

20. Stagg, p. 473 (Madison to Wilson Cary Nicholas, Nov. 25, 1814).

21. Ibid., pp. 477–82.

22. Morison, pp. 147–59.

23. Adams, *Administrations of Madison*, p. 1122.

24. James M. Banner Jr., *To the Hartford Convention: The Federalists and the Origins of Party Politics in Massachusetts, 1789–1815* (New York: Knopf, 1970), p. 349.

25. Morison, p. 151.

26. Adams, *Administrations of Jefferson*, pp. 56–57.

27. Morison, pp. 105–06.

13. Nullification South: John C. Calhoun

1. William W. Freehling, *Secessionists at Bay, 1776–1854*, vol. 1 of *The Road to Disunion* (New York: Oxford University Press, 1990), p. 147.

2. William W. Freehling, *Prelude to Civil War: The Nullification Controversy in South Carolina, 1816–1836* (New York: Harper & Row, 1966), p. 290.
3. Ibid., p. 208.
4. Drew R. McCoy, *The Last of the Fathers: James Madison and the Republican Legacy* (New York: Cambridge University Press, 1989), p. 151.
5. John C. Calhoun, *Exposition and Protest*, in *Union and Liberty: The Political Philosophy of John C. Calhoun*, edited by Ross M. Lence (New York: Library of America, 1992), pp. 346, 348.
6. Ibid., p. 371.
7. Freehling, *Prelude*, p. 263.
8. Richard E. Ellis, *The Union at Risk: Jacksonian Democracy, States' Rights, and the Nullification Crisis* (New York: Oxford University Press, 1987), p. 87.
9. Freehling, *Secessionists*, p. 281.
10. Robert V. Remini, *Andrew Jackson: The Course of American Freedom* (Baltimore: The Johns Hopkins University Press, 1981), p. 233.
11. Freehling, *Secessionists*, pp. 278–79.
12. Freehling, *Prelude*, pp. 274–78.
13. Ibid., pp. 78–80.
14. Alexis de Tocqueville, *Democracy in America*, vol. 1, edited by Phillips Bradley (New York: Knopf, 1976), p. 413.
15. William C. Davis, *Jefferson Davis: The Man and His Hour* (New York: Harper-Collins, 1991), p. 177.
16. Tocqueville, pp. 410–11.
17. Ibid., p. 411.
18. Ibid., pp. 263–65.

14. Academic Nullifiers

1. The professors' arguments, though advanced in a series of articles for the law journals, are most easily found in their books—Amar's *For the People: What the Constitution Really Says About Your Rights*, written with Alan Hirsch (New York: Free Press, 1998), and *The Bill of Rights* (New Haven: Yale University Press, 1998), Ackerman's *We the People, 1: The Foundations* (Cambridge: Harvard University Press, 1991) and *We the People, 2: Transformations* (Cambridge: Harvard University Press, 1998). Professors at other universities (e.g., Sanford Levinson of the University of Texas) agree with many if not all of the Yale men's theses.
2. "Guards at Mall Escape Flogging Indictment," *New York Times*, June 28, 1995, p. A17.
3. "Militias Are Joining Jury-Power Activists to Fight Government," *Wall Street Journal*, May 25, 1995, p. A1.

4. William W. Freehling, *Prelude to Civil War: The Nullification Controversy in South Carolina, 1816–1836* (New York: Harper & Row, 1966), pp. 210–11.
5. Ibid., pp. 271–78.
6. Amar and Hirsch, pp. 109–10.
7. Ibid., pp. 110–12.
8. Andrew Jackson, Proclamation of 1832, in James D. Richardson, *A Compilation of the Messages and Papers of the Presidents, 1789–1897*, vol. 2 (Washington, D.C.: U.S. Government Printing Office, 1899), p. 642.
9. Amar and Hirsch, p. 29.
10. Ackerman, *Foundations*, pp. 54–55.
11. Ibid., p. 271.
12. Ibid., p. 92.

Part IV. Seceders

15. Civil War

1. Lance Banning, "Virginia: Sectionalism and the General Good," in *Ratifying the Constitution*, edited by Michael Allen Gillespie and Michael Lienesch (Lawrence: University Press of Kansas, 1989), pp. 264–66.
2. Gerard H. Clarfield, *Timothy Pickering and the American Republic* (Pittsburgh: University of Pittsburgh Press, 1980), pp. 219–28.
3. Bennett Milton Rich, *The Presidents and Civil Disorder* (Washington, D.C.: Brookings, 1941), p. 44.
4. James D. Richardson, *A Compilation of the Messages and Papers of the Presidents, 1789–1897*, vol. 2 (Washington, D.C.: U.S. Government Printing Office, 1899), p. 1213.
5. William W. Freehling, *Secessionists at Bay, 1776–1854*, vol. 1 of *The Road to Disunion* (New York: Oxford University Press, 1990), pp. 309–52.
6. Ibid., p. 103.
7. James Oakes, *Slavery and Freedom* (New York: Knopf, 1990), p. 101.
8. Don E. Fehrenbacher, *Sectional Crisis and Southern Constitutionalism* (Baton Rouge: Louisiana State University Press, 1995), pp. 147–54.
9. Ibid., pp. 155–56.
10. Ibid., p. 151.
11. Ibid., pp. 156–57.

Part V. Insurrectionists

16. From Daniel Shays to Timothy McVeigh

1. David P. Szatmary, *Shays' Rebellion: The Making of an Agrarian Insurrection* (Amherst: University of Massachusetts Press, 1980), p. 103.
2. Ibid., pp. 108–109.
3. Howard Zinn, *A People's History of the United States, 1492–Present*, 2d ed. (New York: HarperPerennial, 1995), p. 94.
4. Thomas P. Slaughter, *The Whiskey Rebellion: Frontier Epilogue to the American Revolution* (New York: Oxford University Press, 1986), p. 182: "the writs were a bluff."
5. Henry Adams, *The Life of Albert Gallatin* (Philadelphia: Lippincott, 1879), pp. 135–37.
6. Slaughter, p. 200.
7. Ibid., p. 201.
8. James Thomas Flexner, *George Washington* (Boston: Little, Brown, 1969), p. 168.
9. Slaughter, p. 215.
10. Flexner, p. 176.
11. Murray Kempton observed that President Eisenhower had the military sense to know that many troops keep order when he sent a huge contingent of marines in his one overseas commitment of force (in the Lebanon crisis of 1958): "The Underestimation of Dwight D. Eisenhower," *Esquire*, September 1967.
12. Adams, p. 139, and Flexner, p. 175.
13. Slaughter, pp. 223–25.
14. Sarah N. Bradford, *Harriet: The Moses of Her People* (New York: Lockwood, 1897), p. 33.
15. Henry Mayer, *All on Fire: William Lloyd Garrison and the Abolition of Slavery* (New York: St. Martin's, 1998), pp. 408–10.
16. William H. Pease and Jane H. Pease, *The Fugitive Slave Law and Anthony Burns: A Problem in Law Enforcement* (Philadelphia: Lippincott, 1975).
17. Bradford, pp. 122–27.
18. Oswald Garrison Villard, *John Brown, 1800–1859: A Biography Fifty Years After* (Boston: Houghton Mifflin, 1910), pp. 158, 166.
19. Stephen B. Oates, *To Purge This Land with Blood: A Biography of John Brown* (New York: Harper Torchbooks, 1970), pp. 241–42.
20. C. Vann Woodward, "John Brown's Private War," in *America in Crisis: Four-*

teen Crucial Episodes in American History, edited by Daniel Aaron (Hamden, Ct.: Archon, 1971), p. 117.

21. Frederick Douglass, *Autobiographies* (New York: Library of America, 1994), p. 760.
22. Villard, pp. 498–99.
23. Ibid., p. 646.
24. Abraham Lincoln, *Speeches and Writings, 1859–1865* (New York: Library of America, 1989), p. 125.
25. Russell Banks, *Cloudsplitter* (New York: HarperFlamingo, 1998), pp. 596, 621.
26. John Shy and Thomas W. Collier, "Revolutionary War," in *Makers of Modern Strategy: From Machiavelli to the Nuclear Age*, edited by Peter Paret (Princeton: Princeton University Press, 1986), p. 858.
27. Arthur Marwick, *The Sixties* (New York: Oxford University Press, 1998), pp. 749–50.
28. Mark S. Hamm, *Apocalypse in Oklahoma: Waco and Ruby Ridge Revenged* (Boston: Northeastern University Press, 1997), pp. 122–28.
29. Ibid., p. 105.
30. Ibid., pp. 1–5.
31. William Pierce, *The Turner Diaries* (Arlington, Va.: National Vanguard, 1978), p. 2.
32. Richard A. Serrano, *One of Ours: Timothy McVeigh and the Oklahoma City Bombing* (New York: Norton, 1998), p. 218.

17. Academic Insurrectionists

1. Glenn Harlan Reynolds, "To Keep and Bear Arms: An Exchange," *New York Review of Books*, Nov. 16, 1995, p. 62.
2. Ibid., p. 61.
3. Sanford Levinson, "The Embarrassing Second Amendment," *Yale Law Journal* 99 (December 1989), p. 656.
4. Akhil Reed Amar and Alan Hirsch, *For the People: What the Constitution Really Says About Your Rights* (New York: Free Press, 1998), p. 175.
5. Ibid., p. 100.
6. Interview with Amar: Jonathan Mahler, "The Federalist Capers," *Lingua Franca*, September 1998, p. 47.
7. David P. Szatmary, *Shays' Rebellion: The Making of an Agrarian Insurrection* (Amherst: University of Massachusetts Press, 1980), pp. 127–28.
8. Jonathan Elliot, *Debates in the Several Conventions*, vol. 4 (Philadelphia: Lippincott, 1836), Appendix, p. 446.
9. William M. Wiecek, *The Guarantee Clause of the U.S. Constitution* (Ithaca, N.Y.: Cornell University Press, 1972), pp. 39–40.

10. George M. Dennison, *The Dorr War: Republicanism on Trial, 1831–1861* (Lexington: University Press of Kentucky, 1976), pp. 92–96. As had happened with the Whiskey Rebellion, the President *did* send federal troops after the rebels had dispersed.
11. R. Kent Newmyer, *Supreme Court Justice Joseph Story: Statesman of the Old Republic* (Chapel Hill: University of North Carolina Press, 1985), pp. 362–65.
12. Robert V. Remini, *Daniel Webster: The Man and His Time* (New York: Norton, 1997), pp. 640–42.
13. Wiecek, pp. 111–29.
14. Glenn Harlan Reynolds, "A Critical Guide to the Second Amendment," *Tennessee Law Review* (Spring 1995), pp. 466–67.
15. Joseph Story, *A Familiar Exposition of the Constitution of the United States* (New York: American Book, 1840), p. 265.
16. Ibid., p. 261.
17. David C. Williams, "Civic Republicanism and the Citizen Militia: The Terrifying Second Amendment," *Yale Law Journal* 101 (December 1991), p. 584.
18. Madison, *Letters and Other Writings*, edited by William C. Rives and Philip R. Fendall (Washington, D.C.: U.S. Government Printing Office, 1865), vol. 4, p. 80.
19. James D. Richardson, *A Compilation of the Messages and Papers of the Presidents, 1789–1897*, vol. 2 (Washington, D.C.: U.S. Government Printing Office, 1899), p. 1212.
20. David C. Williams, "The Constitutional Right to 'Conservative' Revolution," *Harvard Civil Rights–Civil Liberties Law Review* 32 (Summer 1997), pp. 427–38.
21. Williams, "Civic Republicanism," pp. 597–613.
22. Amar and Hirsch, pp. 138–68.
23. Ibid., p. 162.
24. Sanford Levinson, "To Keep and Bear Arms: An Exchange," *New York Review of Books*, Nov. 16, 1995, p. 61.
25. Wayne LaPierre, *Guns, Crime, and Freedom* (Washington, D.C.: Regnery, 1994), pp. 19–20.
26. Charles J. Dunlap, "Revolt of the Masses: Armed Civilians and the Insurrectionary Theory of the Second Amendment," *Tennessee Law Review* 62 (Spring 1995), pp. 663–66.
27. Amar and Hirsch, pp. 160, 172, 130, 139.

Part VI. Vigilantes

18. Groups: From Regulators to Clinic Bombings

1. Richard Maxwell Brown, *The South Carolina Regulators* (Cambridge: Harvard University Press, 1963), pp. 19–20, 135.
2. Ibid., p. 51. For the undermining of the militia, see pp. 23, 57.
3. Ibid., pp. 58–60.
4. Ibid., pp. 91–92, 204–205.
5. Roger Lotchin argues that California reversed Richard Hofstadter's claim that America was born in the country and moved to town; in California, urban patterns came first and were imposed on the countryside. Lotchin, *San Francisco, 1846–1856: From Hamlet to City* (New York: Oxford University Press, 1974), p. 347.
6. David A. Williams, *David C. Broderick: A Political Portrait* (San Marino, Calif.: Huntington Library, 1969), pp. 11–27.
7. Lotchin, pp. 227–36.
8. Williams, pp. 114–27.
9. Lotchin, pp. 262–63.
10. Ibid., p. 261.
11. Richard Maxwell Brown, *Strain of Violence: Historical Studies of American Violence and Vigilantism* (New York: Oxford University Press, 1975), p. 128.
12. Woodrow Wilson, *A History of the American People*, vol. 9 (New York: Harper & Brothers, 1902), pp. 58–59.
13. Tony Horwitz, *Confederates in the Attic: Dispatches from the Unfinished Civil War* (New York: Pantheon, 1998), p. 153.
14. Allen W. Trelease, *White Terror: The Ku Klux Klan Conspiracy and Southern Reconstruction* (New York: Harper & Row, 1971), p. 294.
15. Wilson, p. 63.
16. Trelease, pp. 3–5.
17. Wilson, p. 60.
18. Jack Hurst, *Nathan Bedford Forrest* (New York: Knopf, 1993), pp. 286–87.
19. Horwitz, p. 153.
20. Hurst, p. 177: "[If] Forrest ordered no massacre, he probably didn't have to; there was enough rancor between his men and the armed former slaves, as well as the Tennessee Unionists, that about all he had to do to produce a massacre was issue no order against one. This seems particularly true in view of the terms of his habitual demand that the enemy should surrender or die."
21. Ibid., p. 313.

22. Ibid., p. 329.
23. Wilson, pp. 62–63.
24. Horwitz, p. 53.
25. Hurst, pp. 330–31, 345–47.
26. Kenneth Stampp, *The Era of Reconstruction, 1865–1877* (New York: Knopf, 1970), pp. 201–203.
27. Edmund Wilson, *Patriotic Gore: Studies in the Literature of the American Civil War* (New York: Oxford University Press, 1962), p. 544.
28. Ibid., p. 546.
29. Ibid., p. xviii.
30. Horwitz, p. 199.
31. Trelease, p. xxi.
32. Helena Huntington Smith, *The War on Powder River* (New York: McGraw-Hill, 1966), pp. 32–33.
33. Ibid., pp. 57–67.
34. Ibid., pp. 121–34.
35. Ibid., pp. 196–219.
36. David Caute, *The Great Fear: The Anti-Communist Purge Under Truman and Eisenhower* (New York: Simon & Schuster, 1978), p. 515.
37. Ellen Schrecker, *Many Are the Crimes: McCarthyism in America* (Boston: Little, Brown, 1998), p. 143.
38. Marcy J. Wilder, "The Rule of Law, the Rise of Violence, and the Role of Morality," in *Abortion Wars: A Half Century of Struggle, 1950–2000*, edited by Rickie Solinger (Berkeley: University of California Press, 1998), p. 82.
39. Ibid.
40. Dallas A. Blanchard and Terry J. Prewitt, *Religious Violence and Abortion* (Gainesville: University Press of Florida, 1993), pp. 39, 116, 122, 144.
41. Ibid., p. 81.
42. Wilder, p. 82.
43. Blanchard and Prewitt, p. 64.
44. James Risen and Judy L. Thomas, *Wrath of Angels: The American Abortion War* (New York: Basic Books, 1998), p. 193.
45. Ibid., pp. 211–12.
46. CNN Interactive, July 15, 1998, p. 1.
47. Risen and Thomas, pp. 343–44, 362–64.
48. *The Abortion Rights Activist*, Nov. 5, 1998, p. 1.
49. Daniel Voll, "The Righteous Man with the Hit List," *Esquire*, February 1999, pp. 111–19. A successful suit was brought against the web site, on the grounds that it was threatening doctors' lives.

19. Individuals: Frontier

1. Joseph G. Rosa, *Taming of the West: Age of the Gunfighter* (New York: Smithmark, 1993), p. 106. Rosa, a British expert on firearms of the nineteenth century, is the source for much of this chapter.
2. Perry D. Jamieson, *Crossing Deadly Ground: United States Army Tactics, 1865–1899* (Tuscaloosa: University of Alabama Press, 1994), p. 55. "Church, William Conant," in *Dictionary of American Biography*, vol. 2, edited by Allen John and Dumas Malone (New York: Scribner's, 1930), pp. 131–32.
3. Martha Derthick, *The National Guard in Politics* (Cambridge: Harvard University Press, 1965), pp. 18, 20, 49, 94.
4. Joseph G. Rosa, *The Gunfighter: Man or Myth?* (Norman: University of Oklahoma Press, 1969), p. 185.
5. Ibid., pp. 125–27.
6. Allen Barra, *Inventing Wyatt Earp: His Life and Many Legends* (New York: Carroll and Graf, 1998), p. 174.
7. Joseph G. Rosa, *They Called Him Wild Bill: The Life and Times of James Butler Hickok* (Norman: University of Oklahoma Press, 1964), pp. 14–30.
8. Rosa, *The Gunfighter*, p. 204.
9. Ibid., pp. 195–96.
10. Ibid., p. 184.
11. Ibid., p. 186.
12. Ibid., pp. 186–88.
13. Ibid., pp. 204–207.
14. Ibid., pp. 197–200.
15. Robert R. Dykstra, *The Cattle Towns* (Lincoln: University of Nebraska Press, 1968), pp. 121–48.
16. Barra, p. 42.
17. Dykstra, p. 134.
18. William H. McNeill, *The Great Frontier: Freedom and Hierarchy in Modern Times* (Princeton: Princeton University Press, 1983), pp. 10–13.
19. Dykstra, pp. 79–82.
20. Jamieson, pp. 13–14, 55, 174. John S. Hutchins, "Mounted Riflemen: The Real Role of Cavalry in the Indian Wars," in *Probing the American West* (Santa Fe: Museum of New Mexico Press, 1962), pp. 79–85. Frank Gilbert Roe, *The Indian and the Horse* (Norman: University of Oklahoma Press, 1955), pp. 229–31. Robert M. Utley, *Frontier Regulars: The United States Army and the Indian, 1866–1891* (New York: Macmillan, 1973), p. 49.
21. Women's suffrage was meant to increase the number of women coming west and to give a greater vote to the stable parts of the community. Wyoming adopted it as a territory in 1869 and as a state in 1890. Kansas adopted it at

the municipal level in 1887, and Colorado (1893), Utah (1896), and Idaho (1896) as state law. In 1914, all states west of the Rocky Mountains but one (New Mexico) had woman suffrage, all states east of the Rockies but one (Kansas) lacked it. By 1917, there were eleven woman suffrage states and eight of them had Prohibition laws. Alan P. Grimes, *The Puritan Ethic and Woman Suffrage* (New York: Oxford University Press, 1967), pp. xi, 131. Aileen S. Kraditor, *The Ideas of the Woman Suffrage Movement, 1890–1920* (Garden City, N.Y.: Anchor, 1971), p. 3.

22. W. Eugene Hollon, *Frontier Violence: Another Look* (New York: Oxford University Press, 1974), pp. 212–13.

23. Ibid., pp. 194–216. Richard A. Bartlett, *The New Country: A Social History of the American Frontier, 1776–1890* (New York: Oxford University Press, 1974), pp. 401–48. Roger D. McGrath, *Gunfighters, Highwaymen, and Vigilantes: Violence on the Frontier* (Berkeley: University of California Press, 1984), pp. 261–71.

24. Ray Allen Billington, *Westward Expansion: A History of the American Frontier*, 3d ed. (New York: Macmillan, 1967), p. 678.

25. Richard E. Lingenfelter, *The Hardrock Miners: A History of the Mining Labor Movement in the American West, 1863–1893* (Berkeley: University of California Press, 1974), p. 23.

26. Robert R. Dykstra, "Field Notes: Overdosing on Dodge City," *Western Historical Quarterly* 27 (Winter 1996), pp. 513–14.

20. Individuals: NRA

1. *The Constitution of the United States of America: Analysis and Interpretation*, edited by Lester S. Jayson (Washington, D.C.: U.S. Government Printing Office, 1973), pp. 1035–36.

2. "Whitehill, Robert," in *Dictionary of American Biography*, vol. 10, edited by Dumas Malone (Charles Scribner's Sons, 1936), pp. 104–05.

3. Bernard Schwartz, *The Bill of Rights: A Documentary History*, vol. 2 (New York: McGraw-Hill, 1971), pp. 1143–54.

4. Stephen P. Halbrook, *That Every Man Be Armed: The Evolution of a Constitutional Right* (Albuquerque: University of New Mexico Press, 1984), p. 219.

5. Articles of Confederation, Articles VII and VIII (R 1.89). For use of the term with the same sense in the drafting process, see R 1.79–81. It had the same meaning in *The Federalist* (F 25.158).

6. Don B. Kates Jr., "Handgun Prohibition and the Original Meaning of the Second Amendment," *Michigan Law Review* 82 (1983), pp. 219, 261.

7. In Shakespeare, civil war is "self-borne arms" (*Richard II*, 2.3.80) and just war is "just-borne arms" (*King John* 2.1.345).

8. Stephen P. Halbrook, *A Right to Bear Arms* (Westport, Ct.: Greenwood, 1989), p. 56.
9. Schwartz, p. 1026.
10. Robert Dowlut, "Federal and State Constitutional Guarantees to Arms," *University of Dayton Law Review* (Spring 1995), p. 69, and Kates, pp. 220, 267.
11. Quotation from seventeenth-century pamphlet in Richard Ashcraft, *Revolutionary Politics and Locke's "Two Treatises of Government"* (Princeton: Princeton University Press, 1986), p. 118.
12. John Trenchard, *An Argument Shewing That a Standing Army Is Inconsistent with a Free Government* (London, 1697), p. 21.
13. Sanford Levinson, "The Embarrassing Second Amendment," *Yale Law Journal* 99 (December 1989), pp. 657-59.

Part VII. Withdrawers

21. Individuals: From Thoreau to Mencken

1. John Quincy Adams, Journal for June 18, 1833.
2. Ralph Waldo Emerson, "Politics," in *Essays and Lectures* (New York: Library of America, 1983), pp. 559–71.
3. For the dependence of Thoreau's civil disobedience essay on Emerson's "Politics," see Raymond Adams, "Thoreau's Sources for 'Resistance to Civil Government,' " *Studies in Philology* 42 (1945), pp. 6422–45.
4. "Civil Disobedience" in *Walden, and Civil Disobedience*, edited by Owen Thomas (New York: Norton, 1966), p. 239. The following quotes from that essay are to be found on pp. 236, 240–41, 243, 241, 238, 239, 232, 229–30, 228–29, 224.
5. Ibid., p. 115. Later quotes from pp. 112–13.
6. Robert D. Richardson, *Henry Thoreau: A Life of the Mind* (Berkeley: University of California Press, 1986), p. 348.
7. Emerson, "Thoreau," in Norton *Walden*, p. 279.
8. Henry Seidel Canby, *Thoreau* (Boston: Houghton Mifflin, 1939), p. 357.
9. Joseph Wood Krutch, *Henry David Thoreau* (New York: Sloane, 1948), p. 194.
10. Ibid., p. 205.
11. Ibid., p. 208.
12. Canby, p. 183.
13. Krutch, p. 139.

14. Canby, pp. 345–53.
15. Henry Adams, *Democracy,* in *Novels* (New York: Library of America, 1983), pp. 7, 99.
16. Henry Adams, *The Education of Henry Adams,* edited by Ernest Samuels (Boston: Houghton Mifflin, 1973), p. 512. Following quotations from pp. 502, 147, 417, 394, 509.
17. Material on Nock, *The Freeman,* and Buckley from John Judis, *William F. Buckley, Jr.: Patron Saint of the Conservatives* (New York: Simon & Schuster, 1988), pp. 44–46, 89, 102, 108, 112, 114, 122–24, 130, 213; George H. Nash, *The Conservative Intellectual Movement in America Since 1945* (Wilmington, Del.: Intercollegiate Studies Institute, 1996), pp. 11–16; and Garry Wills, *Confessions of a Conservative* (Garden City, N.Y.: Doubleday, 1979), pp. 26–37.
18. Albert Jay Nock, *Memoirs of a Superfluous Man* (1943; reprint, Washington, D.C.: Regnery, 1964), p. 138.
19. Albert Jay Nock, *A Journal of These Days* (New York: Morrow, 1934), p. 96.
20. Nock, *Memoirs,* p. 52.
21. Nock, *Journal,* pp. 73–74.
22. Nock, *Memoirs,* p. 126.
23. Ibid., p. 261.
24. Nock, *Journal,* pp. 255–56.
25. Judis, p. 217.
26. For the publication of Mencken's diaries, see Garry Wills, "The Ugly American," *The New Republic,* Feb. 19, 1990, pp. 31–34.
27. Henry L. Mencken, *The Philosophy of Friedrich Nietzsche,* 3d ed. (1913; reprint, Port Washington, N.Y.: Kennikat, 1967), p. 194.
28. Ibid., pp. 167–68.
29. Ibid., p. 177.
30. Ibid., p. 202.
31. Mencken, *In Defense of Women* (1918; Garden City, N.Y.: Garden City Publishing Co., 1922), p. 37.
32. Ibid., p. 174.
33. For Mencken and Bryan, see Garry Wills, *Under God: Religion and American Politics* (New York: Simon & Schuster, 1990), pp. 115–24.
34. Mencken, *Treatise on the Gods* (1930; reprint, New York: Vintage, 1958), p. 228.
35. Ibid., p. 230.

22. Groups: From Brook Farm to Hippie Communes

1. Sydney E. Ahlstrom, *A Religious History of the American People*, vol. 1 (Garden City, N.Y.: Image, 1975), p. 593.
2. Nathaniel Hawthorne, *The Blithedale Romance* (New York: Norton, 1965), p. 61.
3. Ibid., p. 67.
4. Odell Shepard, *Pedlar's Progress: The Life of Bronson Alcott* (Boston: Little, Brown, 1937), pp. 343–50.
5. Mark Holloway, *Heavens on Earth: Utopian Communities in America, 1680–1880* (New York: Dover, 1996), pp. 185–88.
6. Unger, *The Movement: A History of the American New Left* (New York: Dodd, Mead, 1974), pp. 12–13.
7. Ibid., pp. 17–18, 40–42.
8. Richard King, *The Party of Eros: Radical Social Thought and the Realm of Freedom* (Chapel Hill: University of North Carolina Press, 1972), pp. 173–94.
9. Lucy M. Freibert, "Creative Women of Brook Farm," in *Women in Spiritual and Communitarian Societies in the United States*, edited by Wendy D. Chmielewski et al. (Syracuse, N.Y.: Syracuse University Press, 1992), pp. 75–88.
10. Doug Rossinow, *The Politics of Authenticity: Liberalism, Christianity, and the New Left in America* (New York: Columbia University Press, 1998), pp. 297–333.
11. Larry Sloman, *Steal This Dream: Abbie Hoffman and the Countercultural Revolution Against America* (New York: Doubleday, 1998), pp. 87–92.
12. Wini Breines, *Community and Organization in the New Left, 1962–1968: The Great Refusal* (New York: Praeger, 1982), p. 18.
13. Michael S. Sherry, *In the Shadow of War* (New Haven: Yale University Press, 1995).
14. Garry Wills, *Nixon Agonistes: The Crisis of the Self-Made Man* (Boston: Houghton Mifflin, 1970), p. 293.
15. Ralph Waldo Emerson, "The Transcendentalist," in *Essays and Lectures* (New York: Library of America, 1983), p. 193.
16. George R. Fitzgerald, *Communes: Their Goals, Hopes, Problems* (New York: Paulist, 1971), p. 115.
17. Garry Wills, *Lead Time: A Journalist's Education* (Garden City, N.Y.: Doubleday, 1976), pp. 3–10.
18. Sloman, p. 174.
19. James D. Tabor and Eugene V. Gallagher, *Why Waco?: Cults and the Battle for Religious Freedom in America* (Berkeley: University of California Press, 1995), p. 3.

Part VIII. Disobeyers

23. From Dr. King to SDS

1. Henry Seidel Canby, *Thoreau* (Boston: Houghton Mifflin, 1939), p. 231.
2. Carlos Baker, *Emerson Among the Eccentrics: A Group Portrait* (New York: Viking, 1996), p. 269.
3. Henry David Thoreau, "Civil Disobedience," in *Walden, and Civil Disobedience*, edited by Owen Thomas (New York: Norton, 1966), p. 236.
4. Canby, p. 233, and Joseph Wood Krutch, *Henry David Thoreau* (New York: Sloane, 1948), p. 131.
5. Martin Luther King Jr., "Letter From Birmingham City Jail," in *A Testament of Hope: The Essential Writings of Martin Luther King, Jr.*, edited by James Melvin Washington (New York: Harper & Row, 1986), p. 294. The seven rules of civil disobedience are on pp. 290, 294.
6. Baker, p. 269.
7. Odell Shepard, *Pedlar's Progress: The Life of Bronson Alcott* (Boston: Little, Brown, 1937), p. 354.
8. Theodore Baird, "Corn Grows in the Night," in *Walden, and Civil Disobedience*, p. 402.
9. Larry Sloman, *Steal This Dream: Abbie Hoffman and the Countercultural Revolution Against America* (New York: Doubleday, 1998), pp. 48–49.
10. Doug Rossinow, *The Politics of Authenticity: Liberalism, Christianity, and the New Left in America* (New York: Columbia University Press, 1998), pp. 53–60, 85–90, 135–36.
11. Sloman, pp. 27–31.
12. SDS, *The Port Huron Statement* (Chicago: Kerr, 1990), p. 76.
13. Ibid., pp. 74–75.
14. Daniel Berrigan, *The Trial of the Catonsville Nine* (Boston: Beacon, 1970).
15. Garry Wills, *Lead Time: A Journalist's Education* (Garden City, N.Y.: Doubleday, 1976), pp. 11–28.
16. John Judis, *William F. Buckley, Jr.: Patron Saint of the Conservatives* (New York: Simon & Schuster, 1988).
17. J. Bowyer Bell and Ted Robert Gurr, "Terrorism and Revolution in America," in *Violence in America: Historical and Comparative Perspectives*, edited by Hugh Davis Graham and Ted Robert Gurr (Beverly Hills, Calif.: Sage, 1979), pp. 335–36.
18. SDS, p. 11.
19. Ibid., p. 76.

20. Kirkpatrick Sale, *SDS* (New York: Random House, 1973), pp. 60–68.
21. SDS, p. 13.

Part IX. A Necessary Good

24. *The Uses of Government*

1. The extraordinary influence of Locke on our political views has often been noticed. Montesquieu had great influence on the founders, but that effect, unlike Locke's, has seeped out of the folk memory of our culture. Though individual founders were also influenced by other thinkers—Jefferson by Lord Kames, John Adams by Richard Hooker, James Wilson by Jean-Jacques Rousseau—those authors did not supply the philosophical lingua franca that Lockeanism did. Whatever the faults of the 1950s "consensus historians," they were right to think that any consensus in American history would have to be built on Locke (see Louis Hartz, *The Liberal Tradition in America* [New York: Harcourt, Brace, 1955]). The two most discussed recent theories of the state are just a liberal reading of the Lockean contract (John Rawls, *A Theory of Justice* [Cambridge: Harvard University Press, 1971]) and a conservative reading of it (Robert Nozick, *Anarchy, State, and Utopia* [New York: Basic Books, 1974]).
2. Hobbes thought the social contract initiated the moral order when individuals gave up their original right of aggression to a single sovereign. Locke thought there was already moral law in the state of nature, but since everyone was the executor of that law, no one was its *effective* executor. That was created by the investment of liberties in the sovereign people, ruled by a majority. Lockean thinkers who approximate the popular view of him are people like Robert Nozick (favorably) and C. B. Macpherson (unfavorably—see his *The Political Theory of Possessive Individualism* [New York: Oxford University Press, 1962]).
3. Richard Hooker, *Of the Laws of Ecclesiastical Polity* (1593), Book One, ch. 10.
4. Plato, *Symposium* 189–92.
5. G. K. Chesterton, *Orthodoxy* (1909), ch. 9.

25. *The Uses of Fear*

1. Daniel Patrick Moynihan, *Secrecy: The American Experience* (New Haven: Yale University Press, 1998).

2. Ibid., pp. 147–52.
3. James G. Hershberg, *James B. Conant: Harvard to Hiroshima and the Making of the Nuclear Age* (New York: Knopf, 1993), p. 284.
4. Ibid., p. 297.
5. John Ray Skates, *The Invasion of Japan: Alternative to the Bomb* (Columbia: University of South Carolina Press, 1994), p. 80.
6. Hershberg, pp. 294, 300.
7. Stewart Udall, *The Myths of August: A Personal Exploration of Our Tragic Cold War Affair with the Atom* (New Brunswick, N.J.: Rutgers University Press, 1998), p. 229. See Philip L. Fradkin, *Fallout: An American Nuclear Tragedy* (Tucson: University of Arizona Press, 1989).
8. Moynihan, p. 142.
9. Ibid., p. 75.
10. Charles J. Dunlap, "Revolt of the Masses: Armed Civilians and the Insurrection Theory of the Second Amendment," *Tennessee Law Review* 62 (Spring 1995), p. 675.

Index